Mark H

ONE
AHEAD

THE TOP NH HORSES TO FOLLOW FOR **2018/2019**

THE AUTHOR

Mark Howard is 43 and graduated from Manchester University with a BA Honours Degree in History. For the last 25 years, he has written the National Hunt horses to follow book *One Jump Ahead*. He also writes the Flat racing equivalent, *Ahead On The Flat*. In addition, he appears as a pundit on *Racing UK* (Sky Channel 426) and, prior to that, Attheraces. He has also written for *The Irish Field*, *Sports Advisor* and *Racing & Football Outlook* (*Borderer & Trainer File*) and is Ambassador for the successful syndicate ValueRacingClub.co.uk

FRONT COVER: **LAURINA** (Paul Townend) wins the Grade 2 Trull House Stud Mares' Novices' Hurdle at the Cheltenham Festival in March by 18 lengths.

BACK COVER: *Top 40 Prospects* entry **SAMCRO** (Jack Kennedy) makes it eight out of eight in the Grade 1 Ballymore Novices' Hurdle at the Cheltenham Festival with a two and three quarters of a length win.

Front cover photograph supplied by GROSSICK RACING PHOTOGRAPHY. The Steadings, Rockhallhead, Collin, Dumfries. DG1 4JW. Telephone: 01387 750 512.

Published by *Mark Howard Publications Ltd*. 69, Fairgarth Drive,
Kirkby Lonsdale, Carnforth, Lancashire. LA6 2FB.
Telephone: 015242 71826
Email: mark.howard@mhpublications.co.uk
Website: www.mhpublications.co.uk

(Please note: If you are currently NOT on the *Mark Howard Publications* mailing list and you would like to be, and therefore receive all information about future publications then please post / email / phone your name and address to the above).

Printed by H&H REEDS PRINTERS. Southend Road, Penrith, Cumbria. CA11 8JH. Telephone: 01768 864214. www.reeds-printers.co.uk

ISBN: 978-0-9929224-6-7

CONTENTS

INTRODUCTION

Welcome to the 26th edition of *One Jump Ahead*, which is packed with more features and information than ever before and I hope readers will find it useful and informative for the winter ahead. I am fortunate to have been involved with *Racing UK* since its inception in May 2004 and, during the last six months, I have worked alongside one of the greatest ever jump jockeys, namely Ruby Walsh, at both Aintree and Royal Ascot. I will never forget either of those days but arguably the best days racing I have ever covered for the channel came at Cheltenham last March. On day two of the Festival, Samcro, Presenting Percy, Altior and Tiger Roll all gained gold medals at National Hunt racing's Olympics. It doesn't get much better than that - Wednesday 14th March 2018 will be forever etched in my memory.

Talking of the Cheltenham Festival, the home trained runners may have dominated the Champion Hurdle, Queen Mother Champion Chase and Gold Cup, but it was Gordon Elliott (8 winners) and Willie Mullins (7) who monopolized the remainder of the meeting with fifteen winners between them. The following month at Punchestown, Mullins was responsible for a staggering 18 winners, including 9 Grade 1s, with Elliott managing a mere four. The pair haven't rested on their laurels either, recruiting heavily during the summer. The Elliott/Mullins dominance, which was typified by the finish to the Grand National in April, is here for the foreseeable future.

Neither Elliott or Mullins feature in *Talking Trainers* but I am pleased to announce that Kim Bailey, Anthony Honeyball, Donald McCain and Fergal O'Brien are new additions this year. The quartet had stellar campaigns in 2017/2018 with the prospect of even better ones this time around. The way McCain has rebuilt over the last three seasons following the crushing blow of losing the Rooney owned horses is admirable to say the least. His seasonal tallies during that time period have been 53, 80 and 98 and, now with the assistance of newly appointed stable jockey Brian Hughes, the Cheshire based handler is long odds on to train over a hundred winners for the first time since the 2013/2014 campaign. One of the biggest success stories of *OJA* last term was the interview with Tom Lacey. The Herefordshire trainer sent out a brace of winners at Aintree's Grand National meeting during a season which yielded a career best total of 39. Expect more of the same from Lacey who has gradually built up a strong team of youngsters. Sadly, one trainer who is missing from the list is Malcolm Jefferson, who passed away in February at the age of 71. The Malton handler, who was responsible for 4 Cheltenham Festival winners, including two in 2012, trained his first winner at Perth on the 24th September 1981 with Mark Edelson. Malcolm trained some very good horses over the years, including the likes of Cape Tribulation, Cloudy Dream, Kings Measure, Tullymurry Toff and Waiting Patiently.

Leading owner Jared Sullivan has kindly run through his string for the season ahead. The star of the show is undoubtedly Cheltenham Festival winner Laurina. The daughter of Spanish Moon is unbeaten since arriving from France and produced one of the moments of the Festival when blitzing her rivals by upwards of eighteen lengths in the Grade 2 Dawn Run Mares' Novices' Hurdle. She remains a tremendous prospect with Champion Hurdle aspirations.

Finally, thank you to all those who have helped with the production of *One Jump Ahead* - from owners, trainers, jockeys, bloodstock agents, secretaries, photographers, proof readers etc - and subscribers for your continued support, it is much appreciated. I would like to give a special thank you to Mags O'Toole who still found time to provide me with information during such a difficult time following the sad passing of her father Mick in August.

Enjoy the winter.

Mark Howard

FOREWORD
by Nick Luck

Broadcaster of the Year 2007, 2008, 2009, 2011, 2013 & 2014, 2016

Whenever I am lucky enough to work with Mark Howard on *Racing UK*, it rains. Often it rains quite hard; sometimes it is also cold; either way, it *always* rains.

If we are rostered together at Chester in May or York in August, the morning can look quite promising, only for the black clouds to gather in time with the first bar of the opening credits. Mark, invariably without a coat suitable to withstand the elements, complains far less than the southern softie sitting on his left, safe in the knowledge that his subscribers are about to be the grateful recipients of another winner.

Over time, this has reinforced two things: first, that he is extremely well-suited to the more rugged demands of the winter game and, second, that his ability as an accurate forecaster remains peerless. As such, it is hardly surprising that *One Jump Ahead* is more successful than ever after all these years.

I think it is true for many of us that we only really start to re-engage with the jumping season when the leaves start to fall and the *Racing Post* start to publish details of trainers' Open Days. For Mark, sourcing the best horses and most important power bases in National Hunt racing is a year-round labour of love. He is constantly able to take the pulse of jump racing, which is why - for example - a trainer like Tom Lacey was given a full stable tour in last year's edition on the back of a season that had yielded 21 winners without a whole load of fanfare.

Duly, Lacey then pumped out 39 winners at a remarkable 25% strike rate, delivering a level-stakes-profit of £79.80. Similarly, Mark recognised that Olly Murphy's start to his career was so unusual that it needed a prominent position in this book before it was a given that he would become another West Midlands powerhouse. They are featured once again, alongside so many of the *OJA* regulars like Paul Nicholls, Philip Hobbs and Alan King, who have given so generously of their time over the years.

Of other inclusions this time around, it was great to see the burgeoning fortunes of Fergal O'Brien and Anthony Honeyball, to witness the renaissance (reflected here) of the prolific Donald McCain and to see such a depth of quality in the novice hurdling team of Kim Bailey, who arguably has his strongest squad since his mid-90s heyday.

And of course - getting down to brass tacks - Mark can consistently find you quality animals amongst his *Top 40 Prospects*. With such a distillation of quality in the top stables, it is sometimes hard (and foolish) to look beyond the obvious, but here there is always a nugget or two: this time last year, I might only have needed it confirmed that Samcro was the second coming, but I confess to knowing next to nothing about Black Op until I read about him between these covers.

Mark has again produced a belter here - there are few stones unturned and most angles covered. Industry and professionalism shine through again, but most of you already know that - come rain or rain - *One Jump Ahead* will never let you down.

TYPE OF TRACK

AINTREE	National Course	Left-Handed, Galloping
	Mildmay Course	Left-Handed, Tight
ASCOT		Right-Handed, Galloping
AYR		Left-Handed, Galloping
BANGOR-ON-DEE		Left-Handed, Tight
CARLISLE		Right-Handed, Stiff / Undulating
CARTMEL		Left-Handed, Tight
CATTERICK BRIDGE		Left-Handed, Tight / Undulating
CHELTENHAM		Left-Handed, Stiff / Undulating
CHEPSTOW		Left-Handed, Stiff / Undulating
DONCASTER		Left-Handed, Galloping
EXETER		Right-Handed, Stiff / Undulating
FAKENHAM		Left-Handed, Tight / Undulating
FFOS LAS		Left-Handed, Galloping
FONTWELL PARK	Chase Course	Figure of Eight, Tight
	Hurdle Course	Left-Handed, Tight
HAYDOCK PARK	Chase Course	Left-Handed, Galloping
	Hurdle Course	Left-Handed, Tight
HEREFORD		Right-Handed, Tight
HEXHAM		Left-Handed, Stiff / Undulating
HUNTINGDON		Right-Handed, Galloping
KELSO		Left-Handed, Tight / Undulating
KEMPTON PARK		Right-Handed, Tight
LEICESTER		Right-Handed, Stiff / Undulating
LINGFIELD PARK		Left-Handed, Tight / Undulating
LUDLOW		Right-Handed, Tight
MARKET RASEN		Right-Handed, Tight /Undulating
MUSSELBURGH		Right-Handed, Tight
NEWBURY		Left-Handed, Galloping
NEWCASTLE		Left-Handed, Galloping
NEWTON ABBOT		Left-Handed, Tight
PERTH		Right-Handed, Tight
PLUMPTON		Left-Handed, Tight / Undulating
SANDOWN PARK		Right-Handed, Galloping
SEDGEFIELD		Left-Handed, Tight / Undulating
SOUTHWELL		Left-Handed, Tight
STRATFORD-UPON-AVON		Left-Handed, Tight
TAUNTON		Right-Handed, Tight
TOWCESTER		Right-Handed, Stiff / Undulating
UTTOXETER		Left-Handed, Tight / Undulating
WARWICK		Left-Handed, Tight / Undulating
WETHERBY		Left-Handed, Galloping
WINCANTON		Right-Handed, Galloping
WORCESTER		Left-Handed, Galloping

IRELAND

BALLINROBE	Right-Handed, Tight
BELLEWSTOWN	Left-Handed, Tight / Undulating
CLONMEL	Right-Handed, Tight / Undulating
CORK	Right-Handed, Galloping
DOWNPATRICK	Right-Handed, Tight / Undulating
DOWN ROYAL	Right-Handed, Tight / Undulating
FAIRYHOUSE	Right-Handed, Galloping
GALWAY	Right-Handed, Tight / Undulating
GOWRAN PARK	Right-Handed, Tight / Undulating
KILBEGGAN	Right-Handed, Tight / Undulating
KILLARNEY	Left-Handed, Tight
LEOPARDSTOWN	Left-Handed, Galloping
LIMERICK	Right-Handed, Galloping
LISTOWEL	Left-Handed, Tight
NAAS	Left-Handed, Galloping
NAVAN	Left-Handed, Galloping
PUNCHESTOWN	Right-Handed, Galloping
ROSCOMMON	Right-Handed, Tight
SLIGO	Right-Handed, Tight / Undulating
THURLES	Right-Handed, Tight / Undulating
TIPPERARY	Left-Handed, Tight
TRAMORE	Right-Handed, Tight
WEXFORD	Left-Handed, Tight

ACKNOWLEDGEMENTS

I would like to thank all the following Trainers who have given up their time, during the summer, to answer my inquiries:

Talking Trainers: Kim Bailey, Harry Fry, Philip Hobbs, Anthony Honeyball, Alan King, Tom Lacey, Donald McCain, Olly Murphy, Paul Nicholls, Fergal O'Brien, David Pipe, plus Amy Murphy & Venetia Williams. Thank you also to the following secretaries for organising the appointments/answering queries: Hannah Roche & Sarah (Paul Nicholls), James (David Pipe), Lauren (Tom George), Carolyn Harty (Nicky Henderson), Hannah McVeigh (Jonjo O'Neill).

Thank you also to Anthony Bromley, David Minton & Bernice Emanuel (Highflyer Bloodstock), Nick Luck (Foreword), Declan Phelan (Ireland), Jared Sullivan, Graham Wylie, Mags O'Toole, Mick Meagher (Racing Manager for Trevor Hemmings), Rich Ricci, Joe Chambers (Racing Manager for Rich & Susannah Ricci), Chris Richardson (Managing Director Cheveley Park Stud), Joe Foley (Ballyhane Stud), Michael Shinners & Ruairi Stirling (Skybet), Ed Chamberlin (ITV Racing), Jonathan Neesom & Niall Hannity (*Racing UK*), Bruce Jeffryes, James Couldwell (valueracingclub.co.uk).

The TOP 40 PROSPECTS FOR 2018/2019

ACEY MILAN (IRE)

4 b g Milan – Strong Wishes (IRE) (Strong Gale (IRE))
OWNER: OWNERS FOR OWNERS: ACEY MILAN
TRAINER: A.HONEYBALL. Mosterton, Dorset.
CAREER FORM FIGURES: 21114
CAREER WINS: 2017: Dec WINCANTON Soft NHF 2m: 2018: Jan CHELTENHAM Heavy Lstd NHF 1m 6f; Feb NEWBURY Soft Lstd NHF 2m

The 2017/2018 National Hunt season was an excellent one for Dorset trainer Anthony Honeyball. The head of Potwell Farm sent out a personal best tally of 34 winners at an impressive strike-rate of 21%. The stable's total prize-money reached £427,333. Midnight Tune won a Grade 2 mares' novices' hurdle at Sandown and Acey Milan, Duhallow Gesture, Ms Parfois and Regal Encore won half a dozen Listed races between them. The former jockey isn't resting on his laurels either with expensive new recruits Deja Vue (£82,000), Free (€125,000) and Tara West (£100,000) joining the yard during the summer.

Acey Milan was arguably the best bumper horse in the UK last season winning two Listed races at Cheltenham and Newbury before finishing fourth in the championship event at the Festival in March. Bought for €11, 500 as a foal, he is a full-brother to James Ewart's nine times winner Lord Wishes and a half-brother to William's Wishes, an eight times winner for Evan Williams. Beaten nearly four lengths on his racecourse debut in a junior bumper at Exeter (1m 5f) in late October, he learned plenty from that experience, judging by his nine lengths win at Wincanton over an extra quarter of a mile in early December. Acey Milan then headed to Cheltenham on New Year's Day and lifted the Listed four year old bumper by three and three quarters of a length, making all under Aidan Coleman. His most emphatic performance of the season though came at Newbury in February. Eight of the ten horses who lined up in the Listed Best Odds Guaranteed At Betfair Bumper had won last time out. Brian Hughes did the steering and the Milan gelding tore the field apart with an eleven lengths win, denting some lofty reputations in the process. That win booked his place for the Cheltenham Festival and, while he was unable to make it four successive wins, Anthony Honeyball's charge emerged with plenty of credit. Beaten five and a quarter lengths in fourth, Willie Mullins trained the first, second, third, fifth and seventh. Acey Milan held every chance turning for home but lacked the gears of the first three home.

All set to go hurdling, the four year old is likely to reappear over two miles but his trainer feels he will benefit from stepping up in distance later in the season. The Grade 1 Challow Hurdle at Newbury (29th December) is his first major target with a return to Gloucestershire in March hopefully on the agenda.

POINTS TO NOTE:
Probable Best Distance - 2m 4f
Preferred Going - Soft
Connection's Comments: "Acey Milan is a nice horse who has progressed with every run. He goes on any ground. He's got a long raking stride and he could be anything." Anthony HONEYBALL at Newbury (10/2/18)

GOING:	R	W	P	TRACK:	R	W	P
Heavy	1	1	0	Left-Handed	3	2	0
Soft	3	2	0	Right	2	1	1
Good/Soft	1	0	1	Galloping	2	2	0
				Stiff/Undul.	3	1	1

TRIP:	R	W	P	JOCKEY:	R	W	P
1m 5f	1	0	1	A.Coleman	4	2	1
1m 6f	1	1	0	B.Hughes	1	1	0
2m	3	2	0				

ADJALI (GER)

3 b g Kamsin (GER) – Anabasis (GER) (High Chaparral (IRE))
OWNER: Mr SIMON MUNIR & Mr ISAAC SOUEDE
TRAINER: N.J.HENDERSON. Lambourn, Berkshire.
CAREER FORM FIGURES: 213
CAREER WIN: 2018: Apr COMPIEGNE Very Soft Hdle 2m

The Simon Munir and Isaac Souede owned and Nicky Henderson trained We Have A Dream developed into the leading British juvenile hurdler last season winning all five of his starts, culminating in a seven lengths win in Grade 1 company at Aintree. The Martaline gelding, who is rated 156, is likely to be trained with the Champion Hurdle in mind this season.

Ironically, We Have A Dream failed to win in three starts over hurdles in France, prior to being bought by Anthony Bromley for his current connections. Messrs Munir, Souede and Henderson will be hoping lightning strikes twice because they have recruited another potentially smart juvenile hurdler from across the English Channel. Adjali raced three times for Guillaume Macaire and, having finished a length and three quarters runner-up on his jumping debut at Auteuil in April, he then beat Fighter Du Seuil by four lengths at Compiegne nineteen days later. Stepped up in grade, the Kamsin gelding finished a creditable third in the Listed Prix Le Parisien - Prix Stanley Hurdle at Auteuil. Beaten five and a quarter lengths by Arnaud Chaille-Chaille's Beaumec De Houelle, the winner has been placed in Grade 3 company since.

Transferred to Seven Barrows during the summer, the same connections enjoyed Triumph Hurdle success with Soldatino (2010) and Peace And Co (2015) - Henderson has won the race a record breaking six times - and they may have found a prime candidate for the 2019 renewal in Adjali.

POINTS TO NOTE:

Probable Best Distance	-	**2 miles**
Preferred Going	-	**Good/Soft**

GOING:	R	W	P	TRACK:	R	W	P
Very Soft	3	1	1	Left-Handed	3	1	1

TRIP:	R	W	P	JOCKEY:	R	W	P
1m 7f	1	0	1	B.Lestrade	3	1	1
2m	1	1	0				
2m 1f	1	0	0				

ANGELS BREATH (IRE)

4 gr g Shantou (USA) – Mystic Masie (IRE) (Turgeon (USA))
OWNER: WALTERS PLANT HIRE LTD
TRAINER: N.J.HENDERSON. Lambourn, Berkshire.
CAREER FORM FIGURES: 1
CAREER WIN: 2018: Apr MOIRA Soft/Heavy 4YO Mdn PTP 3m

Owner Dai Walters has been associated with some high quality National Hunt horses, including dual Grade 1 winners Oscar Whisky and Whisper. It is early days but the Welshman may have another exciting prospect on his hands in the shape of the once raced winning Irish pointer Angels Breath. A full-brother to Harry Fry's bumper winner Outofthisworld, he created a big impression on pointing fans last spring when winning his only start for Pat Doyle. The grey son of Shantou has joined Nicky Henderson since.

"Fine, big steel grey gelding: purchased by Dai Walters as a store at the 2017 Land Rover sale (€85,000) and sent to Pat Doyle to gain some experience pointing. He turned in a polished winning effort on his one run: at Moira (Soft/Heavy) in April, he moved with authority from the start: jumping to the lead at the second last, he drew clear from a decent field of opponents to record an emphatic twelve lengths success. The dam line of his pedigree is mainly French jumping stock, including Pique Sous. He joins Nicky Henderson and will certainly be one of the more exciting young horses to sport the Walters silks this coming winter. He may distinguish himself in the staying novice hurdle division and may achieve Graded victories. Longer term he can carve a niche as a 140+ staying chaser," believes Irish point-to-point expert Declan Phelan.

POINTS TO NOTE:
Probable Best Distance - 2m 4f – 3 miles
Preferred Going - Soft
Connection's Comments: "He is a lovely horse with a big engine. He was showing us plenty at home and we really fancied him. He has a bright future ahead of him." Pat DOYLE at Moira (14/4/18)

GOING:	R	W	P	TRACK:	R	W	P
Soft/Heavy	1	1	0	Left-Handed	1	1	0

TRIP:	R	W	P	JOCKEY:	R	W	P
3m	1	1	0	J.C.Barry	1	1	0

ASTERION FORLONGE (FR)

4 gr g Coastal Path – Belle Du Brizais (FR) (Turgeon (USA)
TRAINER: W.P.MULLINS. Bagenalstown, Co.Carlow.
CAREER FORM FIGURES: 1
CAREER WIN: 2018: Feb OLDTOWN Soft 4YO Mdn PTP 2m 4f

Willie Mullins became champion trainer in Ireland for a twelfth time last season. On the morning of the first day of the Punchestown Festival, Gordon Elliott led Mullins by €521,413 but things changed dramatically on the second day of the meeting with the head of Closutton being responsible for a 9,802/1 six timer. Over the five days, Mullins sent out 18 winners, 12 second and 9 thirds – 9 of those wins were gained in Grade 1 events. The 62 year old claimed the title by a remarkable €809,524. As discussed, Mullins and Elliott have bought heavily since, especially from the Irish pointing field.

Asterion Forlonge was a six lengths winner of his only start in February before being purchased for a hefty sum four days later at the Cheltenham Sales. **"This grey gelding proved to be a shrewd investment for point handler Pat Doyle as he groomed the €60,000 Land Rover 2017 store purchase into a winning pointer and received £290,000 at Cheltenham February Sales on the back of a win at Oldtown (Soft). In a two and a half miles maiden, Derek O'Connor cushioned him about ten lengths adrift of the leader and took closer order on the downhill run to the third last fence. He responded to a few reminders and he came to challenge for the lead approaching the last, he pinged that fence and quickened away to win in style. His reaction to pressure being exerted was excellent. From a French jumps family packed with winners, he has joined a trainer who has enjoyed plenty of success with stock by the sire Coastal Path. Winning a bumper should be a formality: sure to win Graded races over hurdles (2m 4f to 3m), the only question will be whether he can win at the top Grade 1 level. I think he will be a high win strike rate jumps horse for Mullins, and I would not be surprised to see him line up in a race such as a Ryanair Cheltenham Festival chase in two or three years with a leading chance,"** believes Irish pointing expert Declan Phelan.

POINTS TO NOTE:
Probable Best Distance - 2 miles
Preferred Going - Soft
Connection's Comments: "He's a lovely horse and he did it very well there. He had been doing everything very easily at home so we were very hopeful coming here that he would put in a big performance." Pat DOYLE at Oldtown (11/2/18)

GOING:	R	W	P	TRACK:	R	W	P
Soft	1	1	0	Left-Handed	1	1	0

TRIP:	R	W	P	JOCKEY:	R	W	P
2m 4f	1	1	0	D.O'Connor	1	1	0

BLACK OP (IRE)

7 br g Sandmason – Afar Story (IRE) (Desert Story (IRE))
OWNER: R.S.BROOKHOUSE
TRAINER: T.R.GEORGE. Slad, Gloucestershire.
CAREER FORM FIGURES: 1 – 19 - 41221
CAREER WINS: 2016: Mar LOUGHANMORE Yielding/Soft 5YO Mdn PTP 3m: 2017: Feb DONCASTER Good NHF 2m: 2018: Jan DONCASTER Soft Mdn Hdle 2m 5f; Apr AINTREE Soft Grade 1 NH 2m 4f

"It was a great run and I suppose on that he's the best (at this trip) in this country. He's going to make a cracking chaser next year. It's all about fences with him. He's a big, long striding horse and he's going to make some three mile chaser in due course," enthused Tom George after Black Op had chased home the mighty Samcro in the Grade 1 Ballymore Novices' Hurdle at the Cheltenham Festival. Featured in last year's *Top 40 Prospects*, the Sandmason gelding went on to gain compensation in the Grade 1 Betway Mersey Novices' Hurdle at Aintree a month later. The seven year old, who is rated 152 over hurdles, could make an even better chaser and is a most exciting prospect.

A twenty five lengths point winner for Rodney Ian Arthur before being acquired by Roger Brookhouse for £210,000 in April 2016, he finished fourth over two miles on his hurdling bow at Newbury in December. However, once stepped up to middle distances, the seven year old was a different proposition. A wide margin winner at Doncaster in January, he was unlucky not to win a Grade 2 novice at Cheltenham's Trials meeting when given an overly aggressive ride. Headed close home after a mistake at the last, Black Op was beaten three parts of a length by Santini. Noel Fehily, who partnered him to victory at Town Moor, was reunited at the Cheltenham Festival and he ran a blinder to finish less than three lengths behind Samcro. He pulled five lengths clear of subsequent Grade 1 winner Next Destination. Fehily was seen at his best next time as Tom George's gelding gained a well deserved victory at Aintree. Leading after the fourth last, he wasn't fluent over the next or the last flight but battled on gamely to beat Lostintranslation by half a length.

Yet to race beyond two miles five under Rules, Tom George views Black Op as a three mile chaser in the making and he looks an obvious contender for either the JLT or RSA Chases next spring. It is hoped Noel Fehily retains the ride aboard the Sandmason gelding because the Irishman made a significant difference last spring. Tom George is blessed with some very good young talent and Black Op looks the pick of the crop.

POINTS TO NOTE:
Probable Best Distance - 2m 4f – 3 miles
Preferred Going - Good/Soft
Connection's Comments: "He's a beautiful horse – a staying chaser in the making. We'll have a chat with Roger Brookhouse about whether to go chasing next season but that's what our plan will be." Tom GEORGE at Aintree (14/4/18)

GOING:	R	W	P
Heavy	1	0	1
Soft	4	2	1
Yield/Soft	1	1	0
Good	2	1	0

TRACK:	R	W	P
Left-Handed	8	4	2
Galloping	3	2	0
Stiff/Undul.	2	0	2
Tight	2	1	0

TRIP:	R	W	P
2m	2	1	0
2m 1f	1	0	0
2m 4f	2	1	1
2m 5f	2	1	1
3m	1	1	0

JOCKEY:	R	W	P
N.Fehily	3	2	1
A.Heskin	3	1	0
T.Scudamore	1	0	1
J.McKeown	1	1	0

BREWIN'UPASTORM (IRE)

5 b g Milan – Daraheen Diamond (IRE) (Husyan (USA))
OWNER: Mrs BARBARA HESTER
TRAINER: OLLY MURPHY. Wilmcote, Warwickshire.
CAREER FORM FIGURES: 1 - 14
CAREER WINS: 2017: Apr QUAKERSTOWN Good/Yielding 4YO Mdn PTP 3m: 2018: Jan HEREFORD Soft NHF 2m

Gordon Elliott's former assistant Olly Murphy couldn't have dreamt of a better start to his training career last season. The Warwickshire based handler was responsible for 47 winners from 250 runners at a strike-rate of 19% with his total prize-money reaching £382,935. The ex-Irish gelding Hunters Call provided Murphy with his first big race win when capturing the £85,425 Grade 3 Racing Welfare Handicap Hurdle at Ascot in December. It was the seven year old's first run for the yard.

Murphy's team has been further boosted during the summer with the arrival of three horses owned by Jared Sullivan. Another big spending patron Barbara Hester transferred her string from Dan Skelton to Olly Murphy last Autumn and it included this exciting former Irish pointer.

An eight lengths winner of his only race 'between the flags' for Timmy Hyde in April last year, the Milan gelding was purchased for £250,000 four days later. Unraced for Skelton, he made his Rules debut for his new handler at Hereford in a nine runner bumper in January. Partnered by the yard's conditional rider Fergus Gregory, the five year old pulverised the opposition with a dominant display. A nine lengths from subsequent Grade 2 Aintree bumper winner Portrush Ted, he ploughed through the mud. Less than a month later, Brewin'Upastorm was sent off 3/1 joint favourite for a Listed bumper at Newbury. The field contained eight previous winners and Richard Johnson took over in the saddle. Beaten over thirteen lengths in fourth behind the aforementioned Acey Milan, he was held up early on and never really gave himself a chance of getting involved. The underfoot conditions were testing and trying to make up ground from the rear was never going to be easy.

Given a break since, he remains a highly promising young horse who could develop into Murphy's stable star in years to come. Featured in last year's *Irish Pointers* in *One Jump Ahead*, it is worth recalling Declan Phelan's thoughts on the Milan gelding twelve months ago: **"The Easter maiden for the four year olds at Quakerstown (Good/Yielding) has in the past decade built up quite a reputation as a source of potential stars: Champagne Fever and Bacardys previous winners. Consequently, many trainers are now targeting the race, with the expectation that talent arising from this event will make a premium price. The 2017 renewal was very competitive, attracting a field of fourteen: many were still in contention heading to the third last. Brewin'Upastorm was given a squeeze approaching the second last and in an instant he opened up a lead of five lengths and jumping the last fence neatly, powered away to win by eight lengths. He was one of a handful of pointers to inject pace at a critical juncture in a race this past season and that trait would promote him as an above average sort. He also clocked a commendable time in comparison to previous renewals. He is a rather plain looking individual, though the engine under his bonnet should ensure winning a bumper is a formality, and he may become quite a tasty performer in middle distance novice hurdles and become a player for races such as the Neptune Hurdle: he looks banker material to land at least Grade 3 or better contests over hurdles and fences.**"

POINTS TO NOTE:
Probable Best Distance - 2m – 2m 4f
Preferred Going - Good/Soft
Connection's Comments: "Brewin'Upastorm is a lovely, young horse and he did it very easily." Fergus GREGORY at Hereford (16/1/18)

GOING:	R	W	P
Soft	2	1	0
Good/Yield	1	1	0

TRACK:	R	W	P
Left-Handed	2	1	0
Right	1	1	0
Galloping	1	0	0
Tight	1	1	0

TRIP:	R	W	P
2m	2	1	0
3m	1	1	0

JOCKEY:	R	W	P
F.Gregory	1	1	0
R.Johnson	1	0	0
S.Connor	1	1	0

BULLIONAIRE (IRE)

5 b g Gold Well – Dontcallerthat (IRE) (Anshan)
OWNER: PHIL FRY & CHARLIE WALKER – OSBORNE HOUSE
TRAINER: H.FRY. Seaborough, Dorset.
CAREER FORM FIGURES: 1 - 2
CAREER WIN: 2017: Mar NEWBURY Good/Soft NHF 2m

Provided he learns to settle now his attentions are switched to hurdling, Bullionaire has the ability to develop into a high-class novice and pretensions to becoming a Grade 1 winner for Harry Fry.

Acquired as a three year old for £37,000 at the Doncaster Spring Sales in 2016, he almost recouped his purchase price in one go when winning the Goffs UK Spring Sales Bumper at Newbury on his debut in March last year. Leading with over half a mile to run, the Gold Well gelding maintained a searching gallop to win the first prize of £31,280 by three and a half lengths from Irish raider Midnight Stroll (won twice over hurdles since and is rated 128). Back in seventh position was the subsequent Scottish Champion Hurdle winner Midnight Shadow. Harry Fry elected to shelve his hurdling career for another season and targeted him at the Listed bumper at Ascot's pre Christmas fixture. Ten of the fourteen runners were previous winners and Bullionaire was sent off 3/1 favourite. While he ran well in second, nearly three lengths behind Nick Gifford's Didtheyleaveuoutto, he would have finished closer had he relaxed during the early stages. Having raced keenly during the first mile, he led with two furlongs to run but had no answer to the winner's turn of foot late on. There were some smart horses behind Bullionaire, who missed the rest of the season.

Rather like stablemate If The Cap Fits, one can imagine him starting off at somewhere like Exeter over a stiff two miles. I spoke to Harry in August and his team have reportedly done a lot of work on Bullionaire trying to teach him to settle. Paul Nicholls' former assistant also said that the gelding has done very well physically filling out during the summer.

POINTS TO NOTE:
Probable Best Distance - 2 miles
Preferred Going - Good/Soft
Connection's Comments: "Bullionaire is a lovely, big scopey four year old and we like him a lot. We'll look after him and Noel said he was still green." Harry FRY at Newbury (25/3/17)

GOING:	R	W	P
Good/Soft	2	1	1

TRACK:	R	W	P
Left-Handed	1	1	0
Right	1	0	1
Galloping	2	1	1

TRIP:	R	W	P
2m	2	1	1

JOCKEY:	R	W	P
N.Fehily	2	1	1

COMMANDER OF FLEET (IRE)

4 b g Fame And Glory – Coonagh Cross (IRE) (Saddlers' Hall (IRE))
OWNER: GIGGINSTOWN HOUSE STUD
TRAINER: G.ELLIOTT. Longwood, Co.Meath.
CAREER FORM FIGURES: 11
CAREER WINS: 2018: Mar MOIG SOUTH Yielding/Soft 4YO Mdn PTP 3m; Apr PUNCHESTOWN Yielding/Soft NHF 2m

Ryanair boss Michael O'Leary had his first winner as an owner in the Goffs Land Rover bumper in 2001 courtesy of the David Wachman trained Tuco. Seventeen years later, the head of Gigginstown House Stud was responsible for the first two home (Gordon Elliott trained the first three) in the 2018 running of the valuable prize at the Punchestown Festival in April. Commander of Fleet scored by eight and a half lengths with Elliott saying afterwards: **"He's a lovely horse to have and he's definitely one to look forward to."**

Irish pointing expert Declan Phelan believes: "**With Death Duty nestling in his pedigree, it was no surprise that Gigginstown House Stud bought this bay gelding at the Land Rover store sale of 2017, in fact his price of €47,000 is now looking like a bargain. Another the owner sent to Pat Doyle for pointing: he raced in the four runner geldings maiden at Moig South and the ground was very heavy and tacky. In a slowly run race, the event perked up with four to jump and it soon became apparent that Commander Of Fleet was in his comfort zone and his rivals were struggling. He maintained a constant gallop from three out, and he was left to come home alone as the other three cried enough. In collecting that race, he was also at the time giving his now deceased sire, his first point winner. Gigginstown then made an instant decision to switch the horse to Gordon Elliott and aim at the Land Rover bumper at Punchestown. He was one of five out of the sixteen entries who had race experience and he made it count. Taking the lead with half a mile to race, he gradually upped the ante, and burned off the opposition to win by more than eight lengths. In winning so easily, he certainly gave a boost to the 2018 crop of four year old pointers. With wins at two and three miles already on his record, Commander Of Fleet is likely to be a major force in novice hurdles this winter: I fancy he may be targeted at either the Ballymore (2m4f) or Albert Bartlett (3m) Novices' Hurdles at the Cheltenham Festival. He has illustrated already that he possesses a lethal combination of being a relentless galloper, plus he has some gears, qualities vital in high class staying jumpers.**

Gigginstown House Stud enjoyed a memorable Cheltenham Festival in 2018 with 7 winners and emerged as the leading owners over the four days. In Commander of Fleet they may have unearthed another future Festival winner.

POINTS TO NOTE:
Probable Best Distance - 2m 4f – 3 miles
Preferred Going - Good/Soft
Connection's Comments: "I only got him the week after he won his point-to-point for Pat Doyle. I haven't galloped him, just cantered him away and Pat did all the hard work with him. I'd say the first three are all nice horses." Gordon ELLIOTT at Punchestown (24/4/18)

GOING:	R	W	P	TRACK:	R	W	P
Yield/Soft	2	2	0	Left-Handed	1	1	0
				Right	1	1	0
				Galloping	1	1	0

TRIP:	R	W	P	JOCKEY:	R	W	P
2m	1	1	0	B.O'Neill	1	1	0
3m	1	1	0	J.C.Barry	1	1	0

DICKIE DIVER (IRE)

5 b g Gold Well - Merry Excuse (IRE) (Flemensfirth (USA))
OWNER: J.P.McMANUS
TRAINER: N.J.HENDERSON. Lambourn, Berkshire.
CAREER FORM FIGURES: 1
CAREER WIN: 2017: Dec TEMPLENACARRIGA Heavy 4YO Mdn PTP 3m

"This horse went very well recently in a Fairyhouse schooling hurdle. He was a bit green in front here, but he's a lovely horse with plenty of speed," reported Michael Goff after this gelded son of Gold Well had won by twenty lengths on his point-to-point debut on New Year's Eve. The five year old was subsequently bought by J.P.McManus and has joined the champion trainer at Seven Barrows.

Expert Declan Phelan commented: **"Tall bay gelding with a physical presence: handled by Mick Goff for his point win at Templenacarriga (Heavy) in late December. Confidently ridden from the front, he easily outclassed his rivals as he drew right away on the uphill finish, to record a twenty lengths win in the fastest time of the day (runner up has since franked the form). Dare I say it, there was a touch of the racing exuberance associated with that the likes of Carvills Hill and Denman, in his performance. He commanded a sales price of £210,000 when purchased for J.P. McManus at Goffs UK Sale in January. You find some class acts in his family tree, including Merry Gale and Racing Demon. He could be one of the most exciting pointers that McManus has bought in some time. As a minimum, he will be a major player in the staying novice hurdle division this winter, the Albert Bartlett Novices' Hurdle an obvious target. With big feet, the heavy ground was to his taste at Templenacarriga, a sounder surface for now represents an unknown factor. He could mature into a fine 140+ staying chaser."**

POINTS TO NOTE:
Probable Best Distance - 2m 4f - 3 miles
Preferred Going - Soft
Connection's Comments: "The horse is probably a little bit special for what he did and the way he did it. You'd have to absolutely love him. We loved him from day one. Rumour has it he might go to Mr Henderson, but wherever he goes, he's going to be a very good horse."
Michael GOFF his former trainer at Templenacarriga (31/12/17)

GOING:	R	W	P	TRACK:	R	W	P
Heavy	1	1	0	Right	1	1	0

TRIP:	R	W	P	JOCKEY:	R	W	P
3m	1	1	0	S.Fitzgerald	1	1	0

DLAURO (FR)

5 b g Lauro (GER) - Gergovie De Bussy (FR) (Bad Conduct (USA))
OWNER: LLOYD J.WILLIAMS
TRAINER: JOSEPH P.O'BRIEN. Owning Hill, Co.Kilkenny.
CAREER FORM FIGURES: 1
CAREER WIN: 2018: Feb BELHARBOUR Yielding/Soft 5YO Mdn PTP 3m

Owner Lloyd Williams and trainer Joseph O'Brien combined to win the Irish Derby at the Curragh in June when Latrobe beat Rostropovich by half a length. The pair are also responsible for the potentially very exciting National Hunt horse Dlauro, who was acquired for £410,000 at the

Cheltenham February Sales having won his only Irish point for Donnchadh Doyle eleven days earlier.

Irish point expert Declan Phelan reports: **"A German bred bay gelding with French jumps and Flat winners in his pedigree, he made an instant impact on his point debut at Belharbour (Yielding/Soft) in February. He made all the running and, in what was a virtual time trial, he jumped slickly and his cruising speed could not be matched by his rivals as he won eased down by six lengths without ever being troubled. It was one of those visually appealing performances: substance-wise, he may have beaten a bunch of moderate horses. The manner in which he galloped through the race hinted that he could be effective at a range of distances from two miles to three miles and, as a result, he made plenty of appeal when he turned up at Cheltenham Sales eleven days later. With some of the leading players involved in the bidding, it required a jaw dropping £410,000 to close the bidding, with Joseph O'Brien signing for the horse on behalf of leading Australian owner Lloyd Williams. My verdict on this horse is that a positive will be that he may be versatile to handle a variety of ground conditions and trips. He can win Graded novice hurdles this winter, his ability to win at the highest level may depend on his character and attitude when he is put under pressure, an aspect for now untested."**

The twenty five year old, who also has a Melbourne Cup on his CV, trained two Grade 1 winners over jumps last season, namely Edwulf and Tower Bridge, and he may have another waiting in the wings. Withdrawn from a bumper at the Punchestown Festival due to having a temperature, Dlauro is a horse we are going to be hearing plenty about this winter.

POINTS TO NOTE:
Probable Best Distance - 2 miles – 2m 4f
Preferred Going - Good/Soft
Connection's Comments: "This is a proper horse. He's very exciting and has always pleased us. He is a super jumper; he's one of the nicest horses we've ever had." Donnchadh DOYLE at Belharbour (4/2/18)

GOING:	R	W	P	TRACK:	R	W	P
Yield/Soft	1	1	0	Left-Handed	1	1	0

TRIP:	R	W	P	JOCKEY:	R	W	P
3m	1	1	0	R.James	1	1	0

DOWNTOWN GETAWAY (IRE)

5 b g Getaway (GER) – Shang A Lang (IRE) (Commander Collins (IRE))
OWNER: T.F.P.SYNDICATE
TRAINER: N.J.HENDERSON. Lambourn, Berkshire.
CAREER FORM FIGURES: 1
CAREER WIN: 2017: Dec FAIRYHOUSE Soft NHF 2m

Chomba Womba was a high-class mare who won a couple of bumpers and three times over hurdles for Mags Mullins in Ireland before being bought for £160,000 in April 2007 to join Nicky Henderson. The daughter of Fourstars Allstar subsequently won 5 of her 9 races over timber, including three Grade 2 events. Rated 150, she was a very good mare.

Downtown Getaway hails from the same family and he, too, began his racing career under the guidance of Mags Mullins. A son of Getaway, he made his debut at Fairyhouse's star studded card in early December, which features three Grade 1 contests, in the concluding bumper. Sent off 14/1 and ridden by Katie Walsh, he led with over two furlongs to run before charging clear to win by a dozen lengths. The runner-up Remastered joined David Pipe and won a bumper at Chepstow, while the third Lone Wolf won a similar contest at the Punchestown Festival. Downtown Getaway headed to the Cheltenham Sales less than a fortnight later and was bought on behalf of Nicky Henderson for £350,000. Yet to race for the Seven Barrows team, he looks a smart novice hurdle prospect for this season.

POINTS TO NOTE:
Probable Best Distance - 2m 4f – 3 miles
Preferred Going - Soft
Connection's Comments: "He's unassuming at home and just does what he has to do. He jumps well and does everything lovely. He could be a Cheltenham horse." Mags MULLINS at Fairyhouse (3/12/17)

GOING:	R	W	P	TRACK:	R	W	P
Soft	1	1	0	Right	1	1	0
				Galloping	1	1	0

TRIP:	R	W	P	JOCKEY:	R	W	P
2m	1	1	0	Ms K.Walsh	1	1	0

EL BARRA (FR)

4 br g Racinger (FR) – Oasaka (FR) (Robin Des Champs (FR))
OWNER: Mrs S.RICCI
TRAINER: W.P.MULLINS. Bagenalstown, Co.Carlow.
CAREER FORM FIGURES: 2

Rich and Susannah Ricci, who were leading owners at the Punchestown Festival with 4 winners, tasted Grade 1 success on five occasions last season. The famous pink and green silks will be sported by household names Benie Des Dieux, Douvan, Faugheen, Getabird and Min once again this winter, plus a host of exciting young talent, many of which have been purchased during the last twelve months.

One of their new recruits is the once raced ex-pointer El Barra. Declan Phelan explains: "**The O'Connor brothers, Derek and Paurick stumped up €52,000 for this racy bay athlete at the 2017 Derby Sale: being a half brother to the Cheltenham Festival placed mare Barra, plus coming from a family generously sprinkled with French jump winners, his pedigree alone makes instant appeal. He contested a late season maiden at Dromahane (Good): with Derek riding, the game plan was to educate and finish the race to effect. Held up out the rear, El Barra jumped slickly, he made rapid progress to get within four lengths of Fury Road on the run to the final fence, but with that leader galloping on strongly, El Barra was not punished in the final hundred yards, Derek happy to accept an excellent second to a quality rival, the pair having sped away from the remainder. That race gave the impression of one containing a couple of special jumping recruits, and the general groundswell of opinion was that El Barra would have easily won any ordinary maiden, he was unlucky to have run into Fury Road. That verdict was translated into money at Cheltenham May Sales as Willie Mullins forked out the sales topping price of £280,000 to acquire him for owner Rich Ricci. A leggy rather than robust horse, he has gears and he can win a bumper or two without much bother. He can develop into a Graded class 2m-2m4f chaser and will hold his own in Graded company as a hurdler. He floated on the good ground at Dromahane, it remains to be seen if he will operate on deep winter terrain."**

The Ricci's won the Cheltenham Festival bumper in 2012 courtesy of Champagne Fever but were denied the opportunity in 2016 when the unbeaten and ante-post favourite Getabird suffered an injury a month earlier, which ruled him out. Granted better fortune this time around, they may have another major contender next March.

POINTS TO NOTE:
Probable Best Distance - 2 miles
Preferred Going - Good/Soft

GOING:	R	W	P	TRACK:	R	W	P
Good	1	0	1	Left-Handed	1	0	1

TRIP:	R	W	P	JOCKEY:	R	W	P
3m	1	0	1	D.O'Connor	1	0	1

ENERGUMENE (FR)

4 b g Denham Red (FR) – Olinight (FR) (April Night (FR))
TRAINER: W.P.MULLINS. Bagenalstown, Co.Carlow.
CAREER FORM FIGURES: 1
CAREER WIN: 2018: Jan LARKHILL Good Open Mdn PTP 3m

Relegate provided Willie Mullins with a record breaking ninth win in the Cheltenham Festival bumper last March. Indeed, the head of Closutton ran five horses in the 2018 renewal and they finished first, second, third, fifth and seventh. The fifth home, Blackbow, won his only English point-to-point for Sophie Lacey before being acquired by the Co.Carlow handler.

Ireland's champion National Hunt trainer has returned to the same source and purchased the Larkhill winner Energumene. By the same sire as Mullins' nine times Grade 1 winning chaser Un De Sceaux, the gelded son of Denham Red cost €50,000 as a three year old at the Derby Sales in Ireland. Making his debut in the first division of the open maiden over three miles at the Wiltshire track, he ran out a three and a half lengths winner from Ain't No Limits under Tommie O'Brien. His winning time compared favourably with his stablemate Sebastopol who won the second division thirty five minutes later (1.40 seconds faster). It is also worth noting Energumene was only born on the 13th June 2014 and therefore wasn't even four when making his first public appearance.

When I spoke to Tom Lacey during the summer, he was adamant Energumene is a superior horse to Blackbow, which bodes well for his career under Rules. The Cheltenham Festival bumper therefore looks a realistic aim for the four year old.

POINTS TO NOTE:
Probable Best Distance - 2 miles
Preferred Going - Good/Soft
Connection's Comments: "He is the nicest four year old I have trained to date." Tom LACEY at Larkhill (7/1/18)

GOING:	R	W	P	TRACK:	R	W	P
Good	1	1	0	Right	1	1	0
				Galloping	1	1	0

TRIP:	R	W	P	JOCKEY:	R	W	P
3m	1	1	0	T.O'Brien	1	1	0

ENVOI ALLEN (FR)

4 b g Muhtathir – Reaction (FR) (Saint Des Saints (FR))
OWNER: CHEVELEY PARK STUD
TRAINER: G.ELLIOTT. Longwood, Co.Meath.
CAREER FORM FIGURES: 1
CAREER WIN: 2018: Feb BALLINABOOLA Yielding/Soft 4YO Mdn PTP 2m 4f

Cheveley Park Stud have been associated with so many top-class horses on the Flat with Group 1 winners Medicean (sadly died at the age of 21 in August), Nannina, Peeress, Persuasive, Pivotal and Russian Rhythm. The famous red, white and blue silks are set to be carried by around 20 National Hunt horses this winter with Gordon Elliott, Willie Mullins, Henry De Bromhead, Nicky Henderson, Alan King, Jimmy Moffatt, David Pipe and Sandy Thomson on their trainer's roster.

Based at Duchess Drive in Newmarket, the stud has invested heavily in new jumping stock. Beyondthestorm (£150,000), El Merano (£120,000), Lethal Steps (300,000gns), Malone Road (£325,000), Ontheropes (£240,000) and Pragmatic (£82,000) were all bought at public auctions.

Irish pointer Envoi Allen was acquired for £400,000 at the Cheltenham February Sale. Expert Declan Phelan comments: **"Sparkled at Ballinaboola (Yielding/Soft) in early February as he sluiced in by ten lengths when handled by Colin Bowe. During the race he sat close to the front running favourite (Appreciate It), jumping as if on springs: he settled the issue in a matter of strides between the last two fences and reeked of class. This race was over a trip of two and a half miles and was run at an even gallop and could be considered a fair test. Hailing from a French jumps family on the dam line, I note many of his relations were precocious and failed to train on. For now, one could not but be impressed by his first effort in public, he possesses a fine blend of speed and crisp jumping. He will make his presence felt in track Graded races and it was no surprise that in a season of big transfer fees, he commanded a price of £400,000, with Cheveley Park Stud securing him at Cheltenham February Sales. New handler Gordon Elliott will have little trouble winning a bumper and this bay gelding could be more of a 2m-2m4f specialist than a stayer, he has more natural speed than is the norm for ex-pointers."** Cheveley Park Stud may have recruited a future Grade 1 winning National Hunt horse.

At a much lesser level, Elliott has also taken charge of the former Stuart Crawford, Paul Nicholls and Jimmy Moffatt trained **WESTERN HONOUR**. The six year old was bought for £120,000 by Cheveley Park Stud having won his only Irish point in March 2017 and, having failed to trouble the judge in four starts over hurdles, he is officially rated 112. It will be interesting to see what his new trainer can achieve with the Westerner gelding.

POINTS TO NOTE:
Probable Best Distance - 2m 4f – 3 miles
Preferred Going - Good/Soft
Connection's Comments: "He is a very nice horse, he would be one of the nicer ones that we would have had. He is very straightforward with loads of scope and Barry (O'Neill) said that there is still loads of improvement to come." Colin BOWE at Ballinaboola (4/2/18)

GOING:	R	W	P	TRACK:	R	W	P
Yield/Soft	1	1	0	Left-Handed	1	1	0

TRIP:	R	W	P	JOCKEY:	R	W	P
2m 4f	1	1	0	B.O'Neill	1	1	0

EPATANTE (FR)

4 b f No Risk At All (FR) – Kadjara (FR) (Silver Rainbow)
OWNER: J.P.McMANUS
TRAINER: N.J.HENDERSON. Lambourn, Berkshire.
CAREER FORM FIGURES: 211
CAREER WINS: 2017: Sept LION D'ANGERS Very Soft NHF 1m 4f; Nov SAINT-CLOUD Heavy Grade 1 NHF 1m 4.5f

Multiple champion owner J.P.McManus has once again been busy acquiring new talent from France and is believed to have bought two potentially very smart novice hurdlers for this season. Farid, who is featured in the *French Revolution* section, is a gelded son of Diamond Boy and possible Triumph Hurdle material. Epatante has joined Nicky Henderson having won two of her three starts in AQPS bumpers for Armand Lefeuvre and she looks a very useful filly, indeed.

A half-sister to Alan King's mares' final winner Tante Sissi, she was beaten by the Guy Cherel trained Extra Noire on her debut at Saint-Malo in August. However, the daughter of No Risk At All looked a different proposition three weeks later when beating Enivrante Passion by six lengths at Le Lion D'Angers – the race, the Prix Yann Poirier, is available to watch on *Youtube*. Her final start came over two months later in the Grade 1 Prix Jacques De Vienne at Saint-Cloud and Epatante powered clear to win by three lengths in heavy ground. The runner-up Eveilduboulay had won three times beforehand, including two Grade 3 events. It was a further nine lengths back to third El Martel, who subsequently won over hurdles at Auteuil. The form looks very strong and the legendary owners snapped her up shortly afterwards.

The Dawn Run Mares' Novices' Hurdle at the Cheltenham Festival looks an obvious target as Nicky Henderson attempts to halt Willie Mullins' monopoly of the two miles one event having won all three renewals. It is likely Epatante will mix it with the geldings though as some stage and the four year old may even develop into a leading contender for the Skybet Supreme Novices' Hurdle. J.P.McManus hasn't won the Festival opener since Captain Cee Bee got the better of the same owner's Binocular in 2008.

POINTS TO NOTE:

Probable Best Distance	-	**2 miles**
Preferred Going	-	**Soft**

GOING:	**R**	**W**	**P**
Heavy	**1**	**1**	**0**
Very Soft	**1**	**1**	**0**
Good/Soft	**1**	**0**	**1**

TRACK:	**R**	**W**	**P**
Left-Handed	**2**	**2**	**0**
Right	**1**	**0**	**1**

TRIP:	**R**	**W**	**P**
1m 4f	**1**	**1**	**0**
1m 4.5f	**2**	**1**	**1**

JOCKEY:	**R**	**W**	**P**
A.Bourgeais	**2**	**2**	**0**
J.Cabre	**1**	**0**	**1**

EUXTON LANE (IRE)

6 b g Getaway (GER) – Local Hall (IRE) (Saddlers' Hall (IRE))
OWNER: TREVOR HEMMINGS
TRAINER: O.M.C.SHERWOOD. Upper Lambourn, Berkshire.
CAREER FORM FIGURES: 3572117
CAREER WINS: 2018: Mar FONTWELL Soft Mdn Hdle 2m 1f, NEWBURY Soft NH 2m 4f

Many Clouds provided owner Trevor Hemmings and trainer Oliver Sherwood, plus thousands of National Hunt enthusiasts, with some thrilling moments during his memorable career. The Cloudings gelding, who was bought as a foal for €6,000, won 12 of his 27 career starts earning £928,000 in prize-money. Rated 166 over fences, he won the Grand National in 2015 off a mark of 160, Hennessy Gold Cup (2014) and Grade 2 Argento Chase twice, including when beating King George winner Thistlecrack by a head in January 2017. Sadly, the ten year old passed away shortly after crossing the line but his memories live on.

The same connections' Euxton Lane has a long way to go before he can be mentioned in the same breath as Many Clouds but he embarks on his novice chase career with a higher hurdles rating than his illustrious former stablemate. Rated 139, the Getaway gelding was acquired for €57,000 as a three year old but he didn't make his debut until October last season. Third in a bumper at Bangor, he wasn't sighted on his first couple of outings over hurdles at Market Rasen and Doncaster. However, he showed much more next time when a running on second behind the subsequent Grade 2 Dovecote Novices' Hurdle winner Global Citizen at Southwell in February. The six year old confirmed the promise with victories at Fontwell and Newbury the following month. A seventeen lengths scorer at the former, his rider Leighton Aspell said afterwards: **"Euxton Lane is hopefully a horse with a future. He relaxes now and is showing his potential. His last run was very solid and he came home really well. He came home really well again here."** A three lengths winner at Newbury when tackling two and a half miles for the first time, he beat the 140 rated De Rasher Counter under a penalty. Allowed to take his chance in Grade 1 company at Aintree in April, he held every chance turning for home but couldn't match the likes of Black Op and Lostintranslation thereafter. However, he was far from disgraced in seventh position and the experience won't have been lost on him.

Many Clouds won twice as a novice chaser before finishing second in the Grade 2 Reynoldstown Novices' Chase at Ascot and then being brought down – by the fall of future Gold Cup winner Don Cossack – in the RSA Chase at the Cheltenham Festival. Euxton Lane, who has yet to race beyond two and a half miles, has the credentials to develop into a very useful novice chaser himself.

POINTS TO NOTE:
Probable Best Distance - 2m 4f – 3 miles
Preferred Going - Soft
Connection's Comments: "I've always liked Euxton Lane. My horses didn't fire in the first half of the season and we found a few issues, but he's a lovely looking horse who's showing us what we see at home. I don't mind if he doesn't run again - ground will dictate that - but he's going to be chasing next season and is one to keep an eye on. He's learning how to relax and is neat on his feet; he's just a lovely horse." Oliver SHERWOOD at Newbury (23/3/18)

GOING:	R	W	P
Soft	5	2	1
Good/Soft	1	0	0
Good	1	0	1

TRACK:	R	W	P
Left-Handed	6	2	2
Right	1	0	0
Galloping	2	1	0
Tight	4	1	2
Tight/Undul.	1	0	0

TRIP:	R	W	P	JOCKEY:	R	W	P
2m	3	0	2	L.Aspell	5	2	1
2m 1f	1	1	0	A.Coleman	1	0	0
2m 2f	1	0	0	W.Hutchinson	1	0	1
2m 4f	2	1	0				

FACE THE FACTS (IRE)

4 ch g Nathaniel (IRE) – Aricia (IRE) (Nashwan (USA))
OWNER: ANDREA & GRAHAM WYLIE
TRAINER: W.P.MULLINS. Bagenalstown, Co.Carlow.
CAREER FLAT FORM FIGURES: 2 - 21486210
CAREER FLAT WINS: 2017: Apr NEWBURY Good/Firm Mdn 1m 3f; Sept NEWMARKET Good/Soft Lstd 2m

Eight times Grade 1 winner Nichols Canyon sadly lost his life when falling at the fifth flight in the Christmas Hurdle at Leopardstown on the 28th December last year. The former Stayers' Hurdle winner was the first horse to beat Faugheen when beating his stablemate by half a length in the Grade 1 Morgiana Hurdle at Punchestown in November 2015. A gelding by Authorized, he won 9 of his 20 races over hurdles earning £641,333 in prize-money for his owners Andrea and Graham Wylie.

A Listed winner on the Flat, he started life with John Gosden winning three times and earning an official rating of 111 on the level. Indeed, the dual champion Flat trainer has been a good source of talent for Willie Mullins. Stratum (160,000gns) and Thomas Hobson (£240,000) also plied their trade on the Flat from Clarehaven Stables on the Bury Road in Newmarket before being snapped up by Mullins.

Nichols Canyon's connections will be hoping Face The Facts can follow in his former stablemate's hoofprints. Purchased for 100,000gns at the Newmarket Autumn Sales last October, the Nathaniel gelding was rated 104 on the Flat and, like Nichols Canyon, he was a Listed winner as a three year old. A length winner of the Listed Rose Bowl Stakes at Newmarket in September last year, he beat Nearly Caught by a length. Fifth lengths eighth to the top-class stayer Stradivarius in the Group 2 Queens Vase at Royal Ascot four months earlier, he has winning form on fast and slow ground (runner-up on heavy). Unbeaten over two miles, he stays well and, typically, he has been left off and given time to mature by Mullins since being acquired. Both Graham Wylie and Ruby Walsh are of the opinion Face The Facts should develop into a very good novice hurdler and he is likely to make his jumping bow in October/November.

POINTS TO NOTE:
Probable Best Distance - 2 miles – 2m 4f
Preferred Going - Good/Soft
Connection's Comments: "Face The Facts is genuine and lengthens. He stays well and will have learned a lot. He will go on any ground." John GOSDEN at Newbury (22/4/17)

GOING:	R	W	P	TRACK:	R	W	P
Heavy	1	0	1	Left-Handed	5	1	2
Good/Soft	2	1	1	Right	4	1	1
Good	3	0	1	Galloping	8	2	2
Good/Firm	2	1	0	Stiff/Undul.	1	0	1
Firm	1	0	0				

TRIP:	R	W	P		R	W	P
1m	1	0	1	1m 5f	1	0	0
1m 3f	1	1	0	1m 6f	3	0	1
1m 4f	2	0	1	2m	1	1	0

FEEL MY PULSE (IRE)

4 b g Stowaway - Zenaide (IRE) (Zaffaran (USA))
OWNER: GIGGINSTOWN HOUSE STUD
TRAINER: G.ELLIOTT. Longwood, Co.Meath.
CAREER FORM FIGURES: 1
CAREER WIN: 2018: Mar LISMORE Soft/Heavy 4YO Mdn PTP 3m

"Ken Parkhill is one of the more celebrated National Hunt breeders in Ireland, famous names such as Morley Street and Granville Again count amongst his past productions. Ken bred this tall and powerful bay son of Stowaway and parted with him at the 2017 Derby Sale, with the Monbeg Doyles paying €60,000 to recruit him. Team Monbeg elected to travel to Lismore for the four year old maiden to debut the youngster: this Lismore maiden has a rich tradition as in the past the likes of Florida Pearl and Best Mate used the race as their initial career springboard. From the beginning of the maiden in March on testing soft/heavy ground, Feel My Pulse was encouraged to use his long raking stride and attacking and clearing his fences in style, he soon put his four rivals in trouble. In the end he drew clear for an emphatic fifteen lengths victory and I noted it took the jockey another two furlongs after the winning post to manage to bring the horse to a stop...remarkable as for the remainder of the card, those that finished races were almost down to a walk twenty yards after the finishing post. One could find holes in the race and say that it contained only a handful of runners: yet it was the fastest race of the day (on a card including an above average Open), and it was a proper demolition job. This horse has a real racing presence and a style reminiscent of Denman, what I suppose some would call the "tank" effect. Gigginstown fielded the third in this race (next time out winner Shot To Hell), and the O'Leary team were happy to pay £330,000 at the Cheltenham March Sales to add Feel My Pulse to their Gordon Elliott army. The dam has already bred three siblings with track wins to their name and, as one would expect with Ken Parkhill mares, deeper on the family tree you locate several Graded jump winners. This is a very exciting horse, the sheer power of his gallop could lead to a stellar track future," believes Declan Phelan.

Expect Feel My Pulse to make his Rules debut in a bumper in the Autumn and then a decision is likely to be made whether he goes hurdling or remains in National Hunt Flat races for the rest of the campaign. The Gigginstown House owned youngsters are never rushed by Gordon Elliott and such patience is invariably rewarded in the long-term.

POINTS TO NOTE:

Probable Best Distance	-	**2m 4f - 3 miles**
Preferred Going	-	**Soft**

Connection's Comments: "This is a proper big, good looking horse that has always done everything right and he loved the ground out there today." Donnchadh DOYLE at Lismore (10/3/18)

GOING:	R	W	P	TRACK:	R	W	P
Soft/Heavy	1	1	0	Left-Handed	1	1	0

TRIP:	R	W	P	JOCKEY:	R	W	P
3m	1	1	0	R.James	1	1	0

FURY ROAD (IRE)

4 b g Stowaway – Molly Duffy (IRE) (Oscar (IRE))
OWNER: GIGGINSTOWN HOUSE STUD
TRAINER: G.ELLIOTT. Longwood, Co.Meath.
CAREER FORM FIGURES: 41
CAREER WIN: 2018: May DROMAHANE Good 4YO Mdn PTP 3m

"Gigginstown House Stud have already enjoyed success with Monbeg Worldwide, so it was no surprise when they moved to pay a price of €205,000 for the then unnamed sibling Fury Road at the 2017 Derby Sale: at that tariff, he was the second highest lot at the premier store sale of 2017. A real professional racehorse who oozes quality on physical inspection, Pat Doyle was given the task of teaching him the ropes as a pointer. He debuted at Stowlin (Yielding) in April and finished a close up fourth: Derek O'Connor who was aboard, was not seen at his finest, because he got caught in a pocket away from the second last, and on a tight bend to the last was not able to extract himself to mount a challenge, in effect, an inconclusive outcome. Three weeks later Pat Doyle brought Fury Road to Dromahane (Good) and this time there were no mistakes. With John Barry in the plate, the instructions were to make use of the horse: assuming the lead from the start, he travelled like a dream machine, jumping slickly, and pouring on the pace in the final mile, he burned off all his rivals bar the closing El Barra. John Barry gave Fury Road a squeeze jumping the second last and with the horse hitting top gear, he accelerated and easily held El Barra by four lengths. A top class front running display, capped off by defeating a proper rival. His half brother Monbeg Worldwide is a mudlark requiring a trip, Fury Road is a different beast. He has a high cruising speed, a rapid fire jumping technique and star quality. Pat Doyle has put some class acts through his hands in recent years, many for Gigginstown, including Death Duty and No More Heroes, and he has produced loads of previous Cheltenham Festival winners. Speaking with Pat at the Kinsale Festival at the end of the pointing season (when he was in a relaxed mood), I found it noteworthy that he mentioned that Fury Road was as good as, if not the best four year old he has ever handled. Taking into account, that Gigginstown own the horse and therefore Pat did not need to be hyping the horse for sales purposes, his high regard for the horse added to the Dromahane win recommend that Fury Road will be a proper Graded track horse, more than likely at Grade 1 level. From all the 'pointers' in *One Jump Ahead*, if you are inclined to seek one horse to follow religiously as a fan for the next five to six years, with a high potential win strike rate and the prospect of winning marquee races, then Fury Road would be the horse I would nominate you latch your loyalty to. He will be competitive from two and a half to three miles as a chaser and, in the short term, he could be a top ten bumper horse this winter, if kept to that code," believes Declan Phelan.

POINTS TO NOTE:

Probable Best Distance	-	2m 4f – 3 miles
Preferred Going	-	Good/Soft

Connection's Comments: "Things just didn't pan out right for him at Stowlin the last day. I would say that he's a very good horse." Pat DOYLE at Dromahane (20/5/18)

GOING:	R	W	P	TRACK:	R	W	P
Yielding	1	0	0	Left-Handed	1	1	0
Good	1	1	0	Right	1	0	0

TRIP:	R	W	P	JOCKEY:	R	W	P
3m	2	1	0	J.C.Barry	1	1	0
				D.O'Connor	1	0	0

GAELIK COAST (FR)

4 b g Coastal Path – Gaelika (IRE) (Pistolet Bleu (IRE))
OWNER: T.G.LESLIE
TRAINER: D.McCAIN. Cholmondeley, Cheshire.
CAREER FORM FIGURES: 1
CAREER WIN: 2018: Apr CASTLETOWN-GEOGHEGAN Soft 4YO Mdn PTP 3m

During the last twelve months, Grand National and Cheltenham Festival winning trainer Donald McCain has re-established himself as the northern powerhouse as far as National Hunt racing is concerned. The Cheshire based handler sent out 98 winners last term with his total prize-money reaching £838,514. Testify provided his stable with their first Grade 2 winner for nearly five years when winning the Altcar Novices' Chase at Haydock in January. Following the announcement during the summer that McCain will team up with leading northern rider Brian Hughes, the pair look set to form a formidable partnership this winter and beyond.

The Irish pointing scene has served McCain well over the years, most notably his triple Grade 1 winner Peddlers Cross, who was acquired for £100,000 in April 2009. Nine years later, the same connections paid £110,000 for another unbeaten pointer at the Aintree Grand National Sales. Expert Declan Phelan takes up the story: **"This French bred bay gelding sparkled when posting a winning debut at Castletown (Soft) in April. Held up for the first two miles: he was produced to challenge by Rob James on the climb to the third last. He pinged that fence and landed in front and, from that moment, he proceeded to assert and he jumped the last two fences with poise and in the end won easing down by four lengths. It was a pleasing effort, highlighting that he jumps smartly and has the talent to put a race to bed inside a furlong. Purchased by the Monbeg Doyles for €40,000 at the 2017 Land Rover store sale, this win resulted in a profit as Gaelik Coast made a reasonable £110,000 at Aintree Sales. His sire is proving a source of quality jump horses and his dam line includes several jumps and Flat winners. Possibly his medium stature prevented a bigger sales price: in the current hyper market of pointers, he could well turn out to be a fair buy. McCain is steadily improving his string following some lean years when certain owners deserted the yard. Gaelik Coast joins the stable with a similar profile to Peddlers Cross: on the northern circuits, I would advise keeping on the right side of this new recruit for the next eighteen months as he is likely to win a bumper and hurdle races and should be at least capable of winning at Grade 3 level and probably higher. I would go so far as to say this is the smartest four year old pointer McCain has acquired since that Grade 1 winner Peddlers Cross. The ground at Castletown was not too taxing, so I would imagine this horse could function on most surfaces."**

POINTS TO NOTE:

Probable Best Distance	-	**2 miles – 2m 4f**
Preferred Going	-	**Good/Soft**

GOING:	**R**	**W**	**P**	**TRACK:**	**R**	**W**	**P**
Soft	**1**	**1**	**0**	**Left-Handed**	**1**	**1**	**0**

TRIP:	**R**	**W**	**P**	**JOCKEY:**	**R**	**W**	**P**
3m	**1**	**1**	**0**	**R.James**	**1**	**1**	**0**

GOSHEVEN (IRE)

5 b g Presenting – Fair Choice (IRE) (Zaffaran (USA))
OWNER: The GROCER SYNDICATE
TRAINER: P.J.HOBBS. Minehead, Somerset.
CAREER FORM FIGURES: 535

It is well documented Philip Hobbs endured a tough spell last winter with the Minehead trainer's seasonal tally of 63 winners his lowest total since the 1992/1993 campaign. However, there is every reason to believe normal service will be resumed during the 2018/2019 season with an abundance of talent at Sandhill Stables.

My dark horse for the season is this thrice raced gelded son of Presenting. A half-brother to Vesper Bell who was runner-up in a Grade 1 novice hurdle for Willie Mullins at the Punchestown Festival in 2012, Gosheven made his debut in an eleven runner bumper in bottomless ground at Wincanton on Boxing Day. Green early on, he was soon pushed along by Micheal Nolan but responded to his urgings in the closing stages. Although beaten in excess of twenty lengths, he finished fifth with encouraging signs for the future. With that experience under his belt and sent hurdling for the first time at Kempton in March following an 81 days break, the five year old ran well to finish third behind Alan King's Chosen Path. Champion jockey Richard Johnson took over in the saddle at the Sunbury track and, having been tapped for speed when the tempo lifted after the third last, Gosheven stayed on well and was only beaten around seven lengths by the 132 rated winner. Even more improvement was forthcoming in a hotly contested novice hurdle at Cheltenham last time. Sent off 33/1 in the fourteen runner event over an extended two and a half miles in April, the Presenting gelding stayed on strongly to grab fifth position. Beaten less than seven lengths, the race was won by the 138 rated Diese Des Bieffes. Back in sixth and seventh were Onefortheroadtom (rated 137) and Grade 1 winner Poetic Rhythm (rated 145).

Bred to stay three miles, Philip Hobbs believes Gosheven is one of his leading novice hurdle prospects for this season. Improving with each start, it would be no surprise to see him develop into an Albert Bartlett Novices' Hurdle prospect. He looks to have a bright future.

POINTS TO NOTE:

Probable Best Distance	-	**2m 4f – 3 miles**
Preferred Going	-	**Good/Soft**

GOING:	R	W	P
Heavy	1	0	0
Soft	1	0	1
Good	1	0	0

TRACK:	R	W	P
Left-Handed	1	0	0
Right	2	0	1
Galloping	1	0	0
Stiff/Undul.	1	0	0
Tight	1	0	1

TRIP:	R	W	P
2m	1	0	0
2m 4f	1	0	0
2m 5f	1	0	1

JOCKEY:	R	W	P
R.Johnson	2	0	1
M.Nolan	1	0	0

IF THE CAP FITS (IRE)

6 b g Milan – Derravaragh Sayra (IRE) (Sayarshan (FR))
OWNER: PAUL & CLARE ROONEY
TRAINER: H.FRY. Seaborough, Dorset.
CAREER FORM FIGURES: 114 - 111
CAREER WINS: 2016: Nov PLUMPTON Good/Soft NHF 2m 1f: 2017: Feb TAUNTON Good NHF 2m; Oct EXETER Good NH 2m 2f; Nov BANGOR Soft NH 2m; Dec KEMPTON Good/Soft NH 2m

Noel Fehily, who returned from injury in September having spent four months on the sidelines following a fall at the Punchestown Festival, rode five Grade 1 winners last season, four of which were aboard novice hurdlers. Summerville Boy (Tolworth & Supreme NH), Black Op (Mersey NH) and Draconien (Champion NH at Punchestown) all won at the highest level and yet arguably the best novice hurdler the Irishman partnered during the 2017/2018 campaign was If The Cap Fits. Ironically, Harry Fry's unbeaten novice was ruled out of the spring Festivals due to a setback but is back in full work and could develop into a live Champion Hurdle contender.

Purchased for £30,000 as a three year old, the Milan gelding won two of his three starts in bumpers with his sole defeat coming in the Grade 2 championship event at Aintree in the spring of 2017. Sent hurdling last Autumn, he quickly established himself as one of the leading British novices, claiming three clear cut wins at Exeter, Bangor and Kempton. An eight lengths scorer first time out at the West Country track, he jumped fluently and made all to win hard held. The six year old then quickened up well to beat Solomon Grey by three and a quarter lengths at the North Wales venue under a penalty. Sent off 6/4 favourite for the opening novices' hurdle on Kempton's Boxing Day card, he beat the useful Diese Des Bieffes by five lengths conceding three pounds to Nicky Henderson's three times hurdles winner.

Rated 147, If The Cap Fits hasn't been seen since but he is likely to make his reappearance in the Grade 2 Elite Hurdle at Wincanton (10th November). If all goes to plan, the Grade 2 International Hurdle at Cheltenham (15th December) could be next and then his connections will have a fair idea over whether the Champion Hurdle is a realistic goal. Harry Fry has already been associated with one winner of hurdling's Blue Riband, namely Rock On Ruby, and one gets the impression he feels If The Cap Fits is cut from the same cloth. He is well worth backing ante-post at 33/1, which is available with most bookmakers.

POINTS TO NOTE:
Probable Best Distance - 2 miles
Preferred Going - Good/Soft
Connection's Comments: "If The Cap Fits has been improving all year. Every time when you ask him he quickens up. We have been a bit surprised with the speed he has shown in his last two runs." Jason MAGUIRE, Racing Manager, at Kempton (26/12/17)

GOING:	R	W	P
Soft	1	1	0
Good/Soft	2	2	0
Good	3	2	0

TRACK:	R	W	P
Left-Handed	3	2	0
Right	3	3	0
Stiff/Undul.	1	1	0
Tight	4	3	0
Tight/Undul.	1	1	0

TRIP:	R	W	P
2m	3	3	0
2m 1f	2	1	0
2m 2f	1	1	0

JOCKEY:	R	W	P
N.Fehily	5	4	0
Mr M.Legg	1	1	0

JERRYSBACK (IRE)

6 b g Jeremy (USA) – Get A Few Bob Back (IRE) (Bob Back (USA))
OWNER: J.P.McMANUS
TRAINER: P.J.HOBBS. Minehead, Somerset.
CAREER FORM FIGURES: 42 - F111
CAREER WINS: 2016: Oct LOUGHANMORE Soft 4YO Mdn PTP 3m: 2017: Jan PLUMPTON Heavy NH 2m 4f; Feb WETHERBY Good/Soft NH 2m 3f

Despite the fact he hasn't raced since the 21st February last year and therefore missed the whole of last season, Jerrysback retains his place in the *Top 40 Prospects*. Unbeaten in two starts under Rules for J.P.McManus and Philip Hobbs, the former Irish pointer never satisfied his trainer in his work last term, hence he never ran, plus his stable were under a cloud for the vast majority of the campaign. However, the six year old is back with the Minehead handler following a summer holiday at his owner's Martinstown Stud in Co.Limerick.

The gelded son of Jeremy sauntered to success in two modest novice hurdles at Plumpton and Wetherby during the early part of last year before a minor cut below his knee ruled him out of the rest of the campaign. We are in the dark as to how good he really is but there is no doubting his immense potential.

Trained in Ireland by Colin McKeever, he raced in four point-to-points and was an early faller at Tinahely in October 2016. Returning to the fray a week later at Loughanmore, he was an easy ten lengths winner with his handler saying afterwards: **"In the springtime the penny hadn't dropped with him as he was still a baby, but over the summer he has grown up and improved."** Acquired soon afterwards, Jerrysback was sent off 1/2 favourite for his Rules debut at Plumpton in late January 2017. While his jumping was far from fluent on occasions, he ploughed through the mud to win hard held by four and a half lengths. His rider Barry Geraghty remarked: **"Jerrysback is a big baby. He jumped well and big at times. He was clumsy at the second last. He did as much as he had to."** The six year old then made short work of nine opponents under a penalty at Wetherby less than a month later with Geraghty sitting motionless throughout. A winning margin of a length and a half grossly flattered the runner-up Plus One with previous winner Eaton Hill (had beaten Mount Mews at the same track) back in third. I was working that day for *Racing UK* and speaking to Geraghty afterwards it was evident that he feels the gelding has a big future.

Officially rated 139, it will be interesting to see if he is tested in a valuable handicap hurdle before going chasing. The Grade 3 Silver Trophy Handicap Hurdle at Chepstow (13th October) is a possibility, a race Philip Hobbs has won three times (Lacdoudal (2005), Arthurian Legend (2011) & Lamb Or Cod (2012)). His future lies over the larger obstacles and, regardless of which route he takes during the early part of this season, Jerrysback remains a horse to follow.

POINTS TO NOTE:
Probable Best Distance - 2m 4f – 3 miles
Preferred Going - Good/Soft
Connection's Comments: "Jerrysback is a gorgeous horse who did that very well. I would say he wouldn't go to Cheltenham this year, he'll probably go over fences next season." Barry GERAGHTY at Wetherby (21/2/17)

GOING:	R	W	P
Heavy	2	1	0
Soft/Heavy	1	0	1
Soft	1	1	0
Good/Soft	1	1	0
Good	1	0	0

TRACK:	R	W	P
Left-Handed	3	3	0
Right	3	0	1
Galloping	1	1	0
Tight/Undul.	1	1	0

TRIP:	R	W	P
2m 3f	1	1	0
2m 4f	1	1	0
3m	4	1	1

JOCKEY:	R	W	P
B.Geraghty	2	2	0
D.O'Connor	4	1	1

KALASHNIKOV (IRE)

5 br g Kalanisi (IRE) – Fairy Lane (IRE) (Old Vic)
OWNER: PAUL MURPHY
TRAINER: Miss AMY MURPHY. Newmarket, Suffolk.
CAREER FORM FIGURES: 1 - 11212
CAREER WINS: 2017: Mar WETHERBY Good/Soft NHF 2m; Nov WETHERBY Soft NH 2m; Dec DONCASTER Good/Soft NH 2m: 2018: Feb NEWBURY Soft HH 2m

Twenty six year old Amy Murphy is currently the youngest trainer in Newmarket and in May she moved along the Hamilton Road to Southgate Stables, which houses 60 boxes. Luca Cumani's former assistant has only been training for a couple of seasons but she already has a *Betfair* Hurdle on her burgeoning CV and came within a neck of her first Cheltenham Festival winner last March. Stable star Kalashnikov was headed close home by Summerville Boy in the Skybet Supreme Novices' Hurdle.

Rated 152 over hurdles, the giant son of Kalanisi embarks on a novice chase campaign this season with Arkle Trophy aspirations. Bought as a foal for €35,000, he is a full-brother to five times winner Kalane (preferred decent ground and flat tracks). An impressive winner of his only bumper at Wetherby in March 2017, he returned to the West Yorkshire venue for his hurdles debut last November and produced a powerful display scoring by ten lengths. He then beat Irish Prophecy by the same margin at Doncaster less than a month later before his sights were raised. Ironically, it was Summerville Boy who beat him by four lengths in the Grade 1 Tolworth Hurdle at Sandown in bottomless conditions. Given a mark of 141 as a result, Kalashnikov then became the seventh novice in the last nine years to win the *Betfair* Hurdle at Newbury. Jack Quinlan's mount took over jumping the second last and responded well to fend off the challenge of top weight Bleu Et Rouge to win by four and a half lengths. One of the leading contenders for the Festival opener as a result, the five year old led soon after the third last and still looked the most likely winner jumping the final flight. However, he couldn't withstand the late thrust of Tom George's ex-Irish gelding. **"Kalashnikov ran his heart out. He travelled very sweetly and I'm delighted with him. He's always had a turn of foot and the *Betfair* Hurdle really made a man of him. The hill stops plenty of them and maybe the combination of that and the ground may have just caught him out late on. That will be him done for the season and he'll go novice chasing next season. He can hugely improve for fences. He's a huge horse and next season will be very, very exciting,"** commented his trainer afterwards.

I spoke to Amy in late August and Kalashnikov has reportedly schooled well over fences and he will make his chasing bow at the end of October/early November. While I still have reservations about the Cheltenham hill and feel he will always prove best on a flatter track, the Arkle Trophy is the obvious target. A race such as the Grade 2 Lightning Novices' Chase at Doncaster (26th January) is a likely option en route to a return to Prestbury Park in the spring. Kalashnikov has the size and scope to make a top-class novice chaser.

A couple of unraced bumpers horses set to carry the same colours, those of Amy's father, Paul Murphy, who are worth looking out for include **CAROLE'S TEMPLAR** (3yo ch g Shirocco - Carole's Legacy) and **GENERAL ZHUKOV** (3yo ch g Shirocco - J'y Vole). Both horses are out of top-class mares and are bred to be useful. The pair arrived from Ireland in August.

POINTS TO NOTE:
Probable Best Distance - 2m - 2m 4f
Preferred Going - Good/Soft
Connection's Comments: "We've loved him from day one and he's improved every single time. You can see the size of him and how well he's jumped out of that ground. He's going to be even better over fences. This is a proper jumps bred horse with a huge future over fences. He's very good now, but we hope he'll be even better next year." Jack QUINLAN at Newbury (10/2/18)

GOING:	R	W	P	TRACK:	R	W	P
Heavy	2	0	2	Left-Handed	5	4	1
Soft	2	2	0	Right	1	0	1
Good/Soft	2	2	0	Galloping	5	4	1
				Stiff/Undul.	1	0	1

TRIP:	R	W	P	JOCKEY:	R	W	P
2m	6	4	2	J.Quinlan	6	4	2

LAURINA (FR)

5 b m Spanish Moon (USA) – Lamboghina (GER) (Alkalde (GER))
OWNER: SULLIVAN BLOODSTOCK Limited
TRAINER: W.P.MULLINS. Bagenalstown, Co.Carlow.
CAREER FORM FIGURES: F2 - 1111
CAREER WINS: 2017: Dec TRAMORE Heavy Mdn Hdle 2m: 2018: Jan FAIRYHOUSE Heavy Grade 3 NH 2m 2f; Mar CHELTENHAM Soft Grade 2 NH 2m 1f; Apr FAIRYHOUSE Soft/Heavy Grade 1 NH 2m 4f

Willie Mullins has trained 61 Cheltenham Festival winners during his career, including seven last March. Ireland's champion trainer can't have trained many easier winners at Prestbury Park than Laurina's demolition job in the Grade 2 Trull House Stud Mares' Novices' Hurdle last spring. The ex-French filly sauntered to an eighteen lengths success to maintain Mullins' strangehold on the event – he has won all three renewals of the race. Unbeaten in four runs since arriving from France, Laurina is rated 152 and looks Champion Hurdle material.

Bought as a three year old for only €8,000, she raced twice for Guillaume Macaire. A faller at Fontainebleau in April 2017, she finished runner-up at the same track a fortnight later before being purchased by Harold Kirk on behalf of Jared Sullivan. Sent off a short price favourite on her first run for her new connections at Tramore in December, she barely came off the bridle to brush aside thirteen rivals by upwards of fifteen lengths. Her rider Paul Townend commented: **"She's a bit of a tank of a mare, it's like sitting on a gelding."**An eleven lengths win in Grade 3 company at Fairyhouse swiftly followed and Laurina was immediately installed ante-post favourite for the mares' novices' hurdle at the Festival. With the assistance of stablemate Cut The Mustard at the head of the affairs during the early stages and compromising the chances of market rival Maria's Benefit, the Spanish Moon filly cruised through the race with Paul Townend sitting motionless for much of the two miles one trip. Leading between the final two flights, she powered away to register an emphatic success. Stepped up to two and a half miles for the first time in the Grade 1 Irish Stallion Farms EBF Mares' Novice Hurdle Final at Fairyhouse over Easter, the end result was the same as Laurina handed out an eight and a half lengths beating to Gordon Elliott's Lackaneen Leader. Her trainer said afterwards: **"I wouldn't be worried about trip. She could go out to three miles easily and has enough ability to do two miles."**

The five year old is set to remain over hurdles this season. Willie Mullins has won 9 of the 11 runnings of the David Nicholson Mares' Hurdle over two and a half miles at the Cheltenham Festival. However, he has also trained four of the last eight Champion Hurdle winners, including with another mare Annie Power in 2016. The Closutton yard has been responsible for some top-class mares over the years but Laurina could prove the best of the lot. The 14/1 available about her for hurdling's Blue Riband could look very big by next March.

POINTS TO NOTE:
Probable Best Distance - 2 miles – 2m 4f
Preferred Going - Soft
Connection's Comments: "She's special, very special. She's a fine big mare and has a lovely attitude as well. She's hacked up. She'd be a very good hurdler and has the size and scope to jump a fence. We've always thought she was very, very decent." Willie MULLINS at Cheltenham (15/3/18)

GOING:	R	W	P	TRACK:	R	W	P
Heavy	2	2	0	Left-Handed	3	1	1
Soft/Heavy	1	1	0	Right	3	3	0
Very Soft	2	0	1	Galloping	4	2	1
Soft	1	1	0	Stiff/Undul.	1	1	0
				Tight/Undul.	1	1	0

TRIP:	R	W	P	JOCKEY:	R	W	P
2m	1	1	0	P.Townend	4	4	0
2m 1f	1	1	0	J.Reveley	1	0	1
2m 2f	3	1	1	K.Nabet	1	0	0
2m 4f	1	1	0				

MALONE ROAD (IRE)

4 b g Kalanisi (IRE) – Zaffarella (IRE) (Zaffaran (USA))
OWNER: CHEVELEY PARK STUD
TRAINER: G.ELLIOTT. Longwood, Co.Meath.
CAREER FORM FIGURES: 1
CAREER WIN: 2018: Mar LOUGHANMORE Yielding/Soft 4YO Mdn PTP 3m

Malone Road is the second of three four year old Irish pointers Cheveley Park Stud acquired last spring/summer and sent to Gordon Elliott having shelved out £325,000 for this former Stuart Crawford trained gelding. Purchased at the Aintree Grand National Sale in April, he is related to the Brian Ellison trained pair Ravenhill Road and Windsor Avenue.

Declan Phelan comments: **"County Antrim based trainer Stuart Crawford has mined a seam of riches with progeny of four times winning mare Zaffarella: already former pointers Ravenhill Road and Windsor Avenue have advertised the family on the track after winning points for Crawford: Malone Road continued the trend and, if anything, looked the best of the lot. On Easter Saturday at Loughanmore (Yielding/Soft), he demolished a quality laden field of rivals in spectacular fashion. He quickened twice inside the final half mile, ultimately a decisive burst with 150 yards to race was sufficient to swat away his last threat Soldier At War. Assessed on this performance, including the exceptional time which he clocked, this**

bay gelding already looks like a Graded track winner in waiting. As expected, he topped the Aintree April Sale with Cheveley Park Stud stumping up £325,000 to secure his services. My general opinion on progeny of Kalanisi is that they make better hurdlers than chasers, and one wonders could this trend repeat with Malone Road: he will make a viable contender for a future Cheltenham Festival Ballymore Novices' Hurdle and can win a bumper or two, if that is he selected route this coming winter. A very loose mover, he is nicely balanced and he may be as comfortable operating on soft or good ground."

POINTS TO NOTE:

Probable Best Distance	**-**	**2m 4f – 3 miles**
Preferred Going	**-**	**Good/Soft**

Connection's Comments: "He lost a few lengths jumping on the last circuit, but he picked up going to the last which left him in front and he was as green as grass. Once Mark (O'Hare on Soldier At War) went ahead he came back on the bridle and he took off again on the run in. I told them that I thought he was better than the other two (Ravenhill Road and Windsor Avenue)." Ben CRAWFORD, winning rider at Loughanmore (31/3/18)

GOING:	R	W	P	TRACK:	R	W	P
Yield/Soft	1	1	0	Left-Handed	1	1	0

TRIP:	R	W	P	JOCKEY:	R	W	P
3m	1	1	0	B.Crawford	1	1	0

MIDNIGHT SHADOW

5 b g Midnight Legend – Holy Smoke (Statoblest)
OWNER: Mrs AAFKE CLARKE
TRAINER: Mrs SUE SMITH. High Eldwick, West Yorkshire.
CAREER FORM FIGURES: 127 – 1222U71
CAREER WINS: 2016: Dec NEWCASTLE Soft NHF 1m 6f: 2017: Oct UTTOXETER Soft NH 2m: 2018: Apr AYR Good Grade 2 HH 2m

Midnight Shadow was included in the *Stable Gossip* section of *One Jump Ahead* last season and the five year old rewarded readers by winning twice at Uttoxeter (11/1) and Ayr (25/1). His victory at the latter venue was gained in the Grade 2 Scottish Champion Hurdle. Sue Smith's gelding beat fellow novice Claimantakinforgan by a length and a quarter off a mark of 134. His sights are now set on chasing and the gelded son of Midnight Legend threats to develop into the north's leading two mile novice this season.

Bought for 28,000gns as a three year old at the Goffs UK Spring Sale at Doncaster, Midnight Shadow won a 'junior' bumper by ten lengths at Newcastle on his racecourse debut in December 2016. A creditable seventh behind Bullionaire in the sales bumper at Newbury the following spring, he was sent hurdling last Autumn. For the second consecutive season, Sue Smith's charge won on his reappearance beating Counter Shy by a length and a quarter in a two miles novice at Uttoxeter in October – Diamond Harry won the same race on his hurdles debut in 2008. Runner-up in his next three starts, including in Listed and Grade 2 company at Haydock, he returned to the Merseyside track in March for what appeared a simple task. Sent off 1/4 favourite, Danny Cook's mount was badly hampered leaving the stands with a circuit to run by the errant Keyboard Gangster and lost his rider. A respectable seventh in Grade 1 company at Aintree in April behind Lalor, he then headed to Ayr for his handicap debut and belied his odds to capture the £59,797 first prize and provide his trainer with her first Grade 2 win since Cloudy Too landed the Peter Marsh Chase at Haydock in January 2016. Midnight Shadow struck the front after the third last and, while he wasn't fluent at the final flight, the five year old dug deep to fend off Nicky

Henderson's runner-up with the previous year's winner Chesterfield flashing home in third. Danny Cook commented afterwards: **"He'll go from strength to strength, he's a big raw horse."**

It is ten years since Tidal Bay provided the North with Arkle Trophy success. Rated 140 over timber, Midnight Shadow needs to progress if he is to emulate Howard Johnson's gelding but he looks capable of developing into a live contender. Cloudy Dream was unlucky not to win the Scottish Champion Hurdle off a mark of 133 in 2016 and he chased home Altior in the Arkle Trophy eleven months later.

POINTS TO NOTE:
Probable Best Distance - 2 miles
Preferred Going - Good/Soft
Connection's Comments: "He's a very progressive young horse and will make a lovely chaser next season." Sue SMITH at Ayr (21/4/18)

GOING:	R	W	P	TRACK:	R	W	P
Heavy	3	0	2	Left-Handed	10	3	2
Soft	5	2	0	Galloping	4	2	0
Good/Soft	1	0	0	Tight	5	0	2
Good	1	1	0	Tight/Undul.	1	1	0

TRIP:	R	W	P	JOCKEY:	R	W	P
1m 6f	1	1	0	D.Cook	7	2	2
2m	8	2	2	R.Hogg	3	1	0
2m 1f	1	0	0				

NEVER ADAPT (FR)

3 ch f Anabaa Blue – She Hates Me (IRE) (Hawk Wing (USA))
TRAINER: W.P.MULLINS. Bagenalstown, Co.Carlow.
CAREER FORM FIGURES: 1
CAREER WIN: 2018: Mar COMPIEGNE Heavy Hdle 2m

Guillaume Macaire has been responsible for some top-class horses over the years. The Les Mathes based handler nurtured budding stars Azertyuiop, Laurina, Long Run, Master Minded, and the ill-fated Vautour, during the early part of their careers before being bought for lofty sums and joining high profile British and Irish stables.

Willie Mullins trained the last named to win three times at the Cheltenham Festival before he was tragically killed at home when breaking a leg in November 2016. Ireland's champion trainer has returned to Macaire during the summer and purchased the exciting three year old Never Adapt.

A daughter of Anabaa Blue, she was sent off 12/5 favourite for her hurdling debut in the Prix d'Essai des Pouliches, a newcomers' conditions event, at Compiegne in mid March. Ridden by Kevin Nabet, she ran out an impressive ten lengths winner from Francois Nicolle's Fearless Lady (sixth next time). Bought soon afterwards for a king's ransom, Mullins hasn't won the Triumph Hurdle since Scolardy prevailed in 2002, although Apple's Jade was denied by a length and a quarter by Ivanovich Gorbatov fourteen years later. Never Adapt will hopefully develop into a leading contender for next March's event. French bred horses have won three of the last four renewals.

POINTS TO NOTE:

Probable Best Distance	**-**	**2 miles**
Preferred Going	**-**	**Good/Soft**

GOING:	**R**	**W**	**P**	**TRACK:**	**R**	**W**	**P**
Heavy	**1**	**1**	**0**	**Left-Handed**	**1**	**1**	**0**

TRIP:	**R**	**W**	**P**	**JOCKEY:**	**R**	**W**	**P**
2m	**1**	**1**	**0**	**K.Nabet**	**1**	**1**	**0**

PHOENIX WAY (IRE)

5 b g Stowaway – Arcuate (Arch (USA))
OWNER: J.P.McMANUS
TRAINER: H.FRY. Seaborough, Dorset.
CAREER FORM FIGURES: 1
CAREER WIN: 2018: Jan KILLEAGH Soft 5YO Mdn PTP 3m

J.P.McManus bought Unowhatimeanharry shortly after his one and quarter lengths victory in the Grade 1 Albert Bartlett Novices' Hurdle at the Cheltenham Festival in 2016. Since then, Harry Fry's stable star has won 5 of his 9 subsequent starts, including further Grade 1 victories in the Long Walk Hurdle at Ascot and the Ladbrokes Champion Stayers Hurdle at the Punchestown Festival. Placed in the Stayers' Hurdle at Cheltenham in 2017, the ten year old could only finish tenth in the same championship event last March.

The same owner has sent the unbeaten winning Irish pointer Phoenix Way to Paul Nicholls' former assistant and, according to expert Declan Phelan, the Stowaway gelding could be very good: **"A powerful bay unit: running for the Monbeg stable, he coasted to the lead at the third last and thereafter dominated an above average maiden at Killeagh (Soft) in January. It was a race run at a proper lick and clocked the day's fastest time by over ten seconds. Plenty of point winners have since emerged from the "also rans" to give solid foundations to the form. Pedigree-wise, Phoenix Way is by the popular (recently deceased) Stowaway: the dam introduces Flat speed, as Group 1 performers Colonel Collins and Commander Collins are found in the third generation. This five year old may be the ideal mix of possessing gears added to his obvious athleticism for jumping fences allied to reserves of stamina. Bought by Timmy Hyde on behalf of J.P. McManus for £270,000 at Doncaster January Sales, I would rate him the best five year old that Monbeg had through their hands last season, and quite possibly their smartest pointer in any age group. A career as a Grade 1 or 2 chaser is on the horizon and based on Killeagh, Phoenix Way can win races from two miles to three miles and will be comfortable on most terrains. Winning an ordinary bumper should pose him little trouble."** With Unowhatimeanharry reaching the backend of his illustrious career, Harry Fry may have been sent a ready made replacement.

POINTS TO NOTE:

Probable Best Distance	**-**	**2 miles – 2m 4f**
Preferred Going	**-**	**Soft**

Connection's Comments: "He's a smart horse that does everything very easily in his work at home. He jumped very well out there today." Former trainer Donnchadh DOYLE at Killeagh (14/1/18)

GOING:	**R**	**W**	**P**	**TRACK:**	**R**	**W**	**P**
Soft	**1**	**1**	**0**	**Left-Handed**	**1**	**1**	**0**

TRIP:	R	W	P	JOCKEY:	R	W	P
3m	1	1	0	R.James	1	1	0

POGUE (IRE)

5 gr g Stowaway – Night Palm (IRE) (Great Palm (USA)
OWNER: J.TURNER
TRAINER: D.McCAIN. Cholmondeley, Cheshire.
CAREER FORM FIGURES: 21
CAREER WIN: 2018: May OLDCASTLE Good 5&6YO Mdn PTP 3m

This is the second potentially high-class Irish pointer Donald McCain acquired during the spring. A grey gelding by Stowaway, he won the second of his two races for Colin Bowe before making £100,000 at the Cheltenham May Sales.

"A unique piece of kit: a strapping big grey brute: he has a presence. His full brother, a horse called Maximillian Kolbe was most unlucky in a point during the 2016/17 season: he had a good quality Boulta maiden in the bag only to break a leg on landing over the last and that was the end of him. Pogue the next in the family line raced twice in the month of May: apparently this horse was broken late as a four year old and had only ten weeks preparation with Colin Bowe before his Dawstown (Yielding/Soft) debut: he was in the van for all of the journey for that competitive seventeen runner maiden: leading to the last, he blundered and lost momentum, and failed by a head as he rallied to try and retrieve the race. Inside a fortnight, he lost his maiden tag in style, as he motored up the finishing climb at Oldcastle (Good) to score as he wished. I like him a lot, partly because of his colour (a striking grey), and also because he is a horse with a massive stride. If he remains in one piece, I think he could be the most exciting chase recruit McCain has added to his string since his Halcyon days, costing £100,000 at Cheltenham May Sales. He will be very hard to beat in staying novice hurdles in the north: as a chaser bountiful days lie ahead and he could easily develop into a 140+ chaser: the fact that he has already raced on and handled soft and good ground add an extra dimension to his repertoire," believes Declan Phelan. His Rules debut is therefore eagerly anticipated.

POINTS TO NOTE:

Probable Best Distance	-	2m 4f +
Preferred Going	-	Good/Soft

GOING:	R	W	P	TRACK:	R	W	P
Yield/Soft	1	0	1	Left-Handed	1	1	0
Good	1	1	0	Right	1	0	1

TRIP:	R	W	P	JOCKEY:	R	W	P
3m	2	1	1	B.O'Neill	2	1	1

SAM BROWN

6 b g Black Sam Bellamy (IRE) – Cream Cracker (Sir Harry Lewis (USA))
OWNER: T.C.FROST
TRAINER: A.HONEYBALL. Mosterton, Dorset.
CAREER FORM FIGURES: 11 - 41
CAREER WINS: 2017: Feb WINCANTON Heavy NHF 2m; Mar NEWBURY Soft NHF 2m; Dec PLUMPTON Soft NH 2m 4f

Anthony Honeyball is understandably excited about the prospects of the lightly raced Sam Brown who starts his second season over hurdles with a favourable looking rating of 135. Effective over two and a half miles at present, the six year old threatens to be even better over longer distances this term.

A gelded son of Black Sam Bellamy, he boasts some very strong bumper form with victories gained at Wincanton and Newbury. A length and a quarter scorer at the former track, he beat subsequent Grade 1 winning novice hurdler Lalor (rated 149), and then accounted for the likes of Chef Des Obeaux (rated 149) and the ill-fated Dame Rose (Listed winner - conceded fifteen pounds) at the latter.

Sent hurdling last Autumn, Sam Brown reportedly had an accident at home which resulted in him damaging his spine and tail and therefore wasn't firing on all cylinders when only fourth at Wincanton in late October. Beaten nearly forty lengths by Kim Bailey's useful Red River, he was back to form following a fifty days break (treated for ulcers, too) at Plumpton in December. Making all the running under Aidan Coleman, he wasn't hard pressed to beat New To This Town (rated 125) and Delire D'Estruval (135) by upwards of seven lengths. Another minor setback curtailed the rest of his novice hurdling career but the son of Black Sam Bellamy is back in full work and his trainer is relishing tackling some decent staying handicaps with him. The Grade 3 *Betfair* Stayers' Handicap Hurdle at Haydock Park (24th November) – the race formerly known as the Fixed brush handicap hurdle – has been mooted as a possible target. Given the fact Sam Brown likes to race prominently, he looks tailormade for the extended two miles six event. Six of the last eight winners of the £100,000 event, namely Grands Crus (2010), Dynaste (2011), Gevrey Chambertin (2013), Aubusson (2014), Kruzhlinin (2016) and Sam Spinner (2017), either made all or raced handily throughout.

Regardless of whether Sam Brown heads to Merseyside in late November, there is a big prize to be won with him over hurdles this season before embarking on his chasing career next year. The softer the ground, the better for him.

POINTS TO NOTE:
Probable Best Distance - 2m 4f – 3 miles
Preferred Going - Soft
Connection's Comments: "Sam Brown is a really nice horse and his bumper form was up there with last season's best." Aidan COLEMAN at Plumpton (18/12/17)

GOING:	R	W	P	TRACK:	R	W	P
Heavy	1	1	0	Left-Handed	2	2	0
Soft	2	2	0	Right	2	1	0
Good/Soft	1	0	0	Galloping	3	2	0
				Tight/Undul.	1	1	0

TRIP:	R	W	P	JOCKEY:	R	W	P
2m	2	2	0	H.Cobden	1	1	0
2m 4f	1	1	0	A.Coleman	1	1	0
2m 5f	1	0	0	N.Fehily	1	1	0
				T.Scudamore	1	0	0

SANTINI

6 b g Milan – Tinagoodnight (FR) (Sleeping Car (FR))
OWNER: Mr & Mrs R.KELVIN-HUGHES
TRAINER: N.J.HENDERSON. Lambourn, Berkshire.
CAREER FORM FIGURES: 1 - 1131
CAREER WINS: 2017: Mar DIDMARTON Soft Mdn PTP 3m; Dec NEWBURY Soft NH 2m 4f: 2018: Jan CHELTENHAM Heavy Grade 2 NH 2m 4f; Apr AINTREE Soft Grade 1 NH 3m

"I can't wait to ride him over fences. He's going to be some horse next season. At Cheltenham, we got shuffled back. He's an out and out stayer but I don't necessarily think the ground he had today is what he wants. He's only going to get better and will mature so much more with another summer on his back. He's definitely not yet the finished article," remarked Nico De Boinville after Santini had provided Nicky Henderson with his third win in the Grade 1 Sefton Novices' Hurdle at Aintree in April. The Milan gelding is set to go chasing and looks tailormade for the RSA Chase at next spring's Cheltenham Festival.

A fifteen lengths winner of a Didmarton point-to-point for Polly Gundry in March 2017, the half-brother to Dusky Legend made an instant impression on his Rules debut for Nicky Henderson when beating stablemate Chef Des Obeaux by four and a half lengths at Newbury Winter Festival in early December. **"He jumps and he gallops, and that was terrific, but to be honest life doesn't begin for him until next year. It's all about next year, when he gets a fence,"** commented Henderson afterwards. Elevated in class, Santini reeled in Black Op close home to win a Grade 2 novice hurdle at Cheltenham's Trials meeting in late January. Jeremiah McGrath's mount took full advantage of a last flight mistake by the runner-up as the pair pulled twenty nine lengths clear of the third in testing conditions. Nicky Henderson's charge was sent off 11/4 favourite for the Albert Bartlett Novices' Hurdle at the Festival as a result, and the six year old ran well in third. Keeping on in the closing stages, he was beaten four and a half lengths behind Kilbricken Storm and stablemate Ok Corral. Well backed to gain compensation at Aintree a month later, he stayed on strongly to beat the mare Roksana by a length and a half conceding seven pounds.

Nicky Henderson has won the RSA Chase on three occasions, namely Trabolgan (2005), Bobs Worth (2012) and Might Bite (2017) and the 12/1 which is currently available about Santini for the 2019 renewal makes plenty of appeal. Granted luck, he ought to develop into a top-class staying chaser with Gold Cup aspirations one day.

POINTS TO NOTE:

Probable Best Distance	-	**3 miles**
Preferred Going	-	**Soft**

Connection's Comments: "One day he'll be over fences and you might see something quite special then. He's lovely and he's going to be even more lovely. I see him as a chaser and nothing else; he's big and bold. Santini stays, he gallops and he jumps and he's coped with ground I can't believe he wants. You'd think of him as an RSA horse next year and, if he improves as much as he did from last year to this year, then he'll be an absolute machine - he's a proper horse." Nicky HENDERSON at Cheltenham (27/1/18)

GOING:	R	W	P	TRACK:	R	W	P
Heavy	1	1	0	Left-Handed	5	4	1
Soft	4	3	1	Galloping	2	2	0
				Stiff/Undul.	2	1	1
				Tight	1	1	0

TRIP:	R	W	P	JOCKEY:	R	W	P
2m 4f	2	2	0	N.De Boinville	3	2	1
3m	3	2	1	J.McGrath	1	1	0
				W.Biddick	1	1	0

SEBASTOPOL (IRE)

4 b g Fame And Glory - Knockcroghery (IRE) (Pelder (IRE))
OWNER: BOULTBEE BROOK Ltd
TRAINER: T.LACEY. Woolhope, Herefordshire.
CAREER FORM FIGURES: 11
CAREER WIN: 2018: Jan LARKHILL Good Open Mdn PTP 3m; Apr AYR Good NHF 2m

As discussed, Tom Lacey enjoyed a personal best season last winter with 39 winners from only 158 runners, operating at a remarkable strike-rate of 25%. Jester Jet and Thomas Patrick provided the highlights by capturing big prizes at Aintree's Grand National meeting. The former joined the Herefordshire trainer with an official rating of 98 and won a novices' handicap hurdle at Wetherby on the 21st March 2017 on her first run for Lacey. The Overbury mare is now rated 142 having won 5 of her 12 starts for her current stable.

While the aforementioned stablemate Energumene won the first division of the three miles open maiden point-to-point at Larkhill in early January, Sebastopol followed suit by winning the second division by fifteen lengths under Tommie O'Brien. Left in the lead three out (Elizabeth's Wish fell), he pulverised his remaining four rivals. The gelded son of Fame And Glory, who cost €52,000 as a three year old, was withdrawn from an engagement in a bumper at Kempton (too soft) in March but he made his Rules debut a month later at Ayr's Scottish National meeting. Contesting the same bumper which the brilliant Sprinter Sacre won in 2010, Sebastopol justified strong market support to beat James Ewart's Black Pirate by three and three quarters of a length, in receipt of ten pounds. Having raced keenly early on, Aidan Coleman's mount made smooth headway with two furlongs to run before readily pulling clear. The performance oozed class.

Decent ground may always bring out the best in this unbeaten gelding who has realistic claims of achieving Graded success over hurdles this season. He couldn't be in better hands.

POINTS TO NOTE:
Probable Best Distance - 2m 4f
Preferred Going - Good
Connection's Comments: "Sebastopol is a gorgeous horse. He won his point-to-point by fifteen lengths, but he's got plenty of speed." Tom LACEY at Ayr (21/4/18)

GOING:	R	W	P	TRACK:	R	W	P
Good	2	2	0	Left-Handed	1	1	0
				Right	1	1	0
				Galloping	2	2	0

TRIP:	R	W	P	JOCKEY:	R	W	P
2m	1	1	0	A.Coleman	1	1	0
3m	1	1	0	T.O'Brien	1	1	0

SHADOW RIDER (FR)

4 ch g Martaline – Samansonnienne (FR) (Mansonnien (FR))
OWNER: J.P.McMANUS
TRAINER: W.P.MULLINS. Bagenalstown, Co.Carlow.
CAREER FORM FIGURES: 1
CAREER WIN: 2018: Feb KNOCKANARD Soft/Heavy 4YO Mdn PTP 2m 4f

"Recorded a very impressive debut win at Knockanard (Soft/Heavy) in February. Sited in second place in that competitive two and a half miles race, he quickened smartly approaching the final fence and crossed the finishing line full of beans. Few horses close out their races in such style at Knockanard, due to the concluding Towcester like climb at the end, the last horse I can recall that was as taking at this course, was subsequent Cheltenham bumper winner Missed That. A French bred chestnut who has plenty of toe, he was clumsy at a couple of the jumps. What I must relate is that he is highly strung. He was trained for this point by Colin Bowe (for owner Walter Connors) and the horse was fractious in the parade ring and they had to take him onto the course to mount the horse. He is a full brother to the 130+ Squouateur and for now appears to have more in the talent department than that sibling. What he will have in common with Squouateur is ownership: a swift private sale occurred and Shadow Rider joins Mullins for the J.P. McManus team. Mullins is a master of his profession, in Shadow Rider he has rich raw material, he will have to tweak about with this gelding to get him mentally relaxed and, if he can do so, then this horse can become a Graded winner over hurdles and fences. The extent to which he mentally matures and that temperament can be adjusted (or not) could be the deciding factor in whether he becomes a top class jumper or more of a Grade 2/3 hurdler/chaser. His stride pattern was very smooth and I expect him to cope with good ground as well as softer terrain," comments Declan Phelan.

POINTS TO NOTE:

Probable Best Distance	-	**2 miles**
Preferred Going	-	**Soft**

Connection's Comments: "He won with a bit left in the tank. He's still a bit green." Colin BOWE at Knockanard (17/2/18)

GOING:	R	W	P	TRACK:	R	W	P
Soft/Heavy	1	1	0	Right	1	1	0

TRIP:	R	W	P	JOCKEY:	R	W	P
2m 4f	1	1	0	B.O'Neill	1	1	0

THE BIG BITE (IRE)

5 b g Scorpion (IRE) – Thanks Noel (IRE) (Tel Quel (FR)
OWNER: N.T.GRIFFITH & H.M.HADDOCK
TRAINER: T.R.GEORGE. Slad, Gloucestershire.
CAREER FORM FIGURES: 1 – 10
CAREER WINS: 2017: Mar LINGFIELD Standard NHF 2m; Dec HUNTINGDON Good/Soft NHF 2m

Tom George, who sent out 47 domestic winners last season, trained two top-class novice hurdlers last season, namely Black Op and Summerville Boy, who claimed three Grade 1 victories between them. The Gloucestershire handler once again looks to be blessed with some very useful horses in the same department. New recruit Raya Time and Musselburgh bumper winner Seddon look set to win plenty of races and I have been a big fan of The Big Bite ever since he won an all-weather bumper for Tom Lacey. The gelded son of Scorpion looks a young horse with a bright future.

It is worth recalling Lacey's comments in last year's edition of *One Jump Ahead*: **"From a good family, he was an impressive winner of an all-weather bumper at Lingfield in March. I suppose his victory was a bit of a surprise because we didn't really know what to expect beforehand. Noel Fehily rode him and was very taken by him. We intended running him in the championship bumper at Aintree but he was balloted out. He still has a lot to learn and lacks experience but he is a promising young horse who has the speed for two miles."** Transferred to George last summer/Autumn, he reappeared in another bumper at Huntingdon on Boxing Day. Partnered by Ciaran Gethings, he still looked green but quickened up well inside the final couple of furlongs to beat Oliver Sherwood's Shaughnessy by two and a half lengths. It was a fair performance conceding seven pounds to the runner-up who has won since. Given a break, The Big Bite then ran respectably in the Grade 1 Cheltenham Festival bumper finishing eleventh, less than fifteen lengths behind Willie Mullins' mare Relegate.

Tom George describes The Big Bite as **"a smart young horse who will make a lovely novice hurdler."** It is hard to disagree with that. He is a fine big scopey gelding who will make a cracking chaser one day, too. Tom Lacey is rarely wrong with his assessments.

POINTS TO NOTE:
Probable Best Distance - 2m - 2m 4f
Preferred Going - Good/Soft
Connection's Comments: "The Big Bite is a lovely horse and did it well with a penalty, which is not easy. I think it was a decent bumper run at a good pace." Ciaran GETHINGS at Huntingdon (26/12/17)

GOING:	R	W	P	TRACK:	R	W	P
Standard	1	1	0	Left-Handed	2	1	0
Soft	1	0	0	Right	1	1	0
Good/Soft	1	1	0	Galloping	1	1	0
				Stiff/Undul.	1	0	0
				Tight/Undul.	1	1	0

TRIP:	R	W	P	JOCKEY:	R	W	P
2m	3	2	0	N.Fehily	2	1	0
				C.Gethings	1	1	0

THE VERY MAN (IRE)

4 b g Jeremy (USA) – Mill Meadow (IRE) (Kalanisi (IRE))
OWNER: GIGGINSTOWN HOUSE STUD
TRAINER: G.ELLIOTT. Longwood, Co.Meath.
CAREER FORM FIGURES: F1
CAREER WIN: 2018: May LOUGHANMORE Yielding 4YO Mdn PTP 3m

Dual Grand National winning handler Gordon Elliott became the first trainer to send out all three Grade 1 winners at Fairyhouse meeting in early December last season. Apple's Jade (Hatton's Grace Hurdle), Mengli Khan (Royal Bond Novices' Hurdle) and Death Duty (Drinmore Novices' Chase) all scored on Sunday 3rd December 2017.

Purchased at the Cheltenham May Sales, Elliott will be hoping this former stablemate of Malone Road will develop into a Grade 1 horse himself one day. Expert Declan Phelan reports: "**Medium sized bay gelding with a white blaze on his face: a €28,000 store acquisition for Stuart**

Crawford's yard last autumn, the horse is a member of a rank and file plain jumps family. He contested two points: his debut was inconclusive as he fell before halfway at Moira (Soft/Heavy). On his second run at Loughanmore (Yielding) in May, he was placed last of the twelve remaining runners in a tightly boxed field as they approached the third last. From there he carved his way through the pack, striking the front close to the final fence and he charged up the run in for a mighty six lengths success. The magnitude of the victory resonated at Cheltenham Sales in May as he made a price of £210,000 through the auction ring. I believe he will be an above average bumper horse, capable of winning a couple and possibly a candidate for the Cheltenham Festival bumper and he can hit the target in Graded hurdles/chases."

POINTS TO NOTE:
Probable Best Distance - 2m - 2m 4f
Preferred Going - Good/Soft
Connection's Comments: "He is a serious horse and has plenty of gears. He was unfortunate in Moira making a novicey mistake and was better there today." Stuart CRAWFORD at Loughanmore (12/5/18)

GOING:	R	W	P	TRACK:	R	W	P
Soft/Heavy	1	0	0	Left-Handed	1	0	0
Yielding	1	1	0	Right	1	1	0

TRIP:	R	W	P	JOCKEY:	R	W	P
3m	2	1	0	B.Crawford	2	1	0

TOPOFTHEGAME (IRE)

6 ch g Flemensfirth (USA) - Derry Vale (IRE) (Mister Lord (USA))
OWNER: CHRIS GILES & Mr & Mrs P.K.BARBER
TRAINER: P.F.NICHOLLS. Ditcheat, Somerset.
CAREER FORM FIGURES: 1 - 142 - F412
CAREER WINS: 2016: Mar BELCLARE Yielding/Soft Mdn PTP 3m; Dec ASCOT Good/Soft MH 2m 5f: 2018: Feb SANDOWN Soft HH 2m 7f

On the 5th June 2018 Cheltenham Gold Cup and dual Hennessy Gold Cup winner Denman passed away. The four times Grade 1 winner, who started life in Irish points for Adrian Maguire before joining Paul Nicholls and developing into one of the greatest chasers of his generation, was eighteen. His form figures at the Cheltenham Festival read 211222. Having beaten stablemate Kauto Star in that epic duel in 2008, the Presenting gelding went on to finish second in the next three Cheltenham Gold Cups. His victory in the rescheduled Challow Hurdle at Prestbury Park on New Year's Day 2006 will live long in the memory. Under Rules, he won 14 of his 24 races earning £1,141,347 in prize-money. "The Tank" was a phenomenal horse who was brilliantly handled by P.F.Nicholls and everyone at Ditcheat.

It is highly unlikely Topofthegame will ever match Denman's achievements but the big imposing Flemensfirth gelding retains his place in the *Top 40 Prospects* for the third consecutive year. Denman won the RSA Chase in 2007 and it is hoped this six year old may emulate him twelve years later in March. The ex-winning pointer made his chasing debut at Newbury last November and was still going well when crashing out at the fifth last (cross fence) in a beginners' chase won by Strong Pursuit. Paul Nicholls then decided to switch Topofthegame back to hurdles and, following a break of 65 days, he ran well in the Lanzarote Hurdle at Kempton in January. Beaten less than three lengths in fourth behind William Henry, he then appreciated the step up to nearly three miles in a Grade 3 handicap hurdle at Sandown three weeks later. Taken wide, he travelled strongly under Sam Twiston-Davies before taking over at the penultimate flight. Driven out for a length and a half win off a mark of 142, he then headed to the Cheltenham Festival for the Coral Cup.

Raised eight pounds, he coped with the drop in trip and produced the performance of his career thus far. In front when jumping the last flight, he was run out of it close home by Willie Mullins' Bleu Berry and was denied by a neck. His proud trainer said afterwards: "**It's frustrating but it was an awesome run. Topofthegame won't run again this season but he'll be really exciting when he goes chasing in the autumn.**" Rated 154 over hurdles, it is hoped that experience gained over hurdles last season will stand him in good stead for this year. Topofthegame has the physique and engine to develop into a top flight staying chaser.

POINTS TO NOTE:
Probable Best Distance - 3 miles
Preferred Going - Good/Soft
Connection's Comments: "He's very much the future. He's bigger than Denman; he's huge, enormous, but just needs a bit of time. He stays forever and is the sort of horse who might end up in a National. He's very green and hasn't had many runs; mentally he's a great big baby, but he's got a lot of talent. He'll be a good chaser. I'm not saying he'll win a Gold Cup, but who knows where he'll end up." Paul NICHOLLS at Sandown (3/2/18)

GOING:	R	W	P
Soft	5	1	3
Yield/Soft	1	1	0
Good/Soft	2	1	0

TRACK:	R	W	P
Left-Handed	3	0	1
Right	5	3	2
Galloping	4	2	1
Stiff/Undul.	2	0	1
Tight	1	0	1

TRIP:	R	W	P
2m 3f	1	0	1
2m 4f	1	0	0
2m 5f	3	1	2
2m 6f	1	0	0
2m 7f	1	1	0
3m	1	1	0

JOCKEY:	R	W	P
S.T-Davies	5	2	2
S.Bowen	1	0	1
N.Fehily	1	0	0
R.James	1	1	0

UMNDENI (FR)

4 bb g Balko (FR) – Marie Royale (FR) (Turgeon (USA))
OWNER: ST QUINTON, D.L.WHATELEY & SYDER
TRAINER: P.J.HOBBS. Minehead, Somerset.
CAREER FORM FIGURES: 1
CAREER WIN: 2018: Apr WARWICK Good/Soft NHF 2m

Colin Tizzard is hoping dual Grade 1 runner-up Vision Des Flos (rated 148) develops into a top-class novice chaser this season having chased home Lalor and Draconien at Aintree and Punchestown respectively last spring.

The five year old's full-brother Umndeni looks a horse of similar potential, if his bumper win at Warwick last spring is anything to go by. Bought by Aiden Murphy for €175,000 as a three year old at the Goffs Land Rover Sale in June 2017, the gelded son of Balko made his debut in a seventeen runner event at the Midlands track at the end of April. Sent off 3/1 favourite, Philip Hobbs' charge led with half a mile to travel before staying on too strongly for previous winner Morning Vicar. Admittedly, Richard Johnson's mount was receiving twelve pounds from Nicky Henderson's runner-up, but I will be surprised if the form doesn't work out. The third, Tedham, is a useful sort and one to follow from Jonjo O'Neill's yard. The winning time compared favourably with the second division of the bumper run on the same card, too.

The four year old has reportedly done well during the summer and he will be campaigned in two mile novice hurdles this season. His full-brother finished sixth in the Grade 1 Ballymore Novices' Hurdle at Cheltenham over two miles five but his best performances have been over the minimum trip. Umndeni may follow suit and develop into a high-class novice hurdler himself.

POINTS TO NOTE:
Probable Best Distance - 2m – 2m 4f
Preferred Going - Good/Soft
Connection's Comments: "I'm very pleased with that. Umndeni is a horse who has always shown plenty at home and it was a lovely introduction. He'll be put away now and go novice hurdling next season." Philip HOBBS at Warwick (26/4/18)

GOING:	R	W	P	TRACK:	R	W	P
Good/Soft	1	1	0	Left-Handed	1	1	0
				Tight/Undul.	1	1	0

TRIP:	R	W	P	JOCKEY:	R	W	P
2m	1	1	0	R.Johnson	1	1	0

UPPERTOWN PRINCE

6 b g Strategic Prince – Tarrawarra (IRE) (Kayf Tara)
OWNER: T.G.LESLIE
TRAINER: D.McCAIN. Cholmondeley, Cheshire.
CAREER FORM FIGURES: 61 - 12214
CAREER WINS: 2017: Feb BELHARBOUR Yielding Mdn PTP 3m; Dec BANGOR Soft NH 2m 3f: 2018: Mar AYR Soft NH 2m 4f

Bought for £35,000 at the Cheltenham Sales in February 2017 having won the second of his two Irish points for Donnchadh Doyle, the gelded son of Strategic Prince looks well bought having developed into a smart staying novice hurdler for Donald McCain last winter. Officially rated 140 over timber, his trainer had no hesitation in nominating the six year old as his horse to follow for the winter ahead now his attentions are turned to chasing.

A seven lengths winner from another former Irish pointer The Dellercheckout (£260,000) at Bangor in early December on his hurdles and Rules bow, Uppertown Prince finished runner-up under a penalty at the same track a month later before chasing home Chef Des Obeaux in bottomless ground in Grade 2 company at Haydock in February. He then barely came off the bridle to account for three rivals over two and a half miles at Ayr before his sights were raised once again at Aintree's Grand National fixture. Sent off 40/1 in the Grade 1 Sefton Novices' Hurdle over three miles, he ran a cracker to fill fourth position behind the potentially top-class Santini. Beaten around ten lengths, McCain is understandably excited about the prospect of unleashing Uppertown Prince over fences.

Expect him to reappear over two and a half miles before stepping up in distance as the season progresses. Uppertown Prince looks set to develop into one of the north's leading staying novice chasers.

POINTS TO NOTE:
Probable Best Distance - 2m 4f +
Preferred Going - Soft

GOING:	R	W	P	TRACK:	R	W	P
Heavy	2	0	2	Left-Handed	7	3	2
Soft	4	2	0	Galloping	1	1	0
Yielding	1	1	0	Tight	4	1	2

TRIP:	R	W	P	JOCKEY:	R	W	P
2m 3f	1	1	0	B.Hughes	2	1	0
2m 4f	1	1	0	W.Kennedy	3	1	2
2m 7f	2	0	2	J.O'Rourke	1	1	0
3m	3	1	0	P.J.O'Neill	1	0	0

VISION D'HONNEUR (FR)

4 b g Vision D'Etat (FR) - Hembra (FR) (Croco Rouge (IRE))
OWNER: GIGGINSTOWN HOUSE STUD
TRAINER: G.ELLIOTT. Longwood, Co.Meath.
CAREER FORM FIGURES: 1
CAREER WIN: 2018: Apr FONTAINEBLEU Very Soft 1m 7f

Dortmund Park, who was featured in last year's *Top 40 Prospects*, won three of his six races over hurdles for Gigginstown House Stud and Gordon Elliott last season, culminating in Grade 1 glory at the Punchestown Festival in April. The gelded son of Great Pretender was bought for €230,000 at the Arqana Summer Sale in July 2017 having won both his French bumpers for Fabrice Foucher.

The same connections paid €350,000 for a similar type, Vision D'Honneur, at the Arqana Grand Steeple Auteuil Sale in May. An unbeaten half-brother to Noel Meade's 136 rated chaser Le Martalin, he was trained in France by Robert Collet. The Vision D'Etat gelding was an impressive three and a half lengths winner of the Prix Colonel Bruno De Galbert at Fontainebleu in April, a race restricted to four and five year olds.

Trips around two and a half miles are expected to suit Vision D'Honneur, although his older sibling has gained four career wins over the minimum trip. An exciting addition to Gordon Elliott's yard, the four year old can take high ranks amongst this season's novice hurdlers.

POINTS TO NOTE:
Probable Best Distance - 2 miles - 2m 4f
Preferred Going - Good/Soft
Connection's Comments: "He is a gorgeous stamp of a horse who won very well on his sole start. I came to see him three weeks ago and was very impressed by him, then Gordon (Elliott) and Eddie (O'Leary) saw him this morning and instantly fell in love with him. We think he can develop into a very good horse." Mags O'TOOLE, Bloodstock Agent at the Arqana Sale in July

GOING:	R	W	P	TRACK:	R	W	P
Very Soft	1	1	0	Left-Handed	1	1	0

TRIP:	R	W	P	JOCKEY:	R	W	P
1m 7f	1	1	0	L.Philipperon	1	1	0

MY HORSE TO FOLLOW FOR 2018/2019

Leading Owner

RICH RICCI

ANNAMIX

Racing Manager

JOE CHAMBERS

SALDIER

OWNERS' ENCLOSURE

JARED SULLIVAN

Harry FRY

EROS (FR) 4 b g Diamond Boy (FR) – Madame Lys (FR)
An unraced half-brother to Messire Des Obeaux and Bouvreuil, he was due to run last season but kept tying up at home. Harry (Fry) and Noel (Fehily) both like him and he should be ready to run in a bumper in the Autumn.

Nicky HENDERSON

CHEF DES OBEAUX (FR) 6 b g Saddler Maker (IRE) – O Dame De Gene (FR)
He was a three times winner over hurdles last season, including a Grade 2 event at Haydock in February. However, he disappointed at both Cheltenham and Aintree and it is possible his win at Haydock in bottomless ground left its mark and took the edge off him. We may therefore give him more time between his races this season. A three miles chaser in the making, he will go straight over fences.

DAPHNE DU CLOS (FR) 5 b m Spanish Moon (USA) – Katarina Du Clos (FR)
We are looking forward to seeing her back in action having missed the whole of last season. She looked a very good filly when winning a Listed bumper at Newbury a couple of seasons ago. Unfortunately, she picked up an injury soon afterwards but she is fine now and has developed into a big strong mare. She has had a wind operation since her last run and novice hurdles will be on her agenda. She is a good mare.

DARIUS DES BOIS (FR) 5 b g Great Pretender (IRE) - Palafixe (FR)
A big horse, he benefited from a wind operation last season showing progressive form in the spring. Stepped up to three miles for the first time over hurdles, he won at Newbury and was then unlucky not to follow up at Ayr's Scottish National meeting having made a mistake at the last. Still a young horse, who ran in a couple of Irish point-to-points, he will go novice chasing.

DIESE DES BIEFFES (FR) 5 gr g Martaline (FR) - Chanel Du Berlais (FR)
I must admit he surprised me last season winning three times over hurdles and running well in both the Lanzarote Hurdle at Kempton and the Martin Pipe Conditional Jockeys' Hurdle at the Cheltenham Festival. He produced a very good performance to win at Cheltenham in April appreciating the better ground. Nicky (Henderson) has operated on his wind since and the plan is to send him over fences. He will hopefully develop into a decent novice chaser.

DOUX PRETENDER (FR) 5 b g Great Pretender (IRE) - Lynnka (FR)
He has only raced three times over hurdles winning at Towcester in May, which means he remains a novice for this season. Still quite weak last year, Noel (Fehily) tells me he has really strengthened up during the summer so hopefully he will progress because we have always thought a bit of him.

TURTLE WARS (FR) 5 b g Turtle Bowl (IRE) - Forces Sweetheart
He won over hurdles at Huntingdon in January before finishing fifth in the EBF Final at Sandown. I thought he was unlucky not to finish closer having travelled strongly for a long way. Third in his only Irish point, he will go chasing and could run in a novices' handicap off his mark of 122. I think he's fairly treated.

Willie MULLINS

CHANTE NEIGE (FR) 4 b f Martaline (FR) - Russian Taiga (FR)
Third on her only start over hurdles at Auteuil (Stormy Ireland finished second) when trained by Guillaume Macaire in France, she had an injury last season which kept her off the track. However, Willie (Mullins) has always liked her and we think she is very good. Back in work now, she will be campaigned in mares' novice hurdles and it would be nice to think she could end up at Cheltenham in March.

DENTO DES OBEAUX (FR) 5 gr g Balko (FR) - Quenta Des Obeaux (FR)
Fifth on his only run over hurdles in France a couple of years ago, he has yet to run for us but we have high hopes for him. Willie (Mullins) nearly ran him during the spring/summer but decided to give him more time. We think he could be smart.

DONT HESITATE (FR) 5 b m Diamond Boy (FR) - Quibble (FR)
She ran in eight French bumpers winning twice, including a Grade 3 at Maisons-Laffitte last year. Everytime she was ready to run last season she seemed to pick up a problem but I know Willie likes her a lot. She will be contesting mares' novice hurdles and she could be useful.

DORRELLS PIERJI (FR) 5 br g Coastal Path - Playa Pierji (FR)
A winner of his only point-to-point, he had an injury in the first half of last season hence he didn't run for us until April. Disappointing in his first couple of starts at Tramore and Punchestown, he has come good since winning twice. Both his victories at Wexford and Galway were achieved on better ground, which I think has made a big difference. He carried a penalty at Galway and the winning time was very good, too. It won't be long before he goes hurdling.

DUC DES GENIEVRES (FR) 5 gr g Buck's Boum (FR) - Lobelie (FR)
Placed in Grade 1 company at Naas and Leopardstown on his first two runs for us, he then finished fifth in the Ballymore Novices' Hurdle at the Cheltenham Festival. His form tailed off thereafter at Fairyhouse and Punchestown but we found he was struggling with his wind. He has therefore undergone a breathing operation during the summer and, while no decision has been made, there is every chance he will go novice chasing.

EGLANTINE DU SEUIL (FR) 4 b f Saddler Maker (IRE) - Rixia Du Seuil (FR)
She won her only start in an APQS bumper in France in October and we bought her the following month at the Arqana Sale. Given plenty of time by Willie (Mullins), she won in good style on her hurdling debut at Sligo in August and I know they are excited by her. Her homework has always been very good and she will continue in mares' novice hurdles.

EOLINE JOLIE (FR) 4 b f No Risk At All (FR) - Jolie Catty (FR)
She has been disappointing since arriving from France, where she won on her hurdles debut at Auteuil. Well beaten at Fairyhouse and Punchestown in the spring, she finished fourth at Ballinrobe last time. Willie has operated on her wind since and hopefully that will make a difference. No longer a novice, she will stay over hurdles this season.

ESTELLE MA BELLE (FR) 4 ch f Air Chief Marshall (IRE) - Ozalid (FR)
She is a massive filly measuring seventeen hands. Twice a winner over ten furlongs on the Flat in France, she wasn't disgraced in a Group 2 at Saint-Cloud last time. Unable to run last season due to a setback, I know Harold Kirk, who bought her, is keen on her. She will go novice hurdling.

FAST BUCK (FR) 4 b g Kendargent (FR) - Juvenil Delinquent (USA)
Bought at the Newmarket Horses in Training Sale last Autumn, Willie always gives the three year olds he buys at that time of year plenty of time with a view to going hurdling the following season. Twice a winner over a mile and a half on the Flat in France, he has developed into a big strong four year old and they seem very pleased with him. Two mile novice hurdles are the plan for him.

GETAREASON (IRE) 5 ch g Getaway (GER) - Simple Reason (IRE)
Runner-up in his only Irish point-to-point, he won a bumper at Downpatrick in the spring before finishing third at the Punchestown Festival. Having finished second on his hurdles debut at the Galway Festival in August, he won well next time at Tramore and Ruby (Walsh) liked him. He will continue over hurdles this season but will make a chaser in the long-term.

HOLIDAY WINNER (FR) 5 b m Vision D'Etat (FR) - Holiday Maker
Purchased at the Arqana Sale in May last year, she was due to run over hurdles during the summer but was held up due to a minor problem. She won twice over middle distances on the Flat in France and they seem to think she is quite smart and a good prospect for mares' novice hurdles.

LAURINA (FR) 5 b m Spanish Moon (USA) - Lamboghina (GER)
She is in good form and we are hoping she will develop into a Champion Hurdle contender. Unbeaten in all four starts since arriving from France, she won the Grade 2 mares' novice hurdle at Cheltenham by eighteen lengths and then followed up in a Grade 1 mares' event at Punchestown over two and a half miles. She is a big mare who has done well during the summer and really filled out. We think she is very good and open to further improvement.

REAL STEEL (FR) 5 b g Loup Breton (IRE) - Kalimina (FR)
Runner-up over hurdles in France, he looked good when winning at Thurles in November on his first run for us. He was then in the process of running well when falling at the last in a Grade 1 novice hurdle at Leopardstown over Christmas. His form tailed off thereafter but we found he had an infection, which has been treated with, by antibiotics. We always thought he was very good so hopefully he can show his true form this season. I don't know whether he will remain over hurdles or go chasing.

SAGLAWY (FR) 4 b g Youmzain (IRE) - Spasha
A decent horse on the Flat in France running well in Listed and Group races, he developed into a useful juvenile hurdler last season. Twice a winner, he won a Grade 2 at Fairyhouse over Easter before finishing third in a Grade 1 at Punchestown less than a fortnight later. He then raced twice at Auteuil and I think the plan is for him to stay over hurdles this season. Hopefully, he will continue to progress.

STORMY IRELAND (FR) 4 b f Motivator - Like A Storm (IRE)
A useful filly, but she is inclined to pull hard and race keenly. A wide margin winner at Fairyhouse in December, she was in the process of running well when falling at the last in the Triumph Hurdle at Cheltenham. She made all to win a Listed mares' hurdle at Killarney in May before running a good race in a Grade 3 hurdle at Auteuil over two miles three finishing third. Quite tricky, things have to go right for her but she has plenty of ability and, in all likelihood, she will remain over hurdles for now.

Olly MURPHY

CHARMING ZEN (FR) 6 gr g Youmzain (IRE) - Nioumoun (FR)
I sent three horses to Olly (Murphy) during the summer, including this dual hurdles winner. Disappointing in two runs last season at Kempton and Exeter, he had a few problems and we didn't get a clear run with him. He is likely to go novice chasing this season.

DONCESAR DE PRETOT (FR) 5 gr g Saddler Maker (IRE) - Kobila (FR)
Yet to run for us, he was placed in all three starts over hurdles in France and I know Noel (Fehily) likes him. He has ridden him at home and is keen on him. He will be running in novice hurdles this season.

MONBEG ZENA (IRE) 6 ch m Flemensfirth (USA) - Mandys Gold (IRE)
We bought her at the Cheltenham Festival Sale last year having won her only point-to-point in Ireland by four lengths. Unfortunately, she picked up an injury and couldn't race last season. She is fine now though and has joined Olly with a view to going mares' novice hurdling.

JARED'S HORSE TO FOLLOW: CHANTE NEIGE

TALKING TRAINERS

Kim BAILEY

Stables: Thorndale Farm, Withington Road, Andoversford, Cheltenham, Gloucestershire.
2017/2018: 47 Winners / 292 Runners 16% Prize-Money £472,646
www.kimbaileyracing.com

ALFIE CORBITT (IRE) 5 b g Arakan (USA) – Millanymare (IRE)
A new arrival, he was bought at the Doncaster May Sales and I am delighted to be training for Highclere Thoroughbred Racing for the first time. Very much a chaser in the making, he ran in three Irish points for the recently retired Jim Culloty and, having been placed on his first couple of runs, he won easily last time. It is a case of so far so good and I hope he will make an impact in novice hurdles this season.

ANOTHER VENTURE (IRE) 7 ch g Stowaway – Hard Luck (IRE)
Showed progressive form over fences last season winning at Chepstow and Hereford before finishing third in a Listed chase at Ascot. I hope he will continue to improve and win a decent handicap this winter. He stays well and the softer the better as far as the ground is concerned. There are plenty of good three mile handicap chases we can aim him at.

BALLETICON (IRE) 4 br g Arakan (USA) – Miss Garbo (IRE)
A nice young horse who I was expecting to run very well on his debut in a bumper at Southwell during the spring and he finished second. The form has been franked with the third winning since. It is possible he may have another run in a bumper but I think he's more likely to go straight over hurdles, starting off over two miles. I like him.

CHARBEL (IRE) 7 b g Iffraaj – Eoz (IRE)
He's in good form at home. Despite running well in the Tingle Creek Chase at Sandown in December, he endured a somewhat frustrating season because he wants decent ground and never got his conditions. A faller in the Queen Mother Champion Chase, I think he will benefit from stepping up in trip this time around. It is something I've wanted to do for a while.

CIRANO DE SIVOLA (FR) 6 gr g Vendangeur (IRE) – Wild Rose Bloom (FR)
Yet to run for us, I don't know much about him except he has a good level of form. A winner of a point and a bumper, plus he was third on his only start over hurdles, he had multiple fractures to a leg when he first arrived and has been off for over a year. He is 100% now though and looks a nice horse for novice hurdles this season.

CLOONE LADY (IRE) 6 b m Milan – Cloone Leader (IRE)
Aiden Murphy bought her at the Cheltenham February Sale having won the last of her four runs in Irish points. She didn't show much on her first two starts for us over hurdles on soft ground but then performed a lot better on good ground at Huntingdon in April, which was encouraging. We may send her mares' novice chasing and she will have no trouble staying further than two and a half miles. Indeed, I think she will stay any trip.

COMMODORE BARRY (IRE) 5 br g Presenting – Specifiedrisk (IRE)
A nice looking horse and a very good jumper, he was runner-up in an Irish point-to-point before showing progressive form over hurdles for us last season. A winner at Worcester in May and rated 120, he is eligible for novice events but we also have the option of going chasing at some stage. Suited by two and a half miles, he wants a trip.

CRESSWELL LEGEND 7 b g Midnight Legend - Cresswell Willow (IRE)
A point and bumper winner, he was progressive over hurdles last season winning his first three starts at Ludlow (twice) and Musselburgh before finishing runner-up in a Pertemps qualifier at the latter track in February. He has a preference for racing right-handed and the plan is to send him chasing. We will start him off over two and a half miles but we know he stays three.

DANDY DAN (IRE) 5 b g Midnight Legend - Playing Around
Despite being immature and backward, he has done well winning a bumper and first time out over hurdles. Placed since, we sent him chasing in the spring finishing second at Warwick and third at Stratford. A very good jumper, he stays three miles and likes good ground.

DIAMOND GAIT 5 b m Passing Glance - Milliegait
A well bred mare who won a bumper on her debut at Warwick before finishing runner-up in a Listed event at Huntingdon on Boxing Day. She found the ground too quick on her final start at Cheltenham. We have schooled her over hurdles and she jumps nicely. The plan is to aim her at mares' only novice hurdles over two miles to begin with.

DIVA RECONCE (FR) 5 b m Kap Rock (FR) - Kruscyna (FR)
An impressive winner on her debut in a bumper at Warwick the previous season, she ran well on her hurdles debut at Ludlow before Christmas finishing second. Unfortunately, she banged her knee in the process and hasn't run since. We have given her plenty of time off and she is back cantering now. She is a nice mare who will resume in novice hurdles.

EL PRESENTE 5 b g Presenting - Raitera (FR)
Even though he won on his hurdles debut at Huntingdon and ran some good races in defeat thereafter, he was still very backward last season and can only improve. There is every chance we will send him novice chasing with three miles being his trip.

FIRST FLOW (IRE) 6 b g Primary - Clonroche Wells (IRE)
Back in work, he looks very well but we haven't decided whether to stay over hurdles or go chasing with him. We will school him over fences and then make a decision. If he takes to it, then we will almost certainly go novice chasing. A three times winner over hurdles last season, including the Grade 2 Rossington Main Novices' Hurdle at Haydock in January, things didn't go to plan in the Supreme Novices' Hurdle at Cheltenham. He loves soft ground and, although he is effective over two miles, he will stay further.

HES NO TROUBLE (IRE) 5 b g Scorpion (IRE) - She's No Trouble (IRE)
A nice looking horse who I have been very pleased with since arriving in the spring. Aiden Murphy bought him at the Cheltenham May Sale having won his only Irish point a month earlier. We haven't done a lot with him but I am hoping he will develop into a decent novice hurdler.

IMPERIAL AURA (IRE) 5 b g Kalanisi (IRE) - Missindependence (IRE)
I have always liked him and it didn't surprise me when running well on his debut at Kempton finishing third. He confirmed that promise by winning next time at Ludlow and, even though he has been running well on soft ground, I think he will benefit from racing on a sounder surface. He jumps very well and will go novice hurdling.

MASTEEN (FR) 6 b g Astarabad (USA) - Manson Teene (FR)
Yet to run for us, he finished runner-up in his only bumper at Sedgefield last December before we bought him shortly afterwards. A big horse and very much a chaser in the making, I can't believe Sedgefield would have played to his strengths. We intended running him last season but the ground dried out so we left him off. He gives the impression he will stay well.

MINELLA WARRIOR (IRE) 6 b g King's Theatre (IRE) – Bobbi's Venture (IRE)
A promising horse who finished second in his only Irish point before we bought him. Eighth in a Listed bumper at Ascot the previous season, we were horrified when he got beaten next time at Wetherby but the horse who beat him was Kalashnikov, which represents very strong form. He was then sidelined with a splint problem so we didn't bring him back until May to ensure he was a novice for this season. I was delighted with his win at Warwick and he will continue in two and a half miles plus novice hurdles.

MON PALOIS (FR) 6 b g Muhaymin (USA) – Gastinaise (FR)
Compact, he won twice over hurdles at Ffos Las and Worcester but I think he will improve over fences. He stays well and the plan is to go novice handicap chasing.

MR GREY SKY (IRE) 4 gr g Fame And Glory – Lakil Princess (IRE)
A lovely unraced four year old who was due to run in the spring but the ground changed. He has a good pedigree and is a nice horse to run in a bumper in the Autumn.

MR MACHO (IRE) 6 b g Flemensfirth (USA) – Accordian Rules (IRE)
I have been pleased with him because he has had issues. Sixth on his debut in a bumper at Bangor in the spring, he ran well next time when finishing second on his first start over hurdles at Southwell. He will continue in novice hurdles over a trip.

NEWTIDE (IRE) 5 br g Getaway (GER) – C'Est Fantastique (IRE)
Big and backward last year, he has yet to run for us having been bought at the Punchestown Festival Sale in the spring of 2017. Runner-up in his only point-to-point for Colin Bowe, his form looks strong because the winner (Onefortheroadtom) developed into a 137 rated novice hurdler for Harry Fry last season. He will go novice hurdling.

PEEPING TOM (IRE) 5 b g Morozov (USA) – Orcadian Dawn
A four lengths winner of his third and final Irish point for Shark Hanlon, we bought him cheaply at the Doncaster Spring Sale. It is early days but hopefully he will make an impression in novice hurdles this winter.

POND ROAD (FR) 4 ch g No Risk At All (FR) – Califea (FR)
Unraced, I liked him last year and we were aiming him at the Goffs UK Spring Sale bumper at Newbury in March but the ground was too soft. He is a nice horse who will start off in a bumper in the Autumn.

RED RIVER (IRE) 5 ch g Beneficial – Socker Toppen (IRE)
A useful novice hurdler last season, I think he will benefit from going chasing this time around. Runner-up in his only point-to-point, he was an impressive winner on his first start over hurdles at Wincanton but struggled with his breathing next time when finishing third in a Grade 2 novice at Sandown in December. We therefore operated on his wind and he showed the benefit for it by winning at Musselburgh in February. We were aiming him at the Albert Bartlett Novices' Hurdle at Cheltenham but the ground wasn't suitable and you need to be 100% and everything in your favour at the Festival. Anything he achieved over hurdles was always going to be a bonus and his schooling over fences has gone well. Three miles is his trip.

RHAEGAR (IRE) 7 b g Milan – Green Star (FR)
Despite winning twice last season, including over hurdles at Chepstow, his form was in and out. He looks a different horse now though and there is no doubt he has plenty of ability. Three miles is his trip and he will go over fences. In terms of ground, he won a bumper on good to soft and his hurdles win was gained on heavy, so he appears to be versatile.

ROCKY'S TREASURE (IRE) 7 b g Westerner – Fiddlers Bar (IRE)
A half-brother to Double Shuffle, he is a former point winner and is another who will go novice chasing. Third in a Listed handicap hurdle at Cheltenham in November, I thought he ran well at Warwick last time in the spring. He is a three miler but doesn't want heavy ground.

ROSE TO FAME 4 b f Fame And Glory – Cinderella Rose
She is a nice filly from a very good family and I like her. A full-sister to Twelve Roses, she ran in a couple of bumpers and wasn't beaten far at Ludlow last time. I have been very pleased with her during the summer and I think we will see a big difference this season. We will try and win a bumper with her because it would help her pedigree.

SEA STORY 5 b m Black Sam Bellamy (IRE) – Charlottes Webb (IRE)
A dual bumper winner at Ludlow and Catterick, she did us proud last season and I must admit it surprised us a bit. She has changed a lot during the summer and is a nice mare for novice hurdles over two and a half miles.

SILVER KAYF 6 gr g Kayf Tara – Silver Spinner
He had a good season over hurdles winning at Huntingdon and Ludlow and appears to be suited by flat tracks. We haven't schooled him yet but the intention is to send him novice chasing over two and a half to three miles.

STATION MASTER (IRE) 7 b g Scorpion (IRE) – Gastounette (IRE)
He started off well last season winning staying novice hurdles at Warwick and Southwell but his form tailed off in the second half of the campaign. He stays forever and, having already won a couple of point-to-points in the UK, we are going to send him chasing. In terms of ground, he wants some ease.

SUBWAY SURF (IRE) 4 b f Milan – Dante Rouge (IRE)
I think she is a very nice filly who I like. Successful in her only Irish point, Aiden Murphy bought her at the Cheltenham May Sale. She could go for a mares' bumper before we send her hurdling.

THE LAST SAMURI (IRE) 10 ch g Flemensfirth (USA) – Howaboutthis (IRE)
He ran some good races last season finishing runner-up in the Becher Chase, fourth in the Cotswold Chase and third in the Cross Country chase at the Cheltenham Festival. I need to speak to his owners regarding future plans but there is the option of going hunter chasing with him.

THIBAULT 5 b g Kayf Tara – Seemarye
Third on his debut at Ludlow, he finished fourth next time at Southwell and has had a wind operation since. I am expecting him to improve when he goes novice hurdling.

TIME FOR ANOTHER (IRE) 5 ch g Shantou (USA) – Borleagh Blonde (IRE)
Still weak and backward last season, I thought he ran well on his only start in a bumper at Huntingdon in the spring. A horse with ability, he will go hurdling and I think he is a nice horse.

TWO FOR GOLD (IRE) 5 b g Gold Well – Two of Each (IRE)
Had a good season in bumpers winning two out of three at Southwell and Doncaster and finishing sixth in a Listed contest at Ascot in between. Back cantering at the moment, he is a very good jumper who will want a trip over hurdles this season. I hope he will do well in novice events.

VINNDICATION (IRE) 5 b g Vinnie Roe (IRE) – Pawnee Trail (IRE)
A very promising horse who is unbeaten in four career starts. Having won a bumper at Ludlow on his debut, he won three out of three over hurdles, including the Listed Sidney Banks Memorial Novices' Hurdle at Huntingdon in February. He didn't run again because he had sore shins and there was no point risking him. I have been pleased with him during the summer but no decision has been made whether he stays hurdling or goes novice chasing. Two and a half miles is his trip at the moment and, even though he has only raced right-handed, that is by coincidence rather than by design. I see no reason why he won't be equally effective racing left-handed.

YOUNEVERCALL (IRE) 7 b g Yeats (IRE) – Afarka (IRE)
Missed the whole of last season having suffered a hairline fracture, he finished seventh in a competitive handicap hurdle at the Punchestown Festival in the spring of 2017. He is likely to start off in a three miles handicap hurdle at Perth in September and then we will decide whether to remain over hurdles or go chasing.

TRAINER'S HORSE TO FOLLOW: EL PRESENTE

Harry FRY

Stables: Manor Farm, Seaborough, Beaminster, Dorset.
2017/2018: 53 Winners / 245 Runners 22% Prize-Money £787,617
www.harryfryracing.com

ACTING LASS (IRE) 7 b g King's Theatre (IRE) – Darrens Lass (IRE)
He showed progressive form over fences last season winning his first three races, including a nice prize at Ascot in January. Sent off favourite for the Grade 3 Betdaq Handicap Chase at Kempton the following month, he finished ninth but the ground dried out too much for him because he wants it soft. Rated 149, we are hoping he will develop into a decent second season chaser and we are keen to try him over three miles again. All seven of his career starts have been on right-handed tracks but that is by accident rather than design. He will hopefully be in action by mid November and, being lightly raced, I am hoping he is open to further improvement.

AIR HORSE ONE 7 gr g Mountain High (IRE) – Whisky Rose (IRE)
Despite running some good races in defeat, he didn't have much luck last season. Fourth behind Elgin in a Listed handicap hurdle at Ascot on his reappearance, he was raised a pound as a result but was subsequently raised another three pounds after the winner followed up in the Greatwood Hurdle at Cheltenham. Third next time at Newbury, he was also runner-up in a Graded contest at Ascot and then third in the Grade 2 National Spirit Hurdle at Fontwell. A tough and genuine horse, his jumping isn't always the best, so we will keep him over hurdles for the time being. However, we intend giving him a run or two on the Flat before going back over jumps.

AMERICAN (FR) 8 b g Malinas (GER) – Grande Sultane (FR)
We have kept him ticking over during the summer because he isn't the easiest to train but he is in good form at home. Runner-up in the Grade 2 Cotswold Chase at Cheltenham in January, he looked the winner coming down the hill but still ran a very good race. We haven't made any plans for him yet but I suppose that race again is a possibility and we also have the option of the Ladbrokes Trophy at Newbury (1st December) once again, despite pulling up in it last season. He wants soft ground though and the conditions will dictate his programme.

AMERICAN GIGOLO 6 b g Azamour (IRE) – Sadie Thompson (IRE)
Runner-up on his first start for us in a novice hurdle at Ascot last Autumn, we operated on his wind soon afterwards and brought him back on the Flat on the all-weather in January because he wants better ground. A three times winner at Lingfield, Kempton and Newcastle, he has only had a handful of runs over jumps and will go handicap hurdling.

ANY DRAMA (IRE) 7 b g Gamut (IRE) – Oak Lodge (IRE)
He is back in work having missed the whole of last season due to a stress fracture. Ironically, he would have loved the prevailing soft ground last winter because they are very much his conditions. Twice a winner over hurdles at Market Rasen and Exeter the previous year, he will hopefully develop into a useful novice chaser over two and a half miles plus when the mud is flying.

BAGS GROOVE (IRE) 7 b g Oscar (IRE) – Golden Moment (IRE)
We were expecting him to run well in the Silver Trophy at Chepstow on his reappearance last season and, while he was beaten less than four lengths, he was only eighth in arguably one of the strongest renewals there has been in recent years. However, he won his next two races at Aintree and Kempton. A very consistent horse who prefers decent ground, we dropped him back to two miles for his chasing debut at Uttoxeter in May. Despite the trip being on the sharp side, he ran very well in second only being headed close home. We are looking forward to running him in the Autumn over fences with two and a half miles being his trip at present, although I think he will stay three miles eventually.

BEHIND TIME (IRE) 7 b g Stowaway – She's Got To Go (IRE)
As his name suggests, it has taken a while for the penny to drop but he is a capable horse on his day. He won a good prize over fences at Uttoxeter in March but we then made a mistake by running him back too soon at Haydock. Granted soft ground, I think he will continue to be competitive in three mile handicap chases.

BLACK MISCHIEF 6 b g Black Sam Bellamy (IRE) – Miss Mitch (IRE)
A dual winner over hurdles at Warwick and Kempton, he likes better ground and we may give him one more run over hurdles before going novice chasing. I think two and a half miles is ideal.

BULLIONAIRE (IRE) 5 b g Gold Well – Dontcallerthat (IRE)
He won the Goffs UK Spring Sales bumper at Newbury the previous season and then reappeared in a Listed bumper at Ascot last Christmas. Despite running well in second, he was very keen and we purposely left him off for the rest of the season because there was no point sending him hurdling in the second half of the year and losing his novice status for this winter. We have done a lot of work on him at home trying to teach him to settle and switch off. His owners have been very patient and, provided he settles in his races, he is an exciting prospect for novice hurdles. Physically, he ran up a bit light last year but has really filled out during the summer and is in great form at home. We will start him off over two miles.

CANELIE (FR) 6 b m Gentlewave (IRE) – Medjie (FR)
She joined us halfway through last season having previously been trained by Gordon Elliott. A winner at Taunton in January, she disappointed in her subsequent starts but we found a wind issue, which we have operated on since. She appears to run well fresh and first time out may be the time to catch her. Rated 127, there is every chance we will send her straight over fences over two and a half miles.

CAPTAIN DRAKE (IRE) 5 b g Getaway (GER) – Julika (GER)
Runner-up in his only Irish point for Denis Murphy, we bought him at the Cheltenham December Sales. We sent him to Towcester for a bumper in late March because we knew he stays well and handles slow conditions and he duly won. A lovely big horse who is very much a chaser in the making, he will go novice hurdling over two and a half miles and I think he will cope with good to soft ground having only raced on soft and heavy so far.

CARIBERT (FR) 5 b g Ballingarry (IRE) – Cardamine (FR)
He did us proud last season winning two of his three starts in bumpers, including on his debut at Wincanton in November. I couldn't believe it when he got beaten next time at Exeter but it transpired he was conceding seven pounds to a useful sort (Time To Move On) who has won again since. We then purposely saved him for the Goffs UK Spring Sales Bumper at Newbury in March and it was great to win it for a second time for the same connections. He is a fine big horse who likes to get his toe in. An out and out galloper, I think two and a half miles may prove to be his optimum trip but more than likely we will start him off over a stiff two miles or two and a quarter miles at somewhere like Exeter in the Autumn. He is an exciting prospect for novice hurdles.

CHALONNIAL (FR) 6 ch g Protektor (GER) – Kissmirial (FR)
Sixth on his chasing debut at Sandown in November, he was a bit fresh that day. Unfortunately, he fractured a splint bone and was forced to miss the rest of the season. He is OK now and will resume over fences over two and a half miles. That's where his future lies.

DASHING OSCAR (IRE) 8 b g Oscar (IRE) – Be My Leader (IRE)
Progressive over hurdles last Autumn winning at Fontwell and Bangor. We kept him on the go in the spring because he prefers better ground, although he doesn't want it too quick having suffered with sore shins in the past. He finished fifth on his chasing debut at Uttoxeter and needs to improve in the jumping department. We will try him again over fences but the jury is out whether he is a natural.

DEADRINGERFORLOVE 4 b f Black Sam Bellamy (IRE) – La Perrotine (FR)
An unraced half-sister to Cheltenham Gold Cup winner Sizing John, she is a nice mare who was due to make her debut in a bumper at Towcester at the end of April but the ground was too soft. We will start her off in a bumper and, depending on how she performs on her debut, she could be aimed at a Listed mares' bumper or go hurdling.

DEFINITELYANOSCAR (IRE) 5 b m Oscar (IRE) – Bobs Article (IRE)
She joined us having won a point-to-point by fifteen lengths at Barbury Castle for Chris Barber. A ready winner of a mares' bumper at Market Rasen in late March, she was unlucky not to follow up at Cheltenham in April showing signs of inexperience late on. She got lonely and hung on the run-in and was beaten half a length. She jumps for fun and ought to make a useful mares' novice hurdler. She will start off over two miles.

DRUMCLIFF (IRE) 7 b g Presenting – Dusty Too
I still can't believe he didn't win over hurdles but he took well to chasing last season winning three times. Successful on his chasing debut at Wincanton, he then hacked up at Ascot in January. He found the ground too soft at the Cheltenham Festival before appreciating nicer ground at Uttoxeter in May and winning a good prize in the process. A faller in the Galway Plate in August, we will be aiming him at the decent handicap chases over two and a half to two miles six, provided the ground isn't too soft.

ELEANOROFAQUITAINE (IRE) 5 b m Flemensfirth (USA) – Misty Heather (IRE)
From the family of Rock on Ruby, she took time to come to hand and was a madam on her debut in a bumper at Newton Abbot in June trying to buck her jockey off. However, she shaped with plenty of encouragement for the future running on well to finish second. She returned there a couple of months later and once again finished runner-up. We may give her another run in a mares' bumper before going hurdling.

ENA BAIE (FR) 4 b f Crillon (FR) – Trema Baie (FR)
She won a Grade 3 APQS Flat race in France before arriving here last Autumn. She made her debut for us in the Listed four year old bumper at Cheltenham on New Year's Day. Having travelled well, she didn't quite get up the hill on ground which was slower than ideal finishing fourth. We decided to give her time off after that and let her mature. She is a nice filly who will go novice hurdling over two miles.

GOLDEN BIRTHDAY (FR) 7 b g Poliglote – Gold Or Silver (FR)
Rated 144 over hurdles, he has been running on the Flat during the spring/summer. Narrowly beaten on his chasing debut at Uttoxeter in July, he won next time at Stratford. Due to the fact he wants better ground, he will continue into the Autumn before having a winter break. I hope he will develop into a useful novice chaser.

GREEN DOLPHIN (IRE) 4 b g Oscar (IRE) – Shamrock Miss (IRE)
Unraced, he wasn't forward enough to run in the spring but I have been pleased with him during the summer. I am a big fan of his sire and he ticks all the boxes for a bumper in the Autumn.

HELL'S KITCHEN 7 b g Robin Des Champs (FR) – Mille Et Une (FR)
A big horse who is too exuberant for his own good on occasions. It was great to see him get his head in front over fences at Kempton on Boxing Day beating a subsequent Festival winner in the process. Pulled up at Leopardstown next time, it was all over before it started that day and he never ran his race. Given a break since, he will be campaigned in two and a half miles handicap chases and I hope he will progress further having only raced eight times during his career.

IF THE CAP FITS (IRE) 6 b g Milan – Derravaragh Sayra (IRE)
Unbeaten in three starts over hurdles, he was forced to miss the spring Festivals due to a setback but is back in work with no ill effects. As it transpired, he wouldn't have enjoyed the soft ground at either Cheltenham or Aintree because he appreciates decent ground, although good to soft is OK. Very progressive during the first half of last season, he beat some useful novices in decisive fashion at Kempton, despite still showing signs of inexperience. I hope he will progress again as a second season hurdler before making a chaser later on. He may reappear in something like the Elite Hurdle at Wincanton (10th November).

IMPERIAL ESPRIT (IRE) 4 b g Scorpion (IRE) – Shesourpresent (IRE)
Owned by Imperial Racing, he was bought at the Derby Sales in Ireland as a three year old and is a fine big horse who will start off in a bumper.

JOLLY'S CRACKED IT (FR) 9 b g Astarabad (USA) – Jolly Harbour
He dead-heated in the Ladbroke Hurdle at Ascot in 2015 but hasn't raced since finishing down the field in the same race twelve months later. Back in work, we are hoping he retains plenty of ability and will be campaigned in two mile handicap hurdles.

JUST A STING (IRE) 6 b g Scorpion (IRE) – Shanann Lady (IRE)
Runner-up at Exeter and third a couple of times at Sandown and Ascot, it was frustrating not to get his head in front. I don't think he enjoyed the slow ground but he is a chaser in the making and we will aim him at a novices' handicap over two and a half to three miles.

KING ROLAND (IRE) 4 br g Stowaway – Kiltiernan Robin (IRE)
An impressive ten lengths of his maiden point for Tom Lacey at Larkhill on Easter Saturday, he was bought privately on behalf of Masterson Holdings Limited soon afterwards. He looks a very nice horse who may run in a bumper.

KYLEMORE LOUGH 9 b g Revoque (IRE) – One of The Last
There was a lot of hype surrounding him last year and, unfortunately, things didn't go to plan in the BetVictor Gold Cup at Cheltenham in November on his first run for us. He was going well until leaving his hind legs in the water jump and his chance disappeared after that. His best run came at Warwick in February when he looked like winning until getting headed after the last. I would put a line through his run at Fairyhouse over Easter in Grade 2 company when the ground was bottomless. Two and a half miles is his trip but he will be forced to carry big weights in handicaps off his rating.

LEGENDE DE MINUIT 4 br g Midnight Legend – Chilla Cilla
A nice big unraced four year old who wasn't forward enough to run during the spring. All being well, he will make his debut in a bumper in the Autumn.

LITTERALE CI (FR) 5 b m Soldier of Fortune (IRE) – Cigalia
She had a very good season winning at Ludlow and Stratford and has continued to progress during the spring/summer also scoring at Ffos Las and Newton Abbot. She has formed a terrific rapport with Aine O'Connor, who has partnered her to all four wins. Now rated 138, it will be tougher now off her revised mark but we will continue to campaign her in handicap hurdles over two and a half miles.

MINELLA AWARDS (IRE) 7 b g Oscar (IRE) – Montys Miss (IRE)
When he is at his best, he is very good, although he can be in and out. Restricted to a couple of runs last season, he found the ground much too slow in the valuable handicap hurdle at Haydock in November. Reappearing in the same staying handicap hurdle he had won at the Punchestown Festival twelve months earlier off an eight pounds higher mark, he ran well in seventh only beaten five lengths. We have kept him on the go during the summer and he was a good second in another competitive staying handicap hurdle at Galway in early August. The plan is to send him novice chasing in September/October because he doesn't want the ground too soft. Trips around two miles six and three miles are ideal.

MISTERTON 7 gr g Sagamix (FR) – Mighty Splash
A progressive horse who beat the likes of Elgin in a decent handicap hurdle at Chepstow on his reappearance last October. He was then beaten by a neck by the same rival in the Greatwood Hurdle at Cheltenham the following month from a pound out of the handicap. It was a career best effort. Ninth in the *Betfair* Hurdle at Newbury in February, we gave him some time off after that. Back in work, he may have a run on the Flat before we aim him at something like the Silver Trophy at Chepstow (13th October). He could then go novice chasing. Two or two and a half miles is fine for him.

MOMELLA (IRE) 6 ch m Sholokhov (IRE) – Missing Link (IRE)
She joined us during the summer having shown very good form over hurdles last season. Rated 142 and a three times winner over hurdles, she was third in Grade 1 company at Aintree in April. A winning pointer, we will give her a run over hurdles before going chasing later on. There is a Listed mares' hurdle over two miles at Wetherby (3rd November), which we won three years ago with Blue Buttons. That is an option.

ONEFORTHEROADTOM 5 gr g Fair Mix (FR) – Ifni Du Luc (FR)
A winning pointer, he beat two subsequent Grade 1 winners on his hurdles debut at Exeter, namely Lalor and Kilbricken Storm, in October. Noel (Fehily) liked him that day and, although he won a 'jumpers bumper' at Kempton in March, he didn't progress as much as we had hoped. However, he was still on the weak side and we are hoping with another summer behind him, he will make an impact over fences over two and a half to three miles.

OUTOFTHISWORLD (IRE) 5 bb m Shantou (USA) - Mystic Masie (IRE)
An impressive winner on her debut at Market Rasen in the spring of last year, we intended running her in the Listed mares' bumper at Cheltenham in November but the ground was too soft. We took her to Huntingdon on Boxing Day for a similar event but she boiled over and never ran her race. She was never quite right thereafter hence we gave her a long break and I hope she will be back to form in early Autumn on better ground. Two miles mares' novice hurdles will be on her agenda.

OVER TO SAM 7 b g Black Sam Bellamy (IRE) - Lady Brig
A maiden hurdle winner at Exeter the previous season, he missed the whole of the last campaign due to injury but it may prove a blessing in disguise. He has come back in looking a bigger and stronger horse and we will send him chasing over two and a half miles plus. A former winning English pointer, he will stay three miles.

OVERTOWN EXPRESS (IRE) 10 br g Overbury (IRE) - Black Secret
A good winner at Newbury in early January, he went up the handicap as a result but has come down again following a few subsequent defeats. He loves soft ground and a strong pace over two miles. Rated 145, he may creep into the bottom of the weights in the Haldon Gold Cup at Exeter (6th November).

PHOENIX WAY (IRE) 5 b g Stowaway - Arcuate
Owned by J.P.McManus, he was bought at the Cheltenham January Sale having won his only Irish point by a dozen lengths nine days earlier for Donnchadh Doyle. He looks a very nice prospect.

SAM I (FR) 5 gr g Lord Du Sud (FR) - Blue Girl Star (FR)
Very green on his debut in a bumper at Huntingdon in March, he shaped with plenty of promise staying on well to finish second. Hopefully he will win a bumper before going novice hurdling.

SAMARQUAND 4 bb g Malinas (GER) - Samandara (FR)
He is the one four year old we did manage to get a run into last spring and he beat a smart looking rival (Bold Plan) narrowly at Wincanton in April. The pair pulled clear of the third and both looked very good prospects. A half-brother to Warriors Tale, he is from a chasing family but we may have to look at another bumper for him before going hurdling. Still only four, the Listed bumper at Cheltenham (18th November) is a possibility.

SEROSEVSKY (IRE) 5 b g Morozov (USA) - Be My Rainbow (IRE)
A winning English pointer, he ran OK in bumpers before showing progressive form over hurdles. Successful at Exeter in May on his second start, he then ran a good race under a penalty at Warwick later the same month finishing second. A four and a half lengths winner at Newton Abbot in August, he then finished runner-up behind Litterale Ci at the same track at the start of September. He is still a novice for this season. However, he could go down the handicap route and may be one for the conditional jockeys' handicap hurdle at Cheltenham's November meeting (18th), which we have won for the last three years, depending on his mark by that stage. He prefers decent ground.

SIR IVAN 8 b g Midnight Legend - Tisho
A dual winner last season at Uttoxeter and in a 'jumpers bumper' at Kempton, he threw away another winning opportunity when falling at the second last at Ludlow. We have operated on his wind since, which will hopefully make a difference. He will continue in handicap chases over two miles six plus.

SPACE ODDITY (FR) bb g Al Namix (FR) – Schoune (FR)
Successful on his chasing debut at Uttoxeter, he ran well at Ascot in November when finishing runner-up behind Benatar but didn't appear to get home over two and a half miles at Newbury next time. Runner-up again at Taunton over two miles, I think two and a quarter miles is ideal. He will go handicap chasing.

SUPERB STORY (IRE) 7 b g Duke of Marmalade (IRE) – Yes My Love (FR)
Another new arrival, he is a former County Hurdle winner at the Cheltenham Festival but hasn't been on a racecourse since New Year's Day last year, due to a tendon injury. We will give him plenty of time and hopefully he will retain his ability and we can get him back on track.

THE JITTERBUG 5 b g Sulamani (IRE) – She Likes To Boogy (IRE)
He ran in a couple of English point-to-points and, having unseated his rider on his debut, he won next time by five lengths at Bratton Down in May. Better ground appears to suit him and we may give him a run in a bumper before going novice hurdling.

TOODLEPIP (IRE) 4 b f Robin Des Champs (FR) – Shannon Theatre (IRE)
She is a nice unraced mare who was ready to run in a bumper in the spring but the conditions weren't ideal so we left her off. We will target her at a mares' bumper in the Autumn.

UNOWHATIMEANHARRY 10 b g Sir Harry Lewis (USA) – Red Nose Lady
He made the perfect start to last season winning a two and a half miles conditions hurdle at Aintree. Runner-up next time at Newbury, his form tapered off somewhat and, being a ten year old, he isn't getting any younger. He has been a fantastic horse for us but the Stayers' Hurdle may be beyond him now. However, there are still plenty of good races for him to be aimed at. He could reappear in the West Yorkshire Hurdle at Wetherby (3rd November) or the same conditions hurdle at Aintree a week later (10th November).

WINNINGSEVERYTHING (IRE) 4 b g Flemensfirth (USA) – Baliya (IRE)
Another nice unraced four year old who we decided to give plenty of time to mature last season. He has had a good break and will kick off in a bumper in the Autumn.

WOTZIZNAME (IRE) 8 b g Fruits of Love (USA) – Native Beau (IRE)
Despite winning twice at Exeter and Doncaster over fences, he hasn't looked a natural chaser. We therefore may revert back to hurdles with three miles plus being his trip.

TRAINER'S HORSE TO FOLLOW: IF THE CAP FITS

Philip HOBBS

Stables: Sandhill, Bilbrook, Minehead, Somerset.
2017/2018: 63 Winners / 460 Runners 14% Prize-Money £709,992
www.pjhobbs.com

ARTHUR MAC (IRE) 5 ch g Getaway (GER) – Orchardstown Moss (IRE)
He won first time out in a bumper at Hereford in January and then we let him take his chance in the championship bumper at Aintree's Grand National meeting. I thought he ran OK in eleventh but is a staying type who will be suited by two and a half miles over hurdles this season. I have always liked him and we are expecting him to improve.

BALLOTIN (FR) 7 b g Enrique – Orphee De Vonnas (FR)
Successful in the Bobby Renton Handicap Chase at Wetherby in October on his first start for us, he was also runner-up at Ascot. Rated 141 over fences, the plan is for him to continue in handicaps until going hunter chasing in the New Year for his owner David Maxwell. Two and a half miles appears to suit him.

BROTHER TEDD 9 gr g Kayf Tara – Neltina
Absent since finishing runner-up at Newton Abbot in June last year, due to a tendon injury, he will hopefully be back in action after Christmas, although he doesn't want the ground too soft. Still lightly raced over fences, he will be running in decent two and a half miles handicap chases.

CEDAR VALLEY (IRE) 4 b f Flemensfirth (USA) – Lunar Path (IRE)
She produced a very good performance to win a mares' bumper on her debut at Taunton in the spring. Ninth in the Grade 2 mares' bumper at Aintree in April, she hasn't got a lot of scope in terms of her size but she possesses a very good attitude. There is a possibility we will aim her at the Listed mares' bumper at Cheltenham (17th November) before going over hurdles. She will have no trouble staying two and a half miles.

CHEF D'EQUIPE (FR) 6 b g Presenting – Millesimee (FR)
Like Ballotin, he is owned by David Maxwell and the plan is to send him hunter chasing in the New Year. In the meantime, he will continue in handicap chases over two and a half miles. Only six, he won at Sandown in January and has only raced a handful of times for us.

COTSWOLD WAY (IRE) 5 b g Stowaway – Roses All The Way
Still a maiden over hurdles, he progressed last season and stepped up markedly on his previous performances when finishing runner-up at Wincanton last time. I have always liked him and he is a horse with potential. Two and a half miles is his trip for the time being but I am expecting him to stay further in time. It is possible the better ground at Wincanton suited him.

CROOKS PEAK 5 b g Arcadio (GER) – Ballcrina Girl (IRE)
A six lengths winner on his debut in a bumper at Newton Abbot during the Autumn, the plan was to send him over hurdles next time. However, we decided to run him in the Listed event at Cheltenham's November meeting and he duly won. We therefore then elected to save him for the championship bumper at the Festival in March but he didn't run his race and was well beaten. Given a break since, he undoubtedly has plenty of ability and, given the fact he isn't short of speed, we will start him off over two miles over hurdles.

DARK EPISODE (IRE) 4 b g Getaway (GER) – No Moore Bills
A nice unraced four year old who we liked last season. He showed plenty of ability in his work last Autumn but we decided to give him six weeks off and let him mature. When he came back into work in the spring he wasn't the healthiest so we gave him the summer off. In all likelihood, he will run in a bumper this Autumn.

DEFI DU SEUIL (FR) 5 b g Voix Du Nord (FR) – Quarvine Du Seuil (FR)
Having enjoyed such a successful campaign as a juvenile hurdler the previous year when unbeaten in seven starts, last season proved something of a disaster. Fourth on his return to action in the Ascot Hurdle in November, he was one of the first of our horses to show signs they weren't right. Seventh in the Irish Champion Hurdle at Leopardstown in February on his only other start, we decided to send him back to Martinstown Stud afterwards. There was no point running him again and hopefully one or two issues have been sorted out and he has enjoyed a good summer break. I am inclined to draw a line through last season and still feel he is a very exciting horse. His work has always been good and I would think there is every chance he will go novice chasing this season.

DEISE ABA (IRE) 5 b g Mahler – Kit Massini (IRE)
Mr Hemmings kindly sent us three new horses during the summer, including this winning Irish pointer. A four lengths winner of his only start, he was bought at the Doncaster May Sales. He is a big strong horse with a good outlook and I would imagine he will go straight over hurdles.

DEMOPOLIS (FR) 4 b g Poliglote – Princess Demut (GER)
A winner of his only race over hurdles at Auteuil when trained by Guy Cherel in France, he joined us last summer but has yet to run over here. We were pleased with his work last season but he wasn't the healthiest hence we gave him time. Unfortunately, he isn't a novice and has only raced once which means he won't be the easiest horse to place. We may have to look at a conditions hurdle to start with. A fresh horse, I hope he will do well.

DOSTAL PHIL (FR) 5 b g Coastal Path – Quiphile (FR)
Bought at the Arqana Sale in France in November 2016 having won his only APQS Flat race the previous month, I was disappointed with him when only finishing fourth in a novice hurdle at Bangor on his first run for us last October. He may have found the track too sharp and will probably benefit from stepping up in trip. Not at his best thereafter, we decided to give him the rest of the season off and keep him as a novice for this time around. We may start him off over a stiff two miles before trying him over further in due course.

DUKE DES CHAMPS (IRE) 8 b g Robin Des Champs (FR) – Ballycowan Lady (IRE)
Runner-up and third in a couple of novice handicap chases at Newbury last winter, he had a slight issue with a hind leg afterwards and therefore missed the rest of the campaign. Still a novice over fences and rated 135, he wants two miles six to three miles.

EARTH MOOR (IRE) 4 ch g Ask – Merrylas (IRE)
Despite not winning, he ran well in all three of his bumpers, including when finishing second at Exeter and Worcester. A likeable horse, we may try and win a bumper but I think he is more likely to go straight over hurdles. Two and a half miles ought to suit him to start with because we are expecting him to stay well.

EBONY GALE 4 br g Shirocco (GER) – Glenora Gale (IRE)
I was pleased with him last season and, having shown promise on his debut at Kempton, he won next time at Wincanton showing improved form in the process. He is a nice horse who may run over a stiff two miles over hurdles but will be suited by further in time.

ECU DE LA NOVERIE (FR) 4 b g Linda's Lad – Quat'Sous D'Or (FR)
He raced six times in France winning over fences at Pau in January. Bought soon afterwards by David Maxwell, he has an official mark of 130 over fences. The plan is for David to ride him in novice hurdles this season.

EVIDENCE DE THAIX (FR) 4 b f Network (GER) – Nacre De Thaix (FR)
She is a big strong filly who arrived during the summer. Owned by J.P.McManus, she won two of her three starts in APQS Flat races in France and the form has worked out well. She is one to look forward to over hurdles this season.

FOR GOOD MEASURE (IRE) 7 b g King's Theatre (IRE) – Afdala (IRE)
A full brother to Balthazar King, he is a lovely horse who has only raced twice over fences. Third in the Grade 2 Pendil Novices' Chase at Kempton in February, we didn't run him again because we wanted to preserve his novice status for this season. He will benefit from a step up in trip and, like his brother, he wants decent ground and I think he is on a good mark over fences.

GAELIC PRINCE (FR) 6 b g Martaline (FR) – Gaelic Jane (FR)
He was, unfortunately, hampered and got no further than the first hurdle on his debut at Exeter last November and hasn't run since due to a few issues. A big strong horse, I have always liked him and hopefully he will progress this winter. He will resume in two mile novice hurdles.

GALA BALL (IRE) 8 b g Flemensfirth (USA) – Nuit Des Chartreux (FR)
Absent since the spring of last year due to a leg issue, he will be back in action around Christmas time. Rated 145 over fences, he isn't going to be the easiest horse to place but he remains lightly raced and, if he improves his jumping, he is capable of winning more races. Two and a half miles is his trip.

GARDE LA VICTOIRE (FR) 9 b g Kapgarde (FR) – Next Victory (FR)
Runner-up over hurdles at Auteuil in October, he then finished fourth in the Haldon Gold Cup at Exeter. He wasn't the healthiest during the second half of the season hence he only ran once more in the Grand Annual Chase at the Cheltenham Festival. While he doesn't always hold his form, he is very talented and the handicapper has given him a chance dropping him five pounds since his last run.

GOLDEN SOVEREIGN (IRE) 4 b g Gold Well – Fugal Maid (IRE)
I was pleased with his debut run in a bumper at Chepstow in the spring finishing third. Very much a staying horse for the future, he will go novice hurdling over two and a half miles plus.

GOSHEVEN (IRE) 5 b g Presenting – Fair Choice (IRE)
I think he is one of our best youngsters and is a horse I am very much looking forward to. Still green last year, he improved massively on each start culminating in a very good run at Cheltenham in April in a strongly contested two and a half miles novice hurdle. We ran him there because we didn't want to lose his novice status so late in the season. There is still room for plenty of improvement and he probably only needs to progress another stone before he is competing in the better novice hurdles. We will keep him to two and a half miles for the time being but he will stay three miles in due course.

GUMBALL (FR) 4 gr g No Risk At All (FR) – Good Time Girl (FR)
A three times winner last season, he also finished second in the Grade 1 juvenile hurdle at Aintree in the spring. With a rating of 148, he isn't going to be easy to place but we will probably start him off in the four year old hurdle at Cheltenham (27th October). He appears to prefer better ground and there is a possibility he is more at home on a flat track, although he did win at Chepstow last season.

ICE COOL CHAMPS (IRE) 7 ch g Robin Des Champs (FR) – Last of Many (IRE)
He appreciated the step up to three miles when winning over hurdles at Uttoxeter in November. We then sent him chasing and, while he hasn't got his act together thus far, I think he will improve with experience and his mark looks OK compared to his hurdles rating. Soft ground brings out the best in him.

I'M A GAME CHANGER (IRE) 6 b g Arcadio (GER) – Drinadaly (IRE)
He is a useful horse with plenty of talent. I thought he was impressive when winning at Ludlow in April and then he wasn't beaten far in the Scottish Champion Hurdle. Unlucky last time at Warwick when narrowly denied over two miles three, he was forced to go wide on the hometurn and then made a mistake at the last. He is learning to settle and got the trip well at Warwick. We will probably give him another run over hurdles before making a decision whether to send him chasing.

JERRYSBACK (IRE) 6 b g Jeremy (USA) – Get A Few Bob Back (IRE)
A lovely horse who we are looking forward to seeing running again. He didn't race last season and, while there wasn't anything wrong with him, he never shone in his work and I wasn't happy with him. Unbeaten over hurdles, his future lies over fences but he is capable of winning a decent handicap hurdle, if we decide to continue down that route for the time being. Two and a half miles suits him, although he will stay further.

KALOOKI (GER) 4 b g Martaline (FR) – Karuma (GER)
A half-brother to Kruzhlinin, who we used to train but has now retired, he is a very nice unraced four year old. We did a fair bit of work with him last year but he had a minor issue with lameness behind, which meant we gave him time. I have always liked him and he is one for a bumper in the Autumn.

KAYF ADVENTURE 7 b g Kayf Tara – My Adventure (IRE)
Enjoyed a good first season over fences winning at Newton Abbot and Wincanton before running well at the Cheltenham Festival. Runner-up at Newbury last time, he may be high enough in the ratings off 137 but I think he will be competitive. Two and a half miles is his trip but the key to him is the ground – he copes very well with soft and heavy ground.

KEEP ROLLING (IRE) 5 ch g Mahler – Kayles Castle (IRE)
I think he is a very nice horse who showed plenty in his work last season. We were going to run him in a bumper but he wasn't the healthiest so we backed off him. He was going very well and is one to watch out for in a bumper before going hurdling.

KENSUKES KINGDOM (IRE) 5 b g Stowaway – Hamalata (IRE)
A nice horse who won two of his three Irish points for Thomond O'Mara. Owned in partnership by Martin St Quinton and Tim Syder, he is likely to start off in a bumper before going novice hurdling.

LARKBARROW LAD 5 b g Kayf Tara – Follow My Leader (IRE)
Ran well in three bumpers last season being placed at Southwell, Kempton and Wincanton. There is a possibility he will run in another because he is capable of winning one. However, he is a big tall horse who is still filling his frame and I am expecting him to improve with time. He is a nice horse who will want two and a half miles over hurdles.

LEAPAWAY (IRE) 6 b g Stowaway – Gisela (IRE)
He has made remarkable progress during the spring/summer winning a couple of handicap hurdles at Worcester and Cartmel and then novice hurdles at Stratford and Newton Abbot. The better ground has helped and he is also learning to settle now having raced keenly during his early races. Impressive at Cartmel in a decent handicap, he will continue to run until the ground changes in the Autumn. I am staggered by how much he has improved over the last few months.

LITTLE MISS POET 6 b m Yeats (IRE) – R De Rien Sivola (FR)
Although her form can be a bit in and out, she is a likeable mare who won well at Wincanton in May. Chasing could be on her agenda but she is inclined to be keen so we will probably give her another run over hurdles first.

LITTLE RORY MAC (IRE) 4 b g Yeats (IRE) – Solar Quest (IRE)
A big horse who we thought would run well on his debut in a bumper at Hereford in April. Beaten half a length in second, he is a nice horse who will probably have another run in a bumper before going over jumps. The ground at Hereford was very testing but he is a good moving horse so I would expect him to handle better ground.

LORD DUVEEN (IRE) 5 br g Doyen (IRE) - Afdala (IRE)
I think he could be a very nice horse in the making. A half-brother to Balthazar King and For Good Measure, he was fifth on his debut over hurdles at Exeter before finishing runner-up at Kempton last time. We made a decision to give him the summer off after that and let him mature. Despite his pedigree, he has plenty of speed for two miles and he is a horse I like a lot. Like his older siblings, he may prefer better ground. We will start him off in a suitable maiden hurdle in the Autumn.

LOUIS' VAC POUCH (IRE) 6 b g Oscar (IRE) - Coming Home (FR)
He appreciated the step up to three miles when winning a Pertemps qualifier at Aintree in November. We then purposely saved him for the Final at the Festival but he wasn't at his best during the spring running below par at both Cheltenham and Aintree. Turned away for the summer soon afterwards, he had looked progressive prior to that and there is every chance he will have another run over hurdles before we decide whether to send him chasing.

MCNAMARAS BAND (IRE) 5 b g Getaway (GER) - Katies Pet (IRE)
A nice horse who won a bumper at Worcester on his debut during the summer of last year. He was ready to go hurdling last Autumn but pulled some muscles in his hind quarters. We therefore sent him back to his owners for a month and then decided to save him for this season. He has benefited from the time off and we will send him straight over hurdles.

MELEKHOV (IRE) 4 b g Sholokhov (IRE) - Yorkshire Girl (IRE)
They may not have been the greatest races but he won two out of three in bumpers last season gaining victories at Fakenham and Hexham. I thought it was a good performance at the latter track carrying a penalty. All three of his runs have been on soft ground but I don't envisage a livelier surface being a problem. He is improving and I hope he will continue to go the right way. We will send him hurdling now.

NINTH WAVE (IRE) 4 b g September Storm (GER) - Royale Pearl
A handy horse who won a point-to-point bumper for Philip Rowley before being bought by Mr Hemmings. He joined us during the summer and I have been pleased with him. He goes nicely at home.

NO COMMENT 7 br g Kayf Tara - Dizzy Frizzy
I have always liked him and I think he will do well over fences this season. Not the healthiest last year, he was restricted to a couple of runs. Third in the Grade 1 Scilly Isles Novice Chase at Sandown, he was still in contention at the second last. We then stepped him up to four miles in the National Hunt Chase at the Cheltenham Festival but I don't think he got the trip. Dropped six pounds since to a mark of 139, he is favourably treated over fences compared to hurdles and he is a horse to look forward to. Still a novice, I think three miles is his trip.

OAKLEY (IRE) 5 b g Oscar (IRE) - Tirolean Dance (IRE)
I thought he ran well in both his starts in bumpers at Kempton and Warwick. A horse who shows plenty of speed at home, I didn't think he quite got home on either occasion and will be better over hurdles. There is plenty of room for improvement and he will start off in a two mile novice hurdle.

OZZIE THE OSCAR (IRE) 7 b g Oscar (IRE) - Private Official (IRE)
A very likeable horse who improved out of all recognition last season winning three of his five starts over fences, including a handicap at Warwick last time off a mark of 148. Despite those victories, his jumping wasn't as good as it was at home, which means he could improve again, if he sharpens up in that department on the track. Rated 151, a race like the Haldon Gold Cup at Exeter (6th November) is a possibility, although he doesn't want the ground too soft. Two miles is his trip.

PINEAPPLE RUSH 5 b m Kayf Tara – Celtic Native (IRE)
Out of a very good mare who we trained to win ten races, she is a nice filly who has won two out of three over hurdles. I thought she was on a good mark when she made her handicap debut at Aintree in May but she only finished fifth. Perhaps the ground was quick enough for her. Given a break since, she will continue over hurdles for the time being but will jump fences in due course.

PRECIOUS BOUNTY (IRE) 4 b g Yeats (IRE) – Zaharath Al Bustan
We bought him on behalf of Highclere Thoroughbreds at the Doncaster May Sale having run in two Irish points. Pulled up on his first start, the rein broke and then next time he was only beaten a length and three quarters in third. The winner was subsequently sold for £225,000 and the runner-up for £105,000 so I hope our horse proves a bit of value. His previous trainer Tom Keating suggested we go down the bumper route with him so that is the likely plan. He has a Flat race pedigree on his dam's side.

RAVEN COURT (IRE) 4 b g Court Cave (IRE) – Lady Kate Ellen (IRE)
A lovely unraced four year old belonging to Mr Hemmings, he was bought at the Derby Sales in Ireland last year and had done plenty of work prior to joining us in the summer. He is likely to start off in a bumper.

REIKERS ISLAND (IRE) 5 b g Yeats (IRE) – Moricana (GER)
A winning Irish pointer we acquired at the Cheltenham December Sale, I was delighted with his victory over hurdles at Fontwell on his second run for us. I think he had had enough by the time he ran at Kempton. Still eligible for novice hurdles until the end of October, he will jump fences later on and will stay three miles.

ROCK THE KASBAH (IRE) 8 ch g Shirocco (GER) – Impudent (IRE)
Restricted to only three outings last season due to a few health issues, he won well on his reappearance at Chepstow in a decent handicap chase and ended the campaign with a very good performance at Sandown finishing second in the Bet365 Gold Cup. In between, he pulled up in the Peter Marsh Chase at Haydock, where he didn't appreciate the very soft ground. Rated 147, he is capable of winning a good race. If ready in time, he could reappear at Perth (26th September) or the same race at Chepstow (13th October) which he won last season. We may give him an entry in the Ladbroke Trophy at Newbury (1st December – formerly the Hennessy Gold Cup) and we also have the Grand National at the back of our minds.

ROLLING DYLAN (IRE) 7 ch g Indian River (FR) – Easter Sunday (IRE)
He took well to chasing winning twice at Worcester and Chepstow and finishing second a couple of times. Three miles is his trip and he is suited by small fields. I am hopeful he will continue to be competitive off his mark of 142 because he possesses plenty of ability.

ROYAL REGATTA (IRE) 10 b g King's Theatre (IRE) – Friendly Craic (IRE)
Pulled up in both his starts last season, he had an issue with his breathing which we have hopefully rectified since his last run. A Grade 2 winner, he is ten years old now but has plenty of ability and there is every chance he will run in the Old Roan Chase at Aintree (28th October) once again.

SAMBURU SHUJAA (FR) 5 b g Poliglote – Girelle (FR)
A big strong horse who is open to improvement. I thought he ran well on his first three starts over hurdles before disappointing last time at Chepstow. He stays two and a half miles and, while he will jumps fences in time, he is still only five and will continue over hurdles for now.

SHOW ON THE ROAD 7 b g Flemensfirth (USA) - Roses of Picardy (IRE)
Produced two very good performances to win at Exeter and was runner-up on another three occasions. I didn't think he wanted the ground too soft but it was bottomless on both occasions when he won. Rated 126, he may have another run over hurdles but it won't be long before he is jumping fences. Two miles suits him at the moment but he may want further in time.

SNEAKY FEELING (IRE) 6 b g Oscar (IRE) - Shuil Aris (IRE)
Having done well as a novice hurdler, we had high hopes for him last season but he proved very disappointing in both starts at Aintree and Kempton. There was no real explanation for it either so I can only presume he was under the weather. He wasn't healthy during the second half of the season hence he hasn't run since November. I hope we can get him back on track because we know he is talented. We will start him off in another handicap hurdle and I suppose the Silver Trophy at Chepstow (13th October) is an option.

SPRINGTOWN LAKE (IRE) 6 b g Gamut (IRE) - Sprightly Gal (IRE)
A dual winner over hurdles at Worcester and Leicester, he was also runner-up in a Grade 2 at Sandown in December. He has summered well and come back in looking stronger and I hope he will do well in two and a half miles novice chases this winter. He may stay a bit further, too, if necessary.

STEELY ADDITION (IRE) 6 b g Craigsteel - Blond's Addition (IRE)
He is a likeable horse who showed progressive form last season winning at Wincanton and Chepstow. Unhealthy during the middle part of the season, he returned to action at Cheltenham in April but didn't get the clearest of runs before finishing eighth in a decent handicap hurdle. Three miles is his trip and he copes well with soft ground. A winning pointer, his future lies over fences but I think he is capable of further improvement over hurdles beforehand.

STERNRUBIN (GER) 7 b g Authorized (IRE) - Sworn Mum (GER)
Twice a winner on the Flat last year, he is a very good horse on his day but isn't the easiest to place. We tried him over fences a couple of times last season finishing runner-up on both occasions before he went back over hurdles. Third at Aintree on Grand National day, we will probably go back over fences with him but he must go right-handed.

STRONG PURSUIT (IRE) 8 ch g Flemensfirth (USA) - Loughaderra (IRE)
He is a potentially very nice horse but, unfortunately, he got a leg after winning on his chasing debut at Newbury in November. He therefore won't be in action until after Christmas and is no longer a novice and lacks chasing experience. We will have a look for a suitable Graduation chase and take it from there.

THAT'S A GIVEN (FR) 4 b g Great Pretender (IRE) - Aulne River (FR)
A half-brother to Wait For Me, we have always liked him and therefore it didn't surprise us when he made a winning debut in a bumper at Huntingdon in the spring. A bit disappointing next time in the Land Rover bumper at the Punchestown Festival, it was a messy race and he is better than he showed that day. He possesses the speed for two mile novice hurdles.

TIDAL FLOW 5 b g Black Sam Bellamy (IRE) - Mrs Philip
He is a lovely horse who was bred by my wife Sarah and Richard Johnson. From a family we know well, he was impressive when winning a bumper on his debut at Newbury in November. We made the mistake of not entering him for the DBS bumper at the same track in the spring because he was going very well at home at that time. Reappearing at Wincanton in April, he wasn't at his best that day finishing fourth under a penalty. He is one to look forward to in two and a half mile novice hurdles.

TRUCKIN AWAY (IRE) 5 br g Getaway (GER) – Simons Girl (IRE)
Third in his only Irish point-to-point in March, he was subsequent bought by Ann and Garth Broom of Brocade Racing. We have been very pleased with him since arriving and, while he may contest a bumper, I think he is more likely to go straight over hurdles.

UMNDENI (FR) 4 bb g Balko (FR) – Marie Royale (FR)
An expensive purchase as a three year old at the Land Rover Sale, he is a half-brother to Vision Des Flos. I was delighted with his victory on his debut at Warwick in April and it was no surprise because he has always shown plenty of ability at home. A horse with a very good attitude, I hope he will do well in two mile novice hurdles this season.

VERNI (FR) 9 ch g Sabrehill (USA) – Nobless D'Aron (FR)
Richard (Johnson) gave him a very good ride to win over fences at Uttoxeter in May because he doesn't want to be in front too soon. He is talented but quirky. Lightly raced over fences, he remains a novice for this season and, while he stays further, he ideally wants soft ground over two miles.

VICTARION (IRE) 6 b g Scorpion (IRE) – Gaye Preskina (IRE)
Despite failing to win a bumper, he ran three solid races against some good horses including subsequent Grade 1 and 2 winners Lalor and Portrush Ted respectively the previous season. Sent hurdling last season, he wasn't quite right and I am hoping he will improve this time around. He has a good temperament and we will look for a two and a half miles novices' handicap hurdle off his mark of 115.

VODKA ALL THE WAY (IRE) 6 b g Oscar (IRE) – Fully Focus (IRE)
A winner at Exeter over hurdles last time, he is progressing and going the right way. His jumping could improve but he is suited by three miles on soft ground. He will continue over hurdles but it won't be too long before he goes chasing.

WAIHEKE 5 ch m Black Sam Bellamy (IRE) – Its Meant To Be
A nice mare who won well on her second run at Exeter but was largely disappointing thereafter. She had a tendency to hang to her left, which is something we will hopefully sort out, because she is open to further improvement. I think her mark of 117 is fair, if we can get this issue rectified.

WAIT FOR ME (FR) 8 b g Saint Des Saints (FR) – Aulne River (FR)
We tried him over fences last season and, although he won on his chasing debut at Worcester, he never looked happy so we will keep him over hurdles. Fourth at Haydock and runner-up at Warwick during the spring, he is a very talented horse who appreciates decent ground with three miles being his trip.

WAR SOUND 9 b g Kayf Tara – Come The Dawn
A former Swinton Hurdle winner, he ran some good races in defeat over fences last season and was unlucky not to get his head in front. I think two and a half miles is ideal and he is more than capable of winning races.

WESTEND STORY (IRE) 7 b g Westerner – Sarahall (IRE)
I thought he produced two very good performances to win at Wetherby and Hereford last season and he was also runner-up at Sandown. His jumping hasn't always been great but there is no doubting his ability. A former Irish pointer, he will jump fences soon but we may give him another run or two over hurdles first. The Silver Trophy at Chepstow (13th October) could be an early season target.

WHO'S MY JOCKEY (IRE) 5 b g Yeats (IRE) – Scandisk (IRE)
A half-brother to Hurricane Fly, he won twice over hurdles at Uttoxeter and Kempton. We tried him over three miles at Aintree on his final start but I think he was over the top by that stage and it wouldn't put me off running him again over that trip. Rated 136, he is probably high enough and we may send him chasing. He doesn't want the ground too soft though.

TRAINER'S HORSE TO FOLLOW: GOSHEVEN

Anthony HONEYBALL

Stables: Potwell Farm, Mosterton, Beaminster, Dorset.
2017/2018: 34 Winners / 162 Runners 21% Prize-Money £427,333
www.ajhoneyballracing.co.uk

ACEY MILAN (IRE) 4 b g Milan – Strong Wishes (IRE)
He is in great form at home having had a good summer break following a busy and successful campaign in bumpers last season. I have always liked him and the Listed four year old bumper at Cheltenham on New Year's Day was the plan for sometime with a couple of runs beforehand. He made all at Cheltenham and was then even more impressive when beating a strong field of older horses easily in another Listed bumper at Newbury in February. Sent off favourite for the Cheltenham Festival championship bumper as a result, he finished fourth and I thought it was very satisfactory run. Willie Mullins trained the first three home, plus the fifth, which is an extraordinary achievement. I thought he would run well beforehand and he kept on again in the closing stages. We have done plenty of schooling with him and he enjoys jumping. There is no doubt he has got an engine and the race I have in mind for him during the first half of the season is the Grade 1 Challow Hurdle at Newbury (29th December). We may start him off over two miles, which will help his education, but he will be suited by two and a half miles as the season goes on. He is effective on soft ground but I can't wait to try him on some better ground. I have ridden him at home and he doesn't feel like a soft ground horse. He ought to be in action towards the end of October.

AVOIR DE SOINS (IRE) 4 ch g Flemensfirth (USA) – Garranlea Maree (IRE)
Unraced, we bought him at the Cheltenham December Sale and he is a lovely big long striding horse with plenty of scope. He has already schooled well at home but I envisage him starting off in a soft ground bumper in November and view him as a staying type. He has a good pedigree and is from the family of Albertas Run and Mister Morose.

DEJA VUE (IRE) 4 b f Fame And Glory – Westgrove Berry (IRE)
We are fortunate to have some lovely fillies and mares and we purchased her on behalf of Axom at the Cheltenham April Sale having won her only Irish point the previous month. By Fame And Glory whose stock is very popular at the moment, she is a half-sister to Jetstream Jack and is a very nice scopey filly with a good attitude. We may try and win a bumper with her but I would say she will be jumping hurdles sooner rather than later. She is a fantastic jumper who will go over fences one day but I am hoping she will gain some black type over hurdles beforehand.

DON LAMI (FR) 5 ch g Honolulu (IRE) – Toutamie (FR)
He has already won a point-to-point, bumper and over hurdles and we think he will be an interesting staying horse over fences. Although still eligible for novice hurdles having won at Fontwell in May, the plan is to go chasing and look for a suitable novice handicap off his mark of 121. His only disappointing run came at Hexham during the spring but I would put a line through that. He handles decent ground and we are hoping he will progress over fences.

DROPS OF JUPITOR (IRE) 6 gr m Dylan Thomas (IRE) – Fancy Intense
A winner over hurdles at Exeter last winter, she is inclined to race keenly but I am hoping she will improve over fences. She has got ability and I think she could be suited by small field mares' only novice chases.

DUHALLOW GESTURE (IRE) 6 b m King's Theatre (IRE) – Rare Gesture (IRE)
She is a cracking mare who won a point-to-point and a bumper in the spring of last year before we bought her at the Doncaster May Sales. I rode her a lot at home last season and knew she was spot on for her first run for us in a Listed bumper at Huntingdon on Boxing Day and she

won nicely. A non runner at Sandown in March, we then took her to Aintree for a Grade 2 mares' bumper and, while she ran a stormer in third, I don't think she was at her very best. We will send her hurdling this Autumn and she is likely to start off over two and a half miles because she stays well. Effective on most types of ground, she may not want extremes. Not over big measuring 15.3 hands, I think she will be more of a hurdler than chaser.

HIDEAWAY VIC (IRE) 5 b g Stowaway – Cailin Vic Mo Cri (IRE)
A very nice horse who is an out and out stayer, he will make a lovely chaser one day. In fact, granted luck, he could be a Welsh National type horse in the future. Runner-up behind Caribert in a bumper on his debut at Wincanton, which represents good form, he then won at Plumpton in December before finishing second again at Wincanton last time. We have operated on his wind during the summer and, while he will begin over two or two and a half miles, he will come into his own over three miles because he lacks a gear but handles heavy ground. His jumping at home has been great and he is one for the future.

JEPECK (IRE) 9 b g Westerner – Jenny's Jewel (IRE)
A ten times winning pointer, he joined us during the summer and we are hoping a change of scenery will do him good. Placed in the Devon National at Exeter in February, he is still a maiden over fences but looks a nice horse for staying handicaps. He handles soft ground.

LE COEUR NET (FR) 6 ch g Network (GER) – Silverwood (FR)
Despite only winning one of his seventeen career starts, he is still only six and I am hoping he will progress. I loved him as a store horse when we bought him as a three year old at the Land Rover Sale in Ireland. Consistent at a low level over fences last season, he won at Plumpton and subsequently finished second on three more occasions. He jumps well and copes with heavy ground and, although currently rated 105, I am hoping he could be a 120 horse eventually. Two or two and a quarter miles is ideal.

LECHLADE MAGICIAN (IRE) 5 b g Getaway (GER) – Run Supreme (IRE)
He looked a smart horse when winning by a dozen lengths on his debut in a bumper at Wincanton on Boxing Day. However, he blew out in his next two starts at Newbury in a Listed contest and Uttoxeter but we found he was suffering with ulcers which we have treated. He possesses a good cruising speed and, provided he shows the same level of ability he displayed on his debut at Wincanton, then he will have no trouble winning races over hurdles.

MARILYN MONROE (IRE) 5 b m Scorpion (IRE) – Go On Eileen (IRE)
A ten lengths winner of her second Irish point in May, we bought her at the Cheltenham Sale four days later. She is a half-sister to Regal Encore which obviously attracted us to her. From a family who doesn't want it too soft, we are hoping she will develop into a high-class mare. A forward going mare with plenty of size, we will probably run her in a mares' bumper and then decide whether to go novice hurdling.

MIDNIGHT CALLISTO 3 br f Midnight Legend – Carrigeen Queen (IRE)
She is a nice unraced filly we bought cheaply at the Ascot June Sale as a two year old. Quite a big filly, we have done plenty with her and she is one to watch out for in a bumper during the second half of the season. From a good family, her half-sister Lily The Pink won a point-to-point and bumper earlier this year.

MIDNIGHT TUNE 7 b m Midnight Legend – Harmonic Motion (IRE)
She is another very good mare who baffled us last season and ended up winning three times, including a Grade 2 mares' hurdle at Sandown in February. We were gobsmacked when she won so easily at Wincanton and she thrived thereafter on soft ground. We had schooled her over fences but decided to remain over hurdles after her first win last year. Rated 134 over

hurdles, she will go chasing this winter and when the mud is flying I think she will make a fantastic chaser capable of taking on the geldings at some stage. In the meantime, she will contest mares' only novice chases and her schooling has been very good indeed. Even though her three wins have been gained on right-handed tracks, it won't stop me running her on left-handed ones because I don't think it's a necessity.

MILAN IN MAY (IRE) 3 gr g Milan – Nina Fontenail (FR)
Unraced, he is a lovely horse for the future and one for a bumper in the second half of the season. He has a good pedigree and I like him a lot. Already schooled over easyfix hurdles at home, I have sat on him and he possesses a lovely big stride and I think he will make a nice bumper horse before going jumping.

MONT SEGUR (FR) 3 ch g French Fifteen (FR) – Vie De Reine (FR)
One for the future, he is a very nice three year old we bought at the Doncaster May Sales. Well bred, he is a half-brother to Grade 1 winning novice chaser Terrefort and another useful chaser Vino Griego. We have schooled him already and he jumps well but he will run in a bumper in the New Year and could be targeted at the Goffs UK Spring Sale bumper at Newbury in March.

MS PARFOIS (IRE) 7 ch m Mahler – Dolly Lewis
Useful over hurdles, we always thought she would make a better chaser and she enjoyed a very good season winning three times, including two Listed chases, and finishing second in the Grade 2 Reynoldstown and National Hunt Chases at Ascot and Cheltenham respectively before chasing home Terrefort in the Grade 1 novice chase at Aintree. Rated 146 over fences, she isn't badly handicapped for races such as the Becher Chase (8th December) and Welsh National (27th December) but her owner is keen to aim her at some of the top staying events, granted extreme conditions. If it was heavy ground, I don't think she would disgrace herself in something like the *Betfair* Chase at Haydock (24th November). There is every chance we will enter her, if she is ready. If that doesn't work out, we can always revert back to mares' Listed and Graded chases under a penalty.

MYSTICAL KNIGHT 9 b g Kayf Tara – Dark Diva
We decided to take a punt and bought him cheaply at the Ascot June Sale this summer. A talented horse in his younger days, he has slipped in the ratings but is still low mileage and could be an interesting addition to the team. He looked a good prospect earlier in his career reaching a mark of 139 over fences at one stage. If we have a smooth run, we could have plenty of fun with him and he may even develop into a Saturday horse.

PURE VISION (IRE) 7 b g Milan – Distillery Lane (IRE)
I was pleased with him over fences last season winning at Ffos Las and finishing a close second at Cheltenham in April. Still a baby, I think he has more to offer and it wouldn't surprise me if he developed into an Ultima Handicap Chase at the Cheltenham Festival type horse, or even a Midlands National type. Barry Geraghty always thought he wanted better ground and he got into a lovely rhythm at Cheltenham last time only to be narrowly denied. His jumping is very good and we could aim him at some of those valuable three mile handicap chases at Ascot, which Regal Encore has done so well in.

REGAL ENCORE (IRE) 10 b g King's Theatre (IRE) – Go On Eileen (IRE)
He has been a very good horse for us over the years winning seven races and earning over £188,000 in prize-money. A Listed chase winner at Ascot in February, he also finished third in the Ladbrokes Trophy at Newbury last season. We were preparing him for the Grand National, having finished eighth the previous year, but unfortunately he had some swelling in his hock and was lame which ruled him out. We ran him in the Bet365 Gold Cup at Sandown on the final day of the season but it was very much an afterthought and he wasn't at his best. I am sure

he will be given an entry in the National once again and I would expect him to follow a similar programme. The Ladbrokes Trophy at Newbury (1st December) could also be on his agenda again, plus those good staying handicaps at Ascot.

SAM BROWN 6 b g Black Sam Bellamy (IRE) - Cream Cracker
I think he is a very good horse who had some seriously strong bumper form. He beat subsequent Grade 1 winner Lalor on his debut at Wincanton and then followed up at Newbury from the useful Chef Des Obeaux. This time last year he had a nasty accident at home and hurt his spine and tail. Not right when making his hurdles debut at Wincanton in October, we found he was suffering with ulcers. He was back to form next time though when making all to win easily at Plumpton. Unfortunately, he suffered another setback afterwards and hasn't raced since. Back in work, I am excited about him because I think he is a high-class horse who could be the real deal. A galloper, he handles soft ground very well and will be running over two and a half to three miles. Rated 135, his mark looks very fair and we could aim him at something like the valuable staying handicap hurdle at Haydock (24th November) or we could consider a Pertemps qualifier.

SOJOURN (IRE) 5 b g Getaway (GER) - Toscar (IRE)
He is another exciting young horse who finished fourth on his debut in a bumper at Newbury in November. I was pleased with his run but he wasn't right afterwards so we left him off for the remainder of the season. A big horse with a good attitude, he jumps well and, although he could run in another bumper, I think he is more likely to start off in a two mile novice hurdle. He will go up in trip as the season goes on and it wouldn't surprise me if he ended up in something like the EBF Final at Sandown in March. He may not want it too soft.

TACENDA (IRE) 6 b m Flemensfirth (USA) - Tordasia (IRE)
Lightly raced, I think she could develop into a nice staying handicap chaser this winter. She has had her fair share of setbacks, including fracturing her hind pastern twice, but she has plenty of ability winning over fences at Fontwell before chasing home subsequent Cheltenham Festival winner Benie Des Dieux in a Listed mares' chase at Carlisle. A straightforward mare, she stays well and I can envisage her contesting something like the Tommy Whittle (22nd December) and Peter Marsh Chases at Haydock off a low weight in testing ground. Three miles plus handicap chases will be on her agenda.

TARA WEST 4 b f Kayf Tara - West River (USA)
A very exciting mare who we bought at the Aintree Grand National sale during the spring. Purchased on behalf of the Decimus syndicate, she won her only Irish point for Donnchadh Doyle and I love her. She won by a head and cost £100,000, whereas the runner-up (Little Light) fetched £200,000 at the same sale. I hope she is a black type filly in the making and, while she may have a run in a mares' bumper, it won't be long before she goes novice hurdling because she jumps fantastically. Quite a heavy topped mare, she handled testing ground in her point-to-point and possesses plenty of size and scope.

URCA DE LIMA 5 b m Black Sam Bellamy (IRE) - Dame Fonteyn
She will be suited by two and a half to three mile novice hurdles this season. Noel Fehily rode her to victory on her debut at Uttoxeter in the spring of last year and thought she was very good. Unfortunately, she suffered a setback shortly afterwards and didn't run again until March. Last of eight in a Listed mares' bumper at Sandown, she may have only finished fifth at Hexham next time but Aidan Coleman liked her and said she was a decent mare. I will be disappointed if she doesn't win races over hurdles.

TRAINER'S HORSE TO FOLLOW: ACEY MILAN

Alan KING

Stables: Barbury Castle Stables, Wroughton, Wiltshire.
2017/2018: 58 Winners / 389 Runners 15% Prize-Money £923,496
www.alankingracing.co.uk

ALSA MIX (FR) 6 gr m Al Namix (FR) – Lady Tsana (FR)
A fine big mare who won her only Irish point-to-point by ten lengths in January. We bought her at the Cheltenham Sales the following month but she incurred a setback in the spring with a stress fracture. However, I was delighted with her win in a bumper at Worcester in September. She is likely to go novice hurdling now.

AZZERTI (FR) 6 b g Voix Du Nord (FR) – Zalagarry (FR)
He won over hurdles at Huntingdon in February and finished a good second at Cheltenham's April meeting. We decided to give him a run over fences at Worcester during the summer but he was past his best by then and finished fourth. However, the experience won't have done any harm and we will campaign him in two and a half miles novice chases this season.

BALLYWOOD (FR) 4 b g Ballingarry (IRE) – Miss Hollywood (FR)
Twice a winner over hurdles in France, he joined us halfway through last season. Below form in the Grade 2 Dovecote Novices' Hurdle at Kempton, we have given him a long break and he has summered very well. There is every chance we will send him novice chasing over two and two half miles and try and make use of his age allowance.

BASTIEN (FR) 7 bb g Panoramic – Que Du Charmil (FR)
He is another who is likely to go chasing, although we haven't schooled him yet. Progressive over hurdles, he won at Towcester last season and is suited by two and a half miles plus on soft ground. He looks well following his summer break.

BIG CHIEF BENNY (IRE) 7 ch g Beneficial – Be Airlie (IRE)
A dual winner over hurdles, he missed the whole of last season but is back doing roadwork. We haven't made a decision whether to keep him over hurdles or go chasing but I am looking forward to seeing him back racing. He wants two and a half miles plus.

BRIGADE OF GUARDS (IRE) 4 b g Presenting – Lasado (IRE)
Ran well first time out in a bumper at Kempton finishing fifth but then found the ground too soft in the Goffs UK Spring Sales Bumper at Newbury in March. In all likelihood, he will go hurdling straight away and has shown enough to suggest he will win races.

CANELO (IRE) 5 ch g Mahler – Nobody's Darling (IRE)
A likeable horse who got his act together in the second half of last season winning novice hurdles at Doncaster and Fontwell and finishing a good fourth in the EBF Final at Sandown in between. J.P. (McManus) bought him at the Doncaster Spring Sales and kindly sent him back to us. He will go novice chasing over two and a half to three miles.

CHOSEN PATH (IRE) 5 b g Well Chosen – Karsulu (IRE)
Third in his only Irish point-to-point before we bought him, he was progressive over hurdles last season winning at Fontwell and Kempton. He has strengthened up over the summer and, while we haven't schooled him over fences yet, he could be an interesting prospect for novice chases. Two and a half miles suit him at the moment but I think he will get further in time.

COLDITZ CASTLE (IRE) 4 ch g Getaway (GER) – Stowaway Sue (IRE)
Still quite backward last year, we gave him one run in a bumper at Warwick during the spring. Better than he showed that day, I like him and we may give him another run in a bumper before switching to hurdles.

COSMEAPOLITAN 5 b g Mawatheeq (USA) – Cosmea
He has been running on the Flat this year winning at Kempton in February before finishing fourth at Chester and Windsor. Given a break during the summer, he will have another run or two on the Flat before going jumping again. He has only raced twice over hurdles winning a novice at Newbury a couple of seasons ago. Two mile handicap hurdles will be on his agenda.

CRACKER FACTORY 3 b g Poet's Voice – Pure Song
Well bred being a half-brother to Romsdal, who was placed in the Derby, he has taken well to jumping winning at Aintree and Newton Abbot twice. It has done his confidence the world of good and he will continue in juvenile hurdles in the Autumn before having a winter break. He wouldn't want the ground too soft.

DESIRABLE COURT (IRE) 5 b m Court Cave (IRE) – Desirable Rhythm (IRE)
Successful in her only Irish point-to-point, she has had wind issues which we have operated on, hence she didn't make her hurdles debut until May. Having won well at Newton Abbot, she then finished second a couple of times. Third at Worcester in August, it won't be long before we send her chasing and aim her at mares' only events, although she is another who doesn't want slow ground.

DEYRANN DE CARJAC (FR) 5 b g Balko (FR) – Queyrann (FR)
He is a fine big horse who was placed in a bumper at Chepstow before running well over hurdles at Doncaster and Ayr. He then won in good style at Warwick in May and remains a novice for this season. Immature last year, his owners have been very patient and they are being rewarded now. I think he is one of our better novice hurdle prospects for this season and, while he has the speed for two miles, he will stay further.

DINGO DOLLAR (IRE) 6 ch g Golden Lariat (USA) – Social Society (IRE)
Took well to chasing and had a very good season over fences winning at Newbury and Doncaster before finishing runner-up in a valuable novices' handicap chase at Ayr in April. The Ladbrokes Trophy at Newbury (1st December) is likely to be his first target with one run beforehand and I would imagine he could end the season in the Scottish National. In terms of ground, he doesn't want extremes.

ELYSEES (IRE) 3 ch g Champs Elysees – Queen of Tara (IRE)
He has been progressing on the Flat winning over middle distance and staying trips at Wolverhampton and Sandown. We have schooled him and the plan is to send him juvenile hurdling. He stays well on the Flat.

FIDUX (FR) 5 b g Fine Grain (JPN) – Folle Tempete (FR)
Placed a couple of times over hurdles at Sandown and Warwick last season, he isn't the easiest to predict or win with. Given a break during the summer, we may school him over fences and see how he gets on, although he isn't the biggest.

FULL GLASS (FR) 5 b g Diamond Green (FR) – Full Tune (FR)
A lovely horse who joined us last season from France where he had some smart form over hurdles and fences for Guillaume Macaire. I was very pleased with his run at Ayr in the spring finishing third in a Listed handicap chase on ground which was quick enough for him. The BetVictor Gold Cup at Cheltenham (17th November) could be his first target and he is an exciting prospect for this season and beyond.

GIVING GLANCES 3 b f Passing Glance – Giving
A fine filly who has been doing well on the Flat this summer winning at Lingfield and Leicester over a mile and a half. She has schooled very well over hurdles and is an exciting prospect for juvenile hurdles. A full-sister to Forgiving Glance and Giveaway Glance, the Listed juvenile fillies' hurdle at Aintree (8th December) is a likely target.

GOOD MAN PAT (IRE) 5 b g Gold Well – Basically Supreme (IRE)
Had a good season over hurdles winning at Bangor and Southwell having been placed a few times during the first half of the year. A former winning pointer, he has done particularly well during the winter and will go novice chasing. He stays well.

GREY DIAMOND (FR) 4 b g Gris De Gris (IRE) – Diamond of Diana (FR)
A horse with a big engine, he did plenty of things wrong on his debut in a bumper at Ffos Las but still won. He needs to learn to relax but could be very good. It is possible he will have another run in a bumper but I think he is more likely to go straight over hurdles.

HARAMBE 5 b g Malinas (GER) – Crystal Princess (IRE)
An exciting horse who showed progressive form in bumpers. A winner at Ludlow on his debut, he then finished runner-up under a penalty at Bangor before running very well in third in the Grade 2 championship bumper at Aintree. We will start him off in a two mile novice hurdle but he will stay further, if necessary.

HAREFIELD (IRE) 5 b g Doyen (IRE) – Bobbi's Venture (IRE)
He is a fine big imposing horse who won over hurdles at Warwick last season but also suffered a couple of falls, including in testing conditions back at Warwick on his latest run. His future lies over fences but I will probably give him another run or two over hurdles first to make sure it hasn't knocked his confidence.

HOTTER THAN HELL (FR) 4 ch f No Risk At All (FR) – Ombrelle (FR)
She is a lovely filly who finished runner-up on her debut in the Goffs UK Spring Sales Bumper at Newbury in March. I was delighted with her performance and we will more than likely run her in a mares' bumper and then consider aiming her at some of those Listed mares' bumpers and try and get some black type.

JUST IN TIME 4 b g Excelebration (IRE) – Flying Finish (FR)
A five times winner on the Flat, including at Sandown in July and Goodwood in August, he stays well and appreciates cut in the ground. The plan is to send him novice hurdling after a few more runs on the Flat. He has already schooled and jumps well.

KERROW (IRE) 8 b g Mahler – Olives Hall (IRE)
Back in work having missed the whole of last season. He was a useful staying novice chaser winning twice and running well in the National Hunt Chase over four miles at the Cheltenham Festival. Still lightly raced over fences, we haven't made any plans but we will be aiming him at three miles plus handicap chases.

KOOTENAY RIVER (IRE) 4 ch g Dubai Destination (USA) – Siwaara (IRE)
A likeable sort who won his only English point-to-point by twenty lengths in March. We purchased him a few days later at the Cheltenham Festival Sale and he ran two good races in point-to-point bumpers in the spring. Runner-up at both Exeter and Aintree, he will go novice hurdling over two and a half miles plus.

LABEL DES OBEAUX (FR) 7 b g Saddler Maker (IRE) – La Bessiere (FR)
Ran some good races last season without getting his head in front. Sixth in the Scottish National last time, he will follow a similar programme and continue to run in the decent staying handicaps. The Skybet Chase at Doncaster, in which he finished sixth last season, is likely to be on his agenda again before a return to Ayr in the spring.

LISP (IRE) 4 ch g Poet's Voice – Hora
A half-brother to Coeur De Lion and Thomas Campbell, he did well in juvenile hurdles winning at Plumpton and Fontwell. He was his own worst enemy at times last year though pulling hard but, despite that, he still ran a solid race in the Victor Ludorum Hurdle at Haydock in February. A faller early on in the Fred Winter Juvenile Hurdle at Cheltenham, he will be campaigned in two mile handicap hurdles.

LORD WALSINGHAM 4 b g Shirocco (GER) – Glorious Twelfth (IRE)
I thought he was one of our better bumper horses last season but he was disappointing on his debut at Kempton. He had an issue with one of his knees afterwards though so I am hoping he was still immature last season and will improve. We may run him in another bumper.

MANOR PARK 3 b g Medicean – Jadeel
A horse I really like, he won on the Flat at Windsor in April but hasn't shown what he's capable of yet. Third at Newbury last time, he found the ground too fast and will benefit from racing on an easier surface. The intention is to send him juvenile hurdling later on.

MASTER BLUEYES (IRE) 5 gr g Mastercraftsman (IRE) – Miss Blueyes (IRE)
Absent since running in the Triumph Hurdle in 2017, he was a smart juvenile a couple of seasons ago but missed the whole of last season due to an injury. Back in pre-training, he will either contest handicaps or conditions hurdles.

MIA'S STORM (IRE) 8 b m September Storm (GER) – Letitia's Gain (IRE)
Started her chasing career very well by winning at Chepstow in October and then following up in a Listed mares' event at Market Rasen. However, her season petered out after that because she couldn't handle the soft ground in the Kauto Star Novices' Chase at Kempton on Boxing Day and she was beaten when falling at Ayr last time. We have given her a long break since and she looks very well having enjoyed a good summer. I might give her a run over hurdles to help her confidence before aiming her at the Graded mares' chases. She doesn't want it soft though.

MIDNIGHT MAESTRO 6 b g Midnight Legend – Calamintha
Full-brother to William H Bonney, he was unlucky during the first half of the season but came good in the spring winning over hurdles at Market Rasen in May. Quite late going for his break, he will go novice chasing when he comes back. He handles most types of ground but doesn't want extremes.

MIDNIGHTREFERENDUM 5 b m Midnight Legend – Forget The Ref (IRE)
Another lovely mare who was very progressive in bumpers last season. A winner at Warwick on her second start, she ran really well to finish runner-up in the Grade 2 mares' bumper at Aintree last time. She has a good attitude and her performances didn't surprise us. She is an exciting prospect for mares' novice hurdles.

MR PUMBLECHOOK 4 b g Midnight Legend – Definitely Pip (IRE)
Ran OK in a couple of bumpers last season, including when finishing sixth in the Spring Sales bumper at Newbury in March. He has matured since and may contest another bumper before going hurdling.

MYBOYSAM 4 b g Delegator – Fantastisch (IRE)
I was pleased with his debut run in a bumper at Huntingdon finishing second. Too gassy next time at the same track, he has strengthened up since and will probably go straight over hurdles.

MYSTICAL CLOUDS (IRE) 5 gr g Cloudings (IRE) – Silent Valley
Still a bit weak last year, he had a couple of runs in bumpers but improved when switched to hurdles in the second half of the season. Third at Doncaster and Warwick, he has matured during the summer and I hope he will progress over hurdles before jumping fences eventually.

NAYATI (FR) 4 b g Spirit One (FR) – Smadouce (FR)
A winner on the Flat in France, he won his first two starts over hurdles for us at Newbury and Ascot, albeit in fortunate circumstances at the latter track. I think he had had enough by then because he had been on the go for a while in France. Given a break since his run at Market Rasen in February, he will go handicap hurdling.

NEBUCHADNEZZAR (FR) 3 b g Planteur (IRE) – Trexana
Despite being a maiden on the Flat, he has run some good races. Third at Newbury in June, he found the ground too lively so we gave him a break. He will have another run or two on the Flat but I think he will make an interesting juvenile hurdler. He loves soft ground and will have no problem staying two miles.

NEWTOWN BOY (IRE) 5 b g Beneficial – Tanit Lady (IRE)
A big strong horse who finished second in both his bumpers at Taunton and Southwell during the spring. He works like a very good horse at home and we will start him off over two miles over hurdles because he isn't short of speed.

NOBBY 4 b g Authorized (IRE) – Magic Music (IRE)
Won an English point-to-point over two miles before finishing second in a bumper at Warwick in March on his first run for us. We took him back there a couple of months later and he appreciated the better ground and went one better. He will go novice hurdling.

NOTACHANCE (IRE) 4 b g Mahler – Ballybrowney Hall (IRE)
A fine big four year old who finished second in his only Irish point for Denis Murphy before we acquired him at the Cheltenham February Sale. Yet to run for us, we did a bit with him at home during the spring and he will go novice hurdling over two and a half miles plus.

NYLON SPEED (IRE) 4 b g Campanologist (USA) – Neuquen (IRE)
A winner over middle distances on the Flat in Germany, he didn't run last season because of a few issues, including his wind, which we have operated on. However, he is a horse with a lot of ability and I was delighted with his win on the Flat at Kempton in August. He has schooled well over hurdles but may have another on the Flat before going jumping. I will try and keep him to decent ground because of his breathing issues.

OUR POWER (IRE) 3 b g Power – Scripture (IRE)
Joined us earlier this year, I have been pleased with him. Fourth over ten furlongs at Chepstow on his first run for us, he appreciated the step up to a mile and a half at Ffos Las in August. Despite showing signs of greenness, he won well and the first two pulled seven lengths clear of the third. He then finished runner-up at Chepstow on his handicap debut. Suited by some ease in the ground, we have schooled him and he will go juvenile hurdling in the Autumn.

OUTOFTHEQUESTION 4 b g Delegator – Why Dubai (USA)
Having been placed a few times during the spring, he has really got his act together on the Flat during the summer winning twice at Newbury. Physically, he was still quite weak but has strengthened up and is another who will go juvenile hurdling later on. He has always had ability.

PADDY BOSS (IRE) 6 ch g Gamut (IRE) – Agladora (FR)
He won a bumper at Warwick on his debut in the spring of last year but missed the whole of last season due to injury. Back cantering, he will go novice hurdling.

PASSING CALL 5 b m Passing Glance – Call Me A Legend
She finished second a number of times over hurdles last season having the misfortune to bump into some good rivals. Unlucky not to win at Newton Abbot during the summer, she thankfully won her next three at Worcester, Bangor and Newton Abbot. Still eligible for novice events, we could also go down the handicap route or have a look at some of the better mares' events.

POTTERMAN 5 b g Sulamani (IRE) – Polly Potter
Won twice over hurdles in the spring/summer at Huntingdon and Bangor, he is still a novice for this season. Although he handles soft ground, he doesn't want it too testing because he is quite a good actioned horse. He got bogged down in heavy ground at Bangor last winter. Given a break since his last run, he has benefited from stepping up to two and a half miles.

POTTERS VISION (IRE) 5 b m Getaway (GER) – Peripheral Vision (IRE)
Runner-up in an Irish point-to-point in February, she hadn't been with us for long when finishing fifth in a mares' bumper at Bangor in the spring. She ran OK but I would like to think she is better than she showed that day. We may give her another run in a bumper before going hurdling.

REDICEAN 4 b g Medicean – Red Halo (IRE)
Bought at the Newmarket Horses in Training Sale last Autumn, he did very well over hurdles winning his first three starts at Kempton, including the Grade 2 Adonis Hurdle in February. We then ran him in the Triumph Hurdle at Cheltenham but it completely bottomed him in the testing ground. We ran him back on the Flat at Chester at the end of May but he was still feeling the effects and was below par. Given a two months break, he looks fresh and well and I still think he is a very good horse. Rated 147 over hurdles, we haven't made any plans.

RIVER FROST 6 b g Silver Frost (IRE) – River Test
Fifth in the Silver Trophy at Chepstow on his reappearance, he only raced three times last season. We haven't schooled him yet but I think the intention is to send him novice chasing.

SCARLET DRAGON 5 b g Sir Percy – Welsh Angel
He has enjoyed a good summer break which is his first one for a while. Runner-up in the Grade 2 Dovecote Novices' Hurdle at Kempton on his first run for us, he then ran at Aintree before finishing third in a Group 3 event at Newbury on the Flat in May. Still a novice, we will keep him low key for the time being and try and win a hurdle race before stepping back up in class. I think he wants a sharp track such as Kempton.

SCEAU ROYAL (FR) 6 b g Doctor Dino (FR) – Sandside (FR)
A high-class hurdler, he developed into a very smart two mile novice chaser last season winning four out of five, including the Grade 1 Henry VIII Novices' Chase at Sandown in December. He then won a Grade 2 at Doncaster but picked up a minor niggle before Cheltenham. We could have rushed him back for Aintree but decided to give him more time. Back cantering, the Shloer Chase at Cheltenham (18th November) is a possible starting point.

SENIOR CITIZEN 5 b g Tobougg (IRE) – Mothers Help
He is a lovely horse who finished second in an Irish point before joining us. Third in a bumper at Towcester in February, I was delighted with his run at Ayr in the spring filling the same position. He will go straight over hurdles.

SHANNON HILL 4 b g Kayf Tara - Shannon Native (IRE)
We bought him at the Aintree Grand National Sale in April having won his only English point-to-point by a very wide margin. I don't know a great deal about him other than that, so we will see how he trains before making any plans. I hope he is a promising young horse.

SKIN DEEP (IRE) 5 b m Presenting - Maryota (FR)
From the family of Yanworth, she didn't make her debut until the spring, due to a chip being removed from one of her knees. Placed in bumpers at Wincanton and Southwell, she then won at Worcester in July. Switched to hurdles, she had schooled well prior to her saddle slipping at Bangor in August. However, she made amends next time by winning at Worcester three weeks later. She looks a progressive mare.

SMITH'S BAY 5 b g Midnight Legend - Takotna (IRE)
A horse with a lot of ability, I was pleased with him last season winning a bumper on his debut at Taunton. Over the top by the time he ran again at Doncaster, he will go novice hurdling.

STYLISH MOMENT (IRE) 5 b g Milan - Up The Style (IRE)
Placed in a bumper at Bangor on his debut, he finished third a couple of times over hurdles at Doncaster and Wincanton. He has benefited from his summer break and I am expecting him to pay his way over hurdles. His future lies over fences though.

SULA ISLAND 4 ch f Sulamani (IRE) - Cosmea
Half-sister to Cosmeapolitan and William Hunter, she isn't over big but has schooled well and the plan is to send her hurdling. She has been running consistently on the Flat this year winning at Chepstow during the summer.

TALKISCHEAP (IRE) 6 b g Getaway (GER) - Carrigmoorna Oak (IRE)
He amazed me when he won at Newbury in February because I didn't think he would handle the testing ground. Rated 141 over hurdles, he won three out of three in point-to-points and we are going to send him novice chasing over two and a half miles plus.

THE DEVILS DROP (IRE) 5 b g Court Cave (IRE) - Concernforkillen (IRE)
Has been in good form during the summer winning over hurdles at Southwell twice and Worcester. He ran some decent races in defeat last season but we operated on his wind during the spring. I think a combination of the surgery and racing on better ground has been the key to him. Still a novice, he will continue over hurdles for the time being but it won't be long before he goes chasing.

THE GLANCING QUEEN (IRE) 4 b f Jeremy (USA) - Glancing (IRE)
A lovely filly who I have been very pleased with. She won her only Irish point-to-point for Colin Bowe in March before we bought her a few days later at the Cheltenham Festival Sale. We did some work with her during the spring and she looks a good prospect for mares' novice hurdles over two and a half miles.

THE UNIT (IRE) 7 b g Gold Well - Sovana (FR)
He has got his act together over fences winning twice at Hexham and Newton Abbot in June and August respectively. I thought he won well at the latter track when we reverted back to the old tactics of holding him up. Prior to that, we rode him from the front but it didn't suit him because he raced with the choke out. We will aim him a bit higher now but he doesn't want the ground too soft. Trips around two and a half miles are ideal.

TILLYTHETANK (IRE) 5 b m Stowaway - All Heart
Placed in her two Irish points before we acquired her, she won over hurdles at Exeter in May and therefore remains a novice for this season. Runner-up last time at Stratford, she was beaten by a decent mare. She seems to appreciate better ground.

TIMOTEO (FR) 5 br g Diamond Green (FR) – Goldnella (FR)
He is our Million In Mind horse for this year. Ex-French, he was runner-up twice over hurdles a couple of seasons ago but got a leg at Newbury and missed the whole of last term. Back in work, he is a maiden under all codes and will continue in novice hurdles for the time being.

VOIE DANS VOIE (FR) 5 br g Coastal Path – Peggy Pierji (FR)
A very good looking horse who was a bit unlucky not to win over hurdles last season. Runner-up a couple of times at Towcester and Huntingdon, he has a reasonable level of form and we are going to send him chasing. Rated 121, we will look for a novices' handicap chase over two and a half miles.

WILLIAM H BONNEY 7 b g Midnight Legend – Calamintha
A frustrating horse because he has run some very good races, including in the Greatwood Hurdle at Cheltenham last November when travelling strongly until finishing fifth. He failed to reproduce that in his subsequent starts. He will continue to run in the decent handicap hurdles but, if he is struggling, we have the option of going chasing.

YANWORTH 8 ch g Norse Dancer (IRE) – Yota (FR)
Having won two of his four starts over fences, including the Grade 2 Dipper Novices' Chase at Cheltenham on New Year's Day, he reverted back to hurdles in the spring. Sixth in the Stayers' Hurdle at Cheltenham, he unfortunately picked up a niggle afterwards and therefore won't be in action until the second half of this season. No decision has been made whether he stays over hurdles or goes back chasing.

YESANDNO (IRE) 5 b g Scorpion (IRE) – In Fact (IRE)
A likeable sort who unseated his rider in his only Irish point before we purchased him at the Cheltenham December Sales. I thought he ran well in a bumper in foul conditions at Towcester in the spring finishing third. A big strapping horse, he will go hurdling over two and a half miles.

ZIGA BOY (FR) 9 gr g Califet (FR) – Our Ziga (FR)
Absent since winning the Skybet Chase at Doncaster over eighteen months ago, he is back doing roadwork. His main target is the Grand National and it is a case of working backwards from there. I would imagine we may aim him at the Skybet Chase in January once again en route.

TRAINER'S HORSE TO FOLLOW: GIVING GLANCES

Tom LACEY

Stables: Cottage Field Stables Ltd., Sapness Farm, Woolhope, Herefordshire.
2017/2018: 39 Winners / 158 Runners 25% Prize-Money £359,309
www.cottagefield.co.uk

ALBERTO'S DREAM 9 b g Fantastic Spain (USA) – Molly's Folly
We inherited a very well handicapped horse halfway through last season winning four out of five in just over a month in March/April. Rated 80 when he arrived, it is going to be much tougher off his current mark of 115. Suited by deep ground, he wants three miles plus and, granted such conditions, I hope he will continue to progress.

CONINGSBY 5 ch g Midnight Legend – Motcombe (IRE)
A winning pointer, the plan is to send him over fences and start him off in a novices' handicap chase. Rated 127 over hurdles, he finished second on his first couple of starts at Exeter and Wetherby before disappointing last time at Uttoxeter. We will probably start him off over shorter trips but he will be suited by three miles later on.

DORKING BOY 4 ch g Schiaparelli (GER) - Megasue
He is a lovely young horse who didn't surprise us when winning a bumper on his debut at Market Rasen. His owners are a great sporting bunch and they always have a runner at the Punchestown Festival so we ran him in the Grade 1 championship event and he didn't disgrace himself. I have been pleased with him during the summer and he will go straight over hurdles. We will start him off over a stiff two miles at somewhere like Chepstow and he is one to look forward to. The plan is to get his palate fired before he reappears.

DORKING COCK (IRE) 4 b g Winged Love (IRE) - Kiss Jolie (FR)
Another very nice youngster who has summered really well. Mentally, he is still immature and was fractious before his debut at Newbury in the Goffs UK Spring Sales bumper in March. Despite that, he still ran well to finish fourth and I was very pleased with him. Aidan Coleman partnered him and said it was one of the roughest bumpers he had ridden in. We will take it steady with him because he needs to mature mentally but there is no doubt he possesses plenty of ability. We have the option of running him in another bumper, although I think its more likely he will go hurdling. He will stay two and a half miles but may start off over shorter.

EN MEME TEMPS (FR) 4 b g Saddler Maker (IRE) - Lady Reine (FR)
He made his debut in a bumper at Chepstow in February but tried to do everything in one breath before finishing sixth. Provided he learns to settle, he could be a nice horse who will be suited by two and a half to three miles over hurdles this season.

EQUUS AMADEUS (IRE) 5 b g Beat Hollow - Charade (IRE)
A bumper and hurdles winner last season at Exeter and Uttoxeter respectively, he ran some good races in defeat during the spring/summer. Third at Sandown on the final day of the season, he was unlucky at Market Rasen when encountering traffic problems before finishing fourth in a decent handicap hurdle at Newton Abbot in September. Very much a chaser in the making, I think he will improve over fences because he is learning to settle having been gassy early on. Inclined to pull too hard in his bumpers, he is suited by two and a half miles but I think he will stay three over fences. He should make a lovely chaser.

FLASHING GLANCE 5 b g Passing Glance - Don And Gerry (IRE)
Twice a winner over hurdles at Stratford and Ludlow, he finished third on his chasing debut at Southwell in August. He is likely to continue in novice chases, although we could switch between the two. I think he will respect fences more than hurdles and we will keep him to the minimum trip for the time being.

JESTER JET 8 br m Overbury (IRE) - Hendre Hotshot
She has been a fabulous mare for us winning five times, including three last season. A Grade 3 winner at Aintree's Grand National meeting, she has done nothing but improve and thrives on her work. She is a joy to train. Runner-up at Haydock last time, she didn't appear to stay three miles at Cheltenham in December but I think she will get the trip on a flat track. Versatile in terms of ground, she has schooled well over fences and the plan is to go novice chasing. Rated 142 over hurdles, I hope she will continue to improve.

KATESON 5 gr g Black Sam Bellamy (IRE) - Silver Kate (IRE)
I was delighted with him last season winning first time out at Chepstow and finishing second on three occasions, including in the Grade 2 championship bumper at Aintree in April. This time last year, I thought he might have a couple of outings but he ended up running five times. Out of a decent mare, he has schooled well over hurdles and is likely to start off over a stiff two miles before stepping up in trip in due course. I am expecting him to stay well.

KIMBERLITE CANDY (IRE) 6 b g Flemensfirth (USA) - Mandys Native (IRE)
While not the easiest to catch right, he is a capable horse on his day. Twice a winner over fences last season at Market Rasen and Chepstow, he was badly hampered at Newbury early on, in between. Stepping up to three miles at Chepstow suited him and, if on a going day, I think he will continue to be competitive off his mark of 133.

MEEP MEEP (IRE) 5 ch m Flemensfirth (USA) - Charming Leader (IRE)
I was over the moon with her last season winning first time out at Chepstow before finishing fourth in the Grade 2 mares' bumper at Aintree in April. I thought she would run well beforehand and she wasn't beaten far. She likes soft ground and we will start her off in a mares' only novice hurdle over two miles. I am sure she will stay further but I prefer to start them off over shorter trips rather than burning them out over longer distances early on.

POLYDORA (IRE) 6 b g Milan - Mandysway (IRE)
A half-brother to dual Grade 2 winner Roberto Goldback, he is prone to a dust allergy and is therefore difficult to predict on occasions. He has also suffered with bad feet in the past but they are a lot better now. Twice a winner over hurdles last season at Chepstow and Exeter, he was also runner-up over three miles at Aintree in May. An ex-pointer, he wants two and a half miles plus and will go novice chasing.

SEBASTOPOL (IRE) 4 b g Fame And Glory - Knockcroghery (IRE)
A very exciting prospect who will go novice hurdling in the Autumn. A fifteen lengths winner of the second division of an open maiden point at Larkhill in January, he didn't surprise us when winning a bumper at Ayr's Scottish National meeting. I think he is a good horse who could be competing in some of the better novice hurdles this season. I have been pleased with him during the summer - he has done really well strengthening up. Two miles will be his trip to begin with because he isn't slow. Our best two pointers last season were him and Energumene but this horse has more toe.

SIR EGBERT 5 b g Kayf Tara - Little Miss Flora
Placed a couple of times at Ffos Las and Ludlow, he got his head in front at Taunton last time. Raised six pounds since to a mark of 119, he will go novice handicap chasing and will benefit from a step up to two and a half miles.

SNAPDRAGON FIRE (IRE) 5 b g Getaway (GER) - Global Diamond (IRE)
A maiden over hurdles, he finished runner-up on three occasions, including at Hereford in January and the handicapper raised him seven pounds. Badly handicapped as a result, we will try and win a hurdle race with him before going chasing. Already schooled over fences, I think he will make a better chaser. In terms of trip, he wants less than three miles.

SORAYA 4 b f Black Sam Bellamy (IRE) - Star Ar Aghaidh (IRE)
She is a lovely filly who I really like. Owned by former champion jockey Alastair Crow, she won a two runner point-to-point at Knightswick in late April with her only rival departing at the third fence. It is no easy task for a four year old to go round on her own. We entered her in a bumper at Bangor in May the following month but felt she would benefit from a summer break instead. She has shown enough to suggest she can win a mares' bumper.

THAIS TOIR (FR) 3 b g Diamond Boy (FR) - Scotland Act (FR)
We have a lovely bunch of three year olds, including this three year old we bought at the Tattersalls Derby Sale in June (€80,000). He looks a very nice horse for the future.

THOMAS PATRICK (IRE) 6 b g Winged Love (IRE) – Huncheon Siss (IRE)
He enjoyed a super season winning over hurdles at Exeter in November before switching to fences in the New Year. He was successful in three of his four starts, culminating in victory in a Grade 3 handicap chase at Aintree on Grand National day. Raised nine pounds since to a mark of 148, we still have a lot of thinking to do regarding his future plans. Long-term, I regard him as a Grand National horse one day but he is still only six and a second season novice. The Ladbroke Trophy at Newbury (1st December) is a possibility with the likelihood of one or two races beforehand, possibly over hurdles. The Becher Chase at Aintree (8th December) is an alternative or we could look for something smaller. He wants soft ground, although I don't think he wants it heavy. Richard Johnson has ridden him in all four of his races over fences and I am hoping he will be available to continue the association this season. In terms of appearance, he looks a completely different horse compared to this time last year. Twelve months ago, he took a lot of getting fit and looked like a hunter. He now looks like a racehorse.

VADO FORTE (FR) 5 b g Walk In The Park (IRE) – Gloire (FR)
Very progressive during the second half of last season, he won three times, including the Sussex Champion Hurdle at Plumpton. Still a work in progress last term, he was fractious as a four year old but has grown up a lot since. The Welsh Champion Hurdle at Ffos Las (20th October) and Greatwood Hurdle at Cheltenham (18th November) are possible early season targets and then, depending on how he performs, he is likely to go novice chasing. It would be nice to think he could develop into a contender for the novices' handicap chase over two and a half miles at the Cheltenham Festival in March but he needs to rise in the ratings between now and then.

Unnamed 3 b g Fame And Glory – Westgrove Berry (IRE)
Another potentially very nice unraced three year old we acquired at the Tattersalls Derby Sale in June (€100,000). He is a half-brother to Jetstream Jack.

Unnamed 3 b g Kayf Tara – Megalex
Very well bred being a full-brother to Ballyandy and Megastar, he is another three year old to look forward to.

Below are five promising youngsters Tom sold during the spring/summer and are worth looking out for this winter.

ENERGUMENE (FR) 4 b g Denham Red (FR) – Olinight (FR)
"He bolted up in a point-to-point in the first division of the open maiden at Larkhill in early January. The winning time was quicker than the second division, which Sebastopol won. Subsequently bought privately by **Willie Mullins**, who also purchased Blackbow from us last year, I think he is an absolute weapon."

INTERCONNECTED 4 br g Network (GER) – R De Rien Sivola (FR)
Bought by **Grech & Parkin** for £220,000 at the Cheltenham Festival March Sale, he has joined **Nicky Henderson**.
"He is a spectacular jumper who won the second of his two point-to-points at Larkhill in February. He is a nice horse with a good pedigree and I think he will be capable of winning a bumper because he stays well."

KING ROLAND (IRE) 4 br g Stowaway – Kiltiernan Robin (IRE)
A ten lengths winner of his only point at Larkhill on Easter Sunday, he was subsequently bought privately for **Masterson Holdings Limited** and is now in training with **Harry Fry**.
"I think he is exceptional. He jumps beautifully, stays and gallops. He was very raw and still up behind when he made his debut. With another summer under his belt, he could be anything and possesses the ability to win a bumper."

MUSE OF FIRE (IRE) 4 b g Getaway (GER) – Maria Sophia (IRE)
"A winner of his only point-to-point at Larkhill, he won despite the ground because I think he will be a better horse on decent ground. We sold him to **John Groucott** and is a horse I like."

PORT OF MARS (IRE) 4 b g Westerner – Sarahall (IRE)
He has joined **Olly Murphy** having been bought for £60,000 at the Cheltenham Festival Sale in March.
"A three and a half lengths winner of his sole point at Brocklesby Park in February, he is an out and out galloper. A full-brother to Westend Story, he stays well and it wouldn't surprise me if he won a bumper."

TRAINER'S HORSE TO FOLLOW: SEBASTOPOL

Donald McCAIN

Stables: Bankhouse, Cholmondeley, Cheshire.
2017/2018: 98 Winners / 539 Runners 18% Prize-Money £838,514
www.donaldmccain.co.uk

ALWAYS DU CERISIER (FR) 5 b g Apsis – Tyr Elissa (FR)
A big weak horse we bought cheaply at the Cheltenham June Sale last year having finished third in a couple of Irish points. He did nothing wrong on his first run for us in a bumper at Bangor in the spring. His schooling has gone well and he will be novice hurdling over two and a half to three miles.

ARMATTIEKAN (IRE) 4 b g Arakan (USA) – Serpentine Mine (IRE)
We bought him at the Ascot June Sale having finished fourth in his only point-to-point in Ireland for a small firm. I don't mind his sire and he ran against some nice horses in May. A hardy racy sort, he is a likeable horse who didn't cost very much.

BIRCH VALE (IRE) 6 br m Presenting – Oscar Rebel (IRE)
A genuine mare who was still weak last year but she came good in the spring winning a couple of novice hurdles at Sedgefield and Hexham. We have given her a break since and we will be aiming her at handicap hurdles with a view to going chasing later on. Both her wins have been gained over two miles but she will stay further.

BREAKFAST (IRE) 3 b c Kodiac – Pride Celebre (IRE)
We bought him out of Jamie Osborne's yard after winning a ten furlongs claimer at Leicester in June. I was pleased with his first run for us at Haydock the following month finishing second in a mile and a quarter handicap off a mark of 70. He then made a good start to his hurdling career when winning by nine lengths at Market Rasen in August. He will continue in juvenile hurdles.

BRIGHT SIDE OFLIFE (IRE) 5 ch m Doyen (IRE) – Lough Lein Leader (IRE)
There were a stack of mares who had form with each other in Irish points and she was one of them. Trained by Denis Murphy, she had a couple of runs winning on the second occasion in March. We bought her at the Ascot Sales a few weeks later and I hope there is plenty of improvement in her. A big filly, she still looked raw and immature in her races. By the same sire as Doyly Carte, she may contest a mares' bumper before going hurdling.

CAPTAIN SAM 6 b g Black Sam Bellamy (IRE) – Grande Terre (IRE)
Graham Calder kindly sent me three horses during the summer and this is a good looking type who has only raced three times. Runner-up at Doncaster in a bumper on his debut a few years ago, he has had his share of problems since but hopefully we can have a clear run with him.

CHTI BALKO (FR) 6 br g Balko (FR) – Ina Scoop (FR)
He has been a star for us winning three times over hurdles, including at Haydock last season. Runner-up at the same track behind William of Orange on his latest start, his style of racing means the handicapper is quite hard on him and never relents. Rated 142, we are toying with the idea of sending him over fences but he has become very slick over his hurdles and I am conscious of the fact he made mistakes in his only point-to-point. It is therefore possible he is more of a hurdler. Two miles on heavy ground is ideal and he loves Haydock (1412).

CLASSIC IMPACT (IRE) 6 b m Witness Box (USA) – Tanya Thyne (IRE)
A full-sister to Testify and Wymott she finished second in her only point-to-point for Colin Bowe in March of last year and was with us last season. However, she had a setback so we gave her plenty of time to get over it. A great big filly, she will run in mares' novice hurdles.

CLOUDY DREAM (IRE) 8 gr g Cloudings (IRE) – Run Away Dream (IRE)
Along with Mount Mews, Mr Hemmings kindly sent him to me during the summer and he has settled in really well. Adrian Lane rides him at home everyday and I am delighted with him. He has some very good form and there is every chance we will start him off in the Old Roan Chase at Aintree (28th October), a race in which he finished second last year.

COURT JURADO (IRE) 4 b g Court Cave (IRE) – Glen Eile (IRE)
Successful in his only Irish point for Donnchadh Doyle in April, we acquired him at the Doncaster Spring Sale the following month and I think he will prove good value. It was a fast ground spring point but he won well and is a tough hardy sort.

COUSIN OSCAR (IRE) 6 b g Oscar (IRE) – On The Jetty (IRE)
Twice a winner over hurdles, he is a maiden over fences after three runs but I think he is better than his mark. He has been hobdayed and, if he can recapture the pick of his hurdles form, he is more than capable of winning races over fences. We have given him a break and, while two and a half miles suits him, he isn't slow.

DEAR SIRE (FR) 6 gr g Al Namix (FR) – Polismith (FR)
He has been a wonderful horse for us winning eight times and being placed at Aintree's Grand National meeting. I was very pleased with his chasing debut at Cartmel in July. With the exception of one fence when he got in tight, his jumping was slick and he found more on the run-in when the second came to challenge. He was unlucky next time when going well and falling at the second last a month later at the same track. He is tough and genuine but is inclined to pull up in front when he thinks he has done enough. He stays two and a half miles but is better over shorter trips when they go quicker early on. I hope he will develop into a decent novice chaser, although he doesn't want it too soft.

DEVITO'SREDROBIN (IRE) 5 b m Robin Des Champs (FR) – Koko Rose (IRE)
Bought cheaply at the Cheltenham April Sale, she raced in three Irish points winning her latest start having unseated her rider and then finished second. She is by a good stallion and will go mares' novice hurdling.

FEDERICI 9 b g Overbury (IRE) – Vado Via
A winner at Kelso in November, he was fourth in the Becher Chase at Aintree and fifth in the Skybet Chase at Doncaster. Pulled up in the Cross Country chase at the Cheltenham Festival, he is a very good jumper and will contest the decent long distance handicap chases. The Becher Chase (8th December) could be on his agenda once again.

FIN AND GAME (IRE) 6 b g Oscar (IRE) – Miss Cilla (IRE)
From the family of Peddlers Cross, he is in good form at home and looks great. Twice a winner over hurdles at Wetherby and Bangor, he ran OK at Ayr last time. Despite being fairly treated

over hurdles, he is a big lengthy horse who will go chasing this season. I think he will have more respect for fences and, although he will stay two and a half miles, we will keep him over two miles for the time being. He doesn't want extremes of ground.

FIRST ACCOUNT 4 bb g Malinas (GER) – Kind Nell
A big rangy horse we bought privately for Richard Gilbert having won his only Irish point by six lengths in March for Colin Bowe. We cantered him during the spring and he went nicely. He could make his debut in a bumper.

FLEMENS STORY (IRE) 7 b g Flemensfirth (USA) – Amelia Earhart (IRE)
A winning pointer, he had a couple of runs over hurdles at Kelso last Autumn but then incurred an injury which meant he missed the rest of the season. A nice straightforward horse, we have given him plenty of time and he will continue in staying novice hurdles. Long-term, he wants a fence and will hopefully develop into a solid staying chaser.

GAELIK COAST (FR) 4 b g Coastal Path – Gaelika (IRE)
Purchased on behalf of Tim Leslie at the Aintree Grand National Sale for £110,000, I think he would have cost more if he was slightly bigger, but he is a sharp, racy sort who I like a lot. An impressive four lengths winner of his only point-to-point on the 1st April for Donnchadh Doyle, he was recommended to me and I think he is an exciting prospect. He could run in a bumper before going hurdling.

HENRY'S JOY (IRE) 5 b g Craigsteel – Shocona (IRE)
A funny horse, he has his good and bad days but won a £30,000 series final hurdle race at Sedgefield in March. Still quite immature, he will jump a fence having been placed twice in Irish points. He doesn't want the ground too soft and may benefit from a step up to three miles in due course.

HILLS OF DUBAI (IRE) 9 ch g Dubai Destination (USA) – Mowazana (IRE)
He is fragile having come back from a severe injury and isn't as quick as his half-brother Wells Farhh Go but he is capable of winning more races. He won a couple of small races at Ayr last winter before finishing second at Haydock. If we get a smooth run with him and he encounters his favoured soft ground over three miles at the likes of Ayr, Haydock and Newcastle, he is handicapped to win more races.

KATACHENKO (IRE) 9 b g Kutub (IRE) – Karalee (IRE)
A former winner of the Red Rum Chase at Aintree, he is much more chilled out nowadays and I think he is crying out for a step up to three miles on nice ground. He didn't have much luck last season. Beaten a nose at Aintree in December on ground which was much too soft for him, Brian (Hughes) said he was cantering when falling at the fifth last in a Listed chase at Ayr's Scottish National meeting.

KNOCKROBIN (IRE) 7 bb g Robin Des Pres (FR) – Tudor Style (IRE)
Bought out of a small firm having won his only point-to-point, he is a big horse who has taken a bit of time. However, he won over hurdles at Bangor in March and should have followed up at Sedgefield next time. We are going to send him novice chasing starting off over two and a half miles, although he will want three miles later on.

LASTBUTNOTLEAST (IRE) 8 b m Flemensfirth (USA) – Lakil Princess (IRE)
She won a novice chase at Haydock over Christmas in gruelling conditions and I don't think she ever got over it. Third next time in a Listed mares' chase at Leicester, she twisted a shoe that day which could have been nasty. We gave her a run over hurdles at Kelso in the spring against the geldings with the objective of finding some nicer ground. She ran OK but we will try and keep her to the better mares' staying chases.

LORD SPRINGFIELD (IRE) 5 ch g Well Chosen – Super Thyne (IRE)
A big rangy staying chaser in the making, he looks a nice horse who won his only Irish point in April before we bought him at the Punchestown Festival Sale eleven days later. The runner-up has finished second in a bumper since for Pauline Robson and he is by a sire I like. Purchased for Richard Gilbert, I think he will do well in northern staying novice hurdles.

LOUGH DERG JEWEL (IRE) 7 b g Oscar (IRE) – River Valley Lady (IRE)
An honest straightforward horse who won twice over two and a half miles at Ayr last season, although he stays well and is more of a three miler. Despite winning on heavy ground at Ayr, he doesn't want it too testing. Third at Kelso in the spring, he came back sore behind so we have given him a break.

MOUNT MEWS (IRE) 7 b g Presenting – Kneeland Lass (IRE)
He arrived at the same time as Cloudy Dream and appears to be a very straightforward horse. Cantering away at the moment, we know he has some smart form but he lacks a bit of chasing experience. A winner over fences at Doncaster, he was third in the Grade 2 Reynoldstown Novices' Chase at Ascot and that is the route we will taking with him this season.

MR MCGO (IRE) 7 b g Touch of Land (FR) – La Principal (IRE)
Missed the whole of last season but is back in work and is rated 135 over hurdles. Twice a winner at Bangor and Chepstow, he beat Drumcliff at the former venue. A winning pointer, too, I think he will make a very nice novice chaser this time around. He wants soft ground.

MR MONOCHROME 7 br g Indian Danehill (IRE) – Our Ethel
Lightly raced and a half-brother to Cheltenham Festival winner Attaglance, he is another who arrived during the summer. A winner over hurdles, he has only run once over fences but hasn't been in action since last Autumn. We are still getting to know him.

NEFYN POINT 4 gr g Overbury (IRE) – So Cloudy
A full-brother to Nefyn Bay, who wasn't very big and had his issues, including his wind, but is the most genuine horse I have trained and won nine races. This fella is a bit bigger, has no breathing issues and is a good moving horse. Third on his debut in a bumper at Perth in April, I was pleased with him and the first signs are positive. He may have another run in a bumper before we send him novice hurdling. He could be a nice horse.

ORMESHER 3 b g Sir Percy – Marakabei
Only small, he was placed three times on the Flat and has made a good start to his hurdling career winning at Uttoxeter and Cartmel during the summer. We schooled him as a two year old and his jumping has always been good. The ground at Cartmel in August would have been soft enough for him. Something like the Listed Wensleydale Hurdle at Wetherby (2nd November) could be a possible early season target.

POGUE (IRE) 5 gr g Stowaway – Night Palm (IRE)
A potentially very exciting horse who could be anything. A big tall raw horse, he measures nearly eighteen hands and has plenty of size and scope. By a very good sire, he finished second on his debut in a point-to-point before bolting up next time in May. I watched the video and he was very impressive. Previously trained by Colin Bowe, we bought him on behalf of John Turner at the Cheltenham May Sale. He will go novice hurdling.

POUGNE BOBBI (FR) 7 bb g Protektor (GER) – Amicus
A dual winner over fences for Nicky Henderson, including at Huntingdon in January, we bought him at the Doncaster Spring Sales for Richard Gilbert. A horse with size and scope, he is effective on soft ground and could be ideal for two and a half mile handicap chases at the likes of Ayr and Newcastle.

QUIDS IN (IRE) 5 b g Pour Moi (IRE) – Quixotic
Another we purchased at the Doncaster May Sales, he is a solid horse who I have watched a number of times. A winner over hurdles and placed at the likes of Leicester and Haydock last season, he is tough and handles most types of ground. He appears to have lost his way a bit but I am hoping he will be a fun horse for us in handicap hurdles this winter.

RAISE A SPARK 8 b g Multiplex – Reem Two
A tough hardy horse who has a great way about him. A useful hurdler who has been placed at Aintree's Grand National meeting in the past, he is maturing now and has taken well to chasing winning two of his three starts over fences at Cartmel this summer. Despite not having a chasing pedigree, his jumping has been slick and he was an easy winner in handicap company there in July. Effective on any ground, we have the option of running him in novice chases or continuing in handicap company.

SAME CIRCUS (IRE) 7 b m Brian Boru – Curragh Orpen (IRE)
A nice mare who we took a bit of time to weigh up and, despite winning a point-to-point, she took a while to learn to jump. However, she did well over fences last season winning at Catterick and Bangor. Probably high enough in the ratings off 127, three miles is her trip.

SECRET ESCAPE (IRE) 6 b m Getaway (GER) – Portorosa (USA)
She had some smart bumper form winning twice before finishing fourth in a Listed mares' bumper at Cheltenham and sixth in a Grade 2 at Aintree. Switched to hurdling, she won at Cartmel in July before finishing third at the same track nearly three weeks later. She will be more at home on a galloping track and, on her bumper form, she is well handicapped. Given a break since, we will step her up to two and a half miles.

SHANTALUZE (IRE) 6 b g Shantou (USA) – Nut Touluze (IRE)
A solid straightforward horse who won an Irish point in October before we bought him at the Cheltenham November Sale. A six lengths winner of a bumper at Kelso in January, he was then third at Carlisle under a penalty but came back sick. He will go novice hurdling over two and a half miles plus and I could see him developing into a 120-130 horse.

SNOUGAR (IRE) 5 b g Arakan (USA) – Thorbella
I like him. A winner over hurdles at Ayr in March, he was unlucky at Newcastle last time when falling at the second last. A bit wild and still immature, he is a nice type of horse who should improve. Rated 111, he is on a decent mark and is one for handicap hurdles.

SPIN THE COIN (IRE) 5 b g Witness Box (USA) – Kempinski (IRE)
Runner-up in his only point-to-point for Colin McBratney, he has taken his time to learn his trade. Unlucky at Carlisle in March, he was leading when taking a heavy fall at the last and it really shook him up. He is 100% now though and will continue in novice hurdles before jumping fences later on.

SWASHBUCKLE 5 b g Dashing Blade – Inhibition
A useful staying horse on the Flat for Andrew Balding, we bought him at the Newmarket Horses in Training Sale last Autumn but he has proved disappointing over hurdles. However, I think he is crying out for a step up to three miles. He won a 'jumpers bumper' at Southwell in March but we were trying to pinch races over shorter trips over hurdles. We have also operated on his wind since his last run which will hopefully make a difference. He could be well handicapped.

TAILOR TOM (IRE) 6 b g Fruits of Love (USA) – Anfield Lady (IRE)
A big good looking horse, we weren't sure what to make of him to begin with. His jumping has improved since we schooled him over fences and he won a staying handicap hurdle at Bangor in January. He will be going over fences and we'll start him off in a staying novices' handicap chase.

TESTIFY (IRE) 7 b g Witness Box (USA) – Tanya Thyne (IRE)
A very useful horse who won his first three races over fences, including a Grade 2 at Haydock in January. It didn't happen for him at either Cheltenham or Aintree in the spring but perhaps, like his brother Wymott, he is suited by smaller fields. Effective on bad ground, he wants three miles but could start off in the Colin Parker Memorial Chase at Carlisle (4th November) over two and a half miles.

THE CATTLEJOBBER 6 b g Arvico (FR) – Stillhertoes
His pedigree is a bit of an unknown but he won his only point-to-point by a couple of lengths in April and I loved him when I saw him at the Cheltenham Sales a few days later. Attractive, he is a big horse measuring 16.3 hands and has been brought along quietly. Given the fact he is six, he will almost certainly go straight over hurdles.

THE CON MAN (IRE) 5 b g Oscar (IRE) – Phillis Hill
A lovely horse who has got size and scope, I bought him at the Doncaster August Sale. He won his only point-to-point by six lengths in April for Colin Bowe and I loved the way he did it. I am a big fan of his sire and we have the option of running him in a bumper or going straight over hurdles.

THE GREAT GETAWAY (IRE) 6 b g Getaway (GER) – Park Mist (IRE)
Another big horse who won the last of his four Irish points before we acquired him at Doncaster Sales over a year ago. Fourth in a bumper at Ayr in November, he then won on his hurdles debut at Newcastle but we left him off after that because he had a few growing pains. Rated 118, he could have another run over hurdles but I am tempted to go over fences and run him in a novices' handicap chase.

THE SOME DANCE KID (IRE) 5 b g Shantou (USA) – River Rouge (IRE)
Similar to Shantaluze, we bought him at the Cheltenham November Sale having finished second in one of his two Irish points. He won a bumper first time out for us at Catterick in February before finishing runner-up at Carlisle under a penalty a couple of months later. A good solid horse, he will want a trip over hurdles this winter.

UBALTIQUE (FR) 10 b g Balko (FR) – Ode Antique (FR)
He continues to do us proud winning twice at Haydock last season. Two miles on heavy ground at Haydock wearing blinkers and a tongue tie is the time to catch him.

UPPERTOWN PRINCE (IRE) 6 b g Strategic Prince – Tarrawarra (IRE)
An exciting prospect for novice chasing, I am looking forward to him this season. He was very good over hurdles winning at Bangor and Ayr and finishing runner-up in Grade 2 company at Haydock and fourth in the Grade 1 Sefton Novices' Hurdle at Aintree in April. In fact, he could have been third at Aintree with a clearer run. A winning pointer, he was still immature last year and, while he is effective on slow ground, I think he will handle better ground. We know he stays three miles but we may start him off over two and a half miles over fences.

VAL MOME (FR) 5 b g Turgeon (USA) – Valle Fleurie (FR)
Acquired at the Ascot Sales during the summer, he is a racy type who won the second of his two Irish points. He appeared to benefit from the better ground and I was pleased with his hurdling debut at Bangor in August finishing second. Runner-up again at the same track four weeks later, I hope he will do well over hurdles this season.

WHITEOAK FLEUR 5 b m Black Sam Bellamy (IRE) – Harringay
A well bred mare, she was only beaten a length on her debut in a bumper at Sedgefield and Brian (Hughes) was impressed with her because he couldn't pull her up afterwards. Not quite as sharp at Kelso a month later, I think she is quite useful and we will campaign her in mares' novice hurdles over two and two and a half miles.

WHITEOAK MOLLY 4 b f Flemensfirth (USA) – Whiteoak
She is the third foal out of the dam and, while she is the smallest, I think she is the best. By a very good sire, she ran really well on her debut in a bumper at Bangor finishing third. Still weak and immature at the time, she can only improve and may have another run in a bumper before we start thinking about hurdling.

WILLIAM OF ORANGE 7 b g Duke of Marmalade (IRE) – Critical Acclaim
He is a useful horse on his day but has two ways of running. A five times winner over hurdles, we stepped him up to two and three quarter miles at Cartmel in July and he won a decent prize narrowly. I think he will stay three miles in due course and he is capable of winning more races. We might try schooling him over fences one day, too.

YORVIK 4 b g Yeats (IRE) – Overbranch
From a good family, he is owned by Mr & Mrs Calder and arrived in the summer. Unraced, he is a fine looking horse who may start off in a bumper.

TRAINER'S HORSE TO FOLLOW: UPPERTOWN PRINCE

Olly MURPHY

Stables: Warren Chase Stables, Wilmcote, Stratford Upon Avon.
2017/2018: 47 Winners / 250 Runners 19% Prize-Money £382,935
www.ollymurphyracing.com

BALLINSLEA BRIDGE (IRE) 6 b g Pierre – Feelin' Looser (IRE)
He is a nice horse who showed progressive form over hurdles winning at Market Rasen and Carlisle. Unfortunately, he knocked himself after his last run and won't be in action until after Christmas. However, I feel he is still on a good mark and may be capable of winning a valuable handicap hurdle in the spring. Still a big green horse who I have always liked, he appears to handle any ground and will have no trouble jumping fences one day having won an Irish point-to-point before we bought him.

BEAU SANCY (FR) 6 b g Blue Bresil (FR) – Touquette (FR)
A maiden over hurdles and fences, we bought him cheaply at the Doncaster May Sales and I am hoping he will be a good fun horse. Runner-up over fences at Kelso last spring, we have operated on his wind since he arrived. He seems to want plenty of cut in the ground with two and a half miles plus being his trip.

BLAZER'S MILL (IRE) 4 b g Westerner – Creation (IRE)
A fine big stamp of a horse, he was runner-up in his only Irish point for Warren Ewing before we bought him at the Aintree April Sale. He looks a very nice young horse who will probably run in a bumper before going novice hurdling.

BON CALVADOS (FR) 4 b g Bonbon Rose (FR) – Lamorrese (FR)
He is a lovely unraced horse who belongs to Andrew Brooks. A fine big horse, he is a half-brother to Andrew's high-class novice chaser from last season Saint Calvados. All being well, he will start off in a bumper in the Autumn.

BREWIN'UPASTORM (IRE) 5 b g Milan – Daraheen Diamond (IRE)
We have a very nice team of horses for the winter and I would say this is the one I am most looking forward to. A former winning pointer, his bumper form is very strong. He beat the subsequent Grade 2 Aintree bumper winner Portrush Ted by nine lengths at Hereford in January before finishing fourth in a Listed event at Newbury the following month. All being well, he will start off in a two miles maiden hurdle in October but will benefit from stepping up to two and a half miles later on. We did loads of schooling with him last season and he has always jumped very well. He handles testing ground but is a good moving horse so I don't see why he won't cope with better ground. I have been delighted with him during the summer.

BUBBLES OF GOLD (IRE) 5 b g Gold Well – Bubble Bann (IRE)
A proper old fashioned National Hunt horse and very much a chaser in the making. He won his only point-to-point by eight lengths in March before we bought him at the Cheltenham Festival Sale a few days later. A fine big horse, he looks as though he wants cut in the ground and, while we may run him in a bumper, I think he will want two and a half miles plus over hurdles.

CALIPSO COLLONGES (FR) 6 b g Crossharbour – Ivresse Collonges (FR)
He was most progressive last season winning four out of five for us since arriving from Ireland. Rated 94 when he joined us, he kept surprising us and is now rated 127 over hurdles. I think he could be an interesting staying novice chaser this season because he jumps and stays very well. He loves heavy ground and I have been pleased with his schooling. We may start him off over two and a half miles but it won't be long before he returns to longer trips.

CHEZ HANS (IRE) 4 b g Aizavoski (IRE) – Hidden Reserve (IRE)
A lovely horse, he is a half-brother to Sangha River who showed plenty at home prior to making his debut in a bumper at Bangor in the spring. Only seventh, he was sick afterwards and we have given him a break since. He is a gorgeous horse who could run in another bumper before going novice hurdling.

DORETTE (FR) 5 b m Kingsalsa (FR) – Ombrelle (FR)
She is a sweet filly who had been going well prior to winning on her debut in a mares' bumper at Newton Abbot in August. In all likelihood, she will run in another bumper under a penalty and then go mares' novice hurdling. No star, but she is capable to win more races.

FIGHT COMMANDER (IRE) 9 b g Oscar (IRE) – Creidim (IRE)
A cheap purchase at the Doncaster Spring Sales, I think he will give his syndicate Foxtrot Racing plenty of fun this winter. A winner over fences for Oliver Sherwood, he looks well treated on the pick of his form. Suited by soft ground, we will probably mix and match between hurdles and fences.

FINAWN BAWN (IRE) 5 b g Robin Des Champs (FR) – Kayanti (IRE)
A likeable horse who doesn't show a great deal at home but he won his bumper in good style on his debut at Ayr in May. A proper National Hunt type, he will go straight over hurdles and, while he will want three miles in time, we will start him off over two and a half miles. He is a lovely horse who ought to win plenty of races.

GARRETTSTOWN (IRE) 5 b g Doyen (IRE) – Azur (IRE)
Another lovely big horse who was an impressive winner of his only bumper at Chepstow in the spring. The form is questionable but he had shown plenty of ability at home beforehand. Effective on testing ground, he will go over hurdles and is hopefully a horse with a bright future.

GEORGIATOR (FR) 5 b g Simplex (FR) – Princess Demut (GER)
An impressive winner on his debut at Ffos Las during the summer, he will run in another bumper under a penalty during the Autumn. He doesn't want the ground too soft though and will have a break during the winter.

HUNTERS CALL (IRE) 8 b g Medaaly - Accordiontogelica (IRE)
He is back in work having missed the second half of last season, due to an issue with a near fore joint and a small screw in a cannonbone. He did us proud by winning the valuable Grade 3 Racing Welfare Handicap Hurdle (formerly the Ladbroke Hurdle) at Ascot in December on his only run for us. Raised nine pounds to a rating of 137, I still believe he is on a good mark and he looks fantastic. The plan is to aim him at the Greatwood Hurdle at Cheltenham (18th November) before going back to Ascot (22nd December) for the same race. I think he is capable of winning another big prize over hurdles because he remains lightly raced and open to further improvement. We have the option of going chasing in the New Year, if things don't go to plan at Cheltenham and Ascot.

IMPERIAL KNIGHT (IRE) 6 b g Mahler - And Whatever Else (IRE)
A tough hardy sort, he was unlucky not to win last season being placed in all three of his bumpers. Collared close home at Bangor last time, he is a likeable horse who will go novice hurdling over two miles to begin with. He should have no trouble winning races.

ITCHY FEET (FR) 4 b g Cima De Triomphe (IRE) - Maeva Candas (FR)
Ran well on his debut in a bumper at Fontwell finishing second. Still very green, he is a good moving horse who doesn't want the ground too soft. With that in mind, the plan is to run him in another bumper in September. He is a nice horse.

IT'S O KAY 5 b m Shirocco (GER) - Presenting Copper (IRE)
A well bred mare being related to the likes of Copper Bleu and Copper Kay, I was surprised it took her so long to win a bumper because she has always gone well at home. Fourth on her debut at Doncaster, she was then narrowly beaten at Wetherby before getting off the mark at the third attempt at Sedgefield in April. She has matured during the summer and I will be disappointed if she isn't competitive in mares' novice hurdles this season. The state of the ground doesn't seem to matter to her.

JONES WELL (IRE) 5 b g Gold Well - Mrs Jones (FR)
Runner-up in his only Irish point during the spring, we bought him at the Cheltenham May Sale. He looks a nice staying horse in the making who may contest a bumper on a galloping track before going hurdling.

JUST MINDED (IRE) 7 b g Kayf Tara - Georgia On My Mind (FR)
An interesting horse we bought at the Doncaster Spring Sales. He is a half-brother to Coral Cup winner Diamond King, who I knew very well at Gordon's (Elliott). A maiden over fences, his mark over hurdles looks fair, too, and having watched him a few times last season, he still looks a big raw horse. He doesn't appear to want the ground too soft and will be suited by galloping tracks. We could mix and match between hurdles and fences.

KNOCKGRAFFON (IRE) 8 b g Flemensfirth (USA) - Gleaming Spire
Not the easiest horse to place, he won a good prize at Musselburgh on New Year's Day and there is every chance he will head back there for the same race this time around. I thought he ran well in a Grade 2 handicap chase at Cheltenham in April but was over the top by the time he went to Aintree a month later. The handicapper has dropped him three pounds since to a mark of 139 and we have operated on his wind. Two and a half to three miles is his trip because I think he will stay.

LISHEEN PRINCE (IRE) 7 b g Oscar (IRE) - Dino's Monkey (IRE)
Joined us from Philip Hobbs last season but we haven't found the key to him yet. He raced twice for us last spring, including when running well for a long way at Cheltenham in April. Still lightly raced, he could go novice handicap chasing and I am convinced he is better than he has shown for us thus far.

MON PORT (IRE) 6 b g Scorpion (IRE) – Sounds Charming (IRE)
He has not had the easiest of lives having had a year off but he is a very nice horse who won impressively on his hurdles debut on his first run for us in May. Hatcher, who fell at the last when well held in second, has won four times since. I would like to win another novice hurdle with him and perhaps aim him at the Persian War Novices' Hurdle at Chepstow (14th October). Despite the fact he won over two miles, I think two and a half miles will prove to be his trip. I like him a lot.

OXFORD BLU 4 b g Aqlaam – Blue Zealot (IRE)
An easy winner on his hurdles debut at Fakenham, he went on to finish second at Market Rasen before taking his chance in the Fred Winter Juvenile Hurdle at the Cheltenham Festival. Hampered early on, he never got involved but is better than he showed that day. Previously trained on the Flat by Sir Mark Prescott, he never got a break last year and has benefited from a holiday this summer. We have operated on his wind and I think he will be competitive in handicap hurdles off his mark of 123.

PEACHEY (IRE) 4 b g Robin Des Champs (FR) – Zita Hall (IRE)
A nice horse who has been very backward. I thought he ran a good race on his debut in a bumper at Market Rasen finishing fifth. Only beaten around two lengths, he has summered well and, while we will start him off over two miles over hurdles, he will benefit from further in time.

PERFECT MAN (IRE) 7 b g Morozov (USA) – Garrisker (IRE)
A three times winner over hurdles in Ireland, we bought him at the Doncaster May Sales. I was delighted with his win at Market Rasen on his first run for us in August. Raised ten pounds since to a mark of 124, he stays well and seems to handle any ground.

PIRI MASSINI (IRE) 7 b g Pierre – Lady Doctor (IRE)
A big strong horse who surprised us when winning on his hurdles debut at Fakenham in January beating our other horse Rio Quinto in the process. Runner-up at Newcastle last time, he will go chasing and is a stayer who wants three miles plus. A former winning Irish pointer, he jumps well and ought to win races over fences.

PORT OF MARS (IRE) 4 b g Westerner – Sarahall (IRE)
A full-brother to Westend Story, he is a tough, likeable horse we purchased at the Cheltenham March Sale. Successful in his only English point-to-point in February for Tom Lacey, he is a nice type and I have been pleased with him since he arrived. He could run in a bumper before going hurdling.

RIO QUINTO (FR) 5 b g Loup Breton (IRE) – Seal of Cause (IRE)
Had a somewhat in and out season winning at Fakenham in December and then finishing second on three occasions. Despite running in a couple of point-to-points prior to us buying him, he was still backward last year. We have operated on his wind since his last run and the plan is to send him over fences. I think he could make a nice staying novice chaser.

ROBIN ROE (IRE) 7 b g Robin Des Champs (FR) – Talktothetail (IRE)
A high-class novice hurdler for Dan Skelton a couple of seasons ago, he hasn't raced since falling in the Grade 1 Challow Hurdle in December 2016. He has obviously had his problems but I am delighted to be training him and he is back in work. It is early days and he has a long way to go but he could return in a conditions/handicap hurdle before going chasing later on.

SANGHA RIVER (IRE) 5 br g Arcadio (GER) – Hidden Reserve (IRE)
I think the world of him and he is very much one to look forward to. He is a very good moving horse who appreciates nice ground and therefore isn't one for the middle of the winter. He won a bumper at Doncaster on his first run for us and was then unlucky not to follow up at Lingfield.

Quite a keen going sort, I told David England to switch him off early on but he met trouble in running before finishing strongly in second. He then missed the remainder of the season due to a blip but is back in work and will go novice hurdling over two miles.

SEEMINGLY SO (IRE) 5 br g Dubai Destination (USA) – Jane Hall (IRE)
A lovely big horse we purchased at the Cheltenham February Sale having finished runner-up in his only Irish point. He is the first horse we have trained for Clive Boultbee-Brooks. Very much a staying chaser in the making, there is every chance he will have a run in a bumper before embarking on his novice hurdle career.

SMACKWATER JACK (IRE) 4 b g Flemensfirth (USA) – Malachy's Attic (IRE)
Beaten a nose on his debut in a bumper at Fakenham in the spring, he was unlucky because it wouldn't have been his track, plus he shied away from something close home. We may give him another run in a bumper on a more galloping track and then send him hurdling.

SUPERYACHT (IRE) 5 b g Fastnet Rock (AUS) – Olympienne (IRE)
A fine big horse who is very well bred being a half-brother to Patkai and Saptapadi. A Ballymacoll Stud homebred, he raced three times on the Flat for Sir Michael Stoute finishing second and third at Haydock in the spring of 2016. Absent since, he has settled in well and will go novice hurdling.

THE VERY THING (IRE) 4 b g Getaway (GER) – Katie Quinn (IRE)
Fourth on his first start in a bumper on the all-weather at Newcastle in April, I thought he should have won but I gave Aidan (Coleman) the wrong instructions. He shows plenty at home and is good enough to win a bumper before turning his attentions to jumping hurdles. I have been pleased with him since and he has summered well.

THOMAS DARBY (IRE) 5 b g Beneficial – Silaoce (FR)
Still a big baby last season, he is a lovely horse and a half-brother to Muirhead. I was delighted with his debut win in a bumper at Huntingdon and the runner-up has won twice since. Following a good summer break, he will go novice hurdling and, while he may start off over two miles, he will be suited by further later on.

VAMANOS (IRE) 4 b g Fame And Glory – Bean Ki Moon (IRE)
I thought he ran a lovely race on his debut at Market Rasen. Even though he finished seventh, he wasn't beaten far and was still a big weak horse last year. He has strengthened up since and is another who will go novice hurdling. I think he will leave that run behind him this season.

WEEBILL 6 b g Schiaparelli (GER) – Wee Dinns (IRE)
A horse with plenty of ability, he was green last year but still managed to win twice at Fakenham and Ayr. We were aiming him at the Silver Trophy at Chepstow (13th October) but he suffered a blip during the summer and it may come too soon. Open to further improvement, he will be campaigned in two and a half miles handicap hurdles but it won't be long before he goes novice chasing.

YENSIR 5 ch g Sir Percy – Yensi
Bought at the Newmarket Horses in Training Sale last Autumn, he has proved a revelation this summer winning four out of five over hurdles. Effective over two and two and a half miles and decent ground, he could be aimed at the Persian War Novices' Hurdle at Chepstow (14th October).

TRAINER'S HORSE TO FOLLOW: BREWIN'UPASTORM

Champion Trainer 2005/2006, 2006/2007, 2007/2008, 2008/2009, 2009/2010, 2010/11, 2011/12, 2013/2014, 2014/2015 & 2015/2016

Paul NICHOLLS

Stables: Manor Farm Stables, Ditcheat, Somerset.
2017/2018: 127 Winners / 576 Runners 22% Prize-Money £2,513,233
www.paulnichollsracing.com

ADRIEN DU PONT (FR) 6 b g Califet (FR) – Santariyka (FR)
A winner on his chasing debut at Fontwell, he ran some good races in defeat thereafter. He doesn't appear to want the ground too testing and will be at his best in middle distance handicaps when they go a good gallop.

AMOUR DE NUIT (IRE) 6 b g Azamour (IRE) – Umthoulah (IRE)
Twice a winner over hurdles last season and also runner-up in the Grade 2 Persian War Novices' Hurdle at Chepstow, we sent him chasing in the spring. Having warmed to his task at Kempton in May, he won nicely in the end. Given a break since, he will run in a novice chase in early October because he prefers decent ground.

ART MAURESQUE (FR) 8 b g Policy Maker (IRE) – Modeva (FR)
Ran some solid races in defeat last season, including when runner-up in a Grade 2 chase at Sandown in April. He is suited by small field conditions chases on decent ground. Two and a half miles is his trip, although he stays three miles.

ASK FOR GLORY (IRE) 4 b g Fame And Glory – Ask Helen (IRE)
A big backward four year old who we bought at the Doncaster May Sales having won his only Irish point-to-point by ten lengths. Quite lean and light when he arrived, we are going to give him a good long break and plenty of time to mature. He is very much a chaser for the future.

BIRDS OF PREY (IRE) 4 b g Sir Prancealot (IRE) – Cute
He is a nice horse who won twice on the Flat for John Oxx in Ireland. Yet to run over hurdles, we have been running him on the Flat during the spring/summer and, having finished fourth a couple of times at Kempton, he was beaten a short head at Haydock in August in a twelve furlongs handicap. We schooled him last year and he jumps well. I think he will make a decent novice hurdler in the Autumn.

BLACK CORTON (FR) 7 br g Laverock (IRE) – Pour Le Meilleur (FR)
He has been a great horse for us, who enjoyed a fantastic season over fences winning eight times, including the Grade 1 Kauto Star Novice Chase at Kempton on Boxing Day and the Grade 2 Reynoldstown Novice Chase at Ascot in February. Rated 153, he may run in the Intermediate chase at Newton Abbot (12th October) which he won last year. There is also a Listed Intermediate chase at Sandown (11th November), which we will consider, and then we will aim him at the Ladbrokes Trophy at Newbury (1st December).

BLACKJACK KENTUCKY (IRE) 5 b g Oscar (IRE) – My Name's Not Bin (IRE)
Trained by Colin Bowe in Ireland to win the second of his two point-to-points, we bought him at the Cheltenham December Sale. Still backward, we gave him a break since arriving with a view to sending him hurdling in the Autumn.

BLU CAVALIER 8 b g Kayf Tara – Blue Ride (IRE)
He hasn't been the easiest horse to train but I was pleased with him last season winning three times over hurdles in the spring earning a mark of 143. We may aim him at the Persian War Novices' Hurdle at Chepstow (14th October) before he goes chasing.

BRAQUEUR D'OR (FR) 7 b g Epalo (GER) - Hot D'Or (FR)
Successful over fences at Stratford, Newton Abbot and Ludlow last season, we have operated on his wind since his last run. He wants fast ground and is capable of winning a decent staying handicap chase.

BREWERS PROJECT (IRE) 4 b g Aizavoski (IRE) - Shaylee Wilde (IRE)
A five lengths winner of his only Irish point in March, we purchased him at the Cheltenham Festival Sale a few days later. He is another we have given lots of time to mature since arriving. He will spend this season in novice hurdles.

BRIO CONTI (FR) 7 gr g Dom Alco (FR) - Cadoulie Wood (FR)
He won on his chasing debut at Carlisle in November but unfortunately picked up an injury in the process and missed the rest of the season. All being well, he will be back in action after Christmas and we will be aiming him at Graduation chases over two and a half miles plus.

CAPITAINE (FR) 6 gr g Montmartre (FR) - Patte De Velour (FR)
Looked very good on his first two starts over fences, winning at Newton Abbot and Market Rasen. He then hurt himself when falling at the second last in the Grade 1 Henry VIII Novices' Chase at Sandown in December. We gave him a couple of runs over hurdles in the spring and he has had surgery on a back problem which means he won't be running until a bit later on. The plan is to go back over fences and I think he will be worth a try over two and a half miles at some stage.

CAPTAIN CATTISTOCK 5 b g Black Sam Bellamy (IRE) - Pearl Buttons
A lovely horse who won an English point-to-point for Jack Barber before joining us last season. A three times winner over hurdles, he improved with every run and had every chance at Cheltenham last time when making a mistake at the last. We could aim him at something like the Silver Trophy at Chepstow (13th October) before going chasing.

CASKO D'AIRY (FR) 6 b g Voix Du Nord (FR) - Quaska D'Airy (FR)
A French bumper winner and runner-up over hurdles at Auteuil, we bought him a couple of seasons ago but he has yet to run for us due to setbacks. It has been frustrating because he has a lot of ability. Hopefully we will get a clear run with him in novice hurdles this winter.

CHAMERON (FR) 5 b g Laveron - Chamanka (FR)
I don't know how he managed to win twice over hurdles at Auteuil before he joined us because he has been such a big backward horse. Still only five, he was runner-up on his chasing debut at Exeter last November and will continue over fences. I think he will benefit from stepping up in trip.

CHIEF CRAFTSMAN 4 b g Mastercraftsman (IRE) - Eurolink Raindance (IRE)
Placed three times on the Flat for Luca Cumani and rated 77, he was in training with us last season but we decided to give him time and he will go two miles novice hurdling this Autumn.

CLAN DES OBEAUX (FR) 6 b g Kapgarde (FR) - Nausicaa Des Obeaux (FR)
He is a very nice horse who won a Graduation chase at Haydock before finishing second at Cheltenham in a valuable handicap in December. We were aiming him at the Festival but he threw a splint. Forced to miss Cheltenham, we rushed him back for Aintree and, while he ran well in third in the Grade 1 Betway Bowl, he would have been much closer with a better preparation. He is in good form at home and his first target could be the Charlie Hall Chase at Wetherby (3rd November). I think he is a very good horse.

CLIFFS OF DOVER 5 b g Canford Cliffs (IRE) - Basanti (USA)
A smart juvenile hurdler a couple of seasons ago winning six times, he was off the track for nearly fifteen months through injury. Pulled up on soft ground in the Kingwell Hurdle at Wincanton in February, he has been running well on the Flat since winning three times, including by twelve lengths at Haydock in August under my daughter Megan. He will go back over hurdles and I think he will stay two and a half miles, although he doesn't want it too soft.

CYRNAME (FR) 6 b g Nickname (FR) - Narquille (FR)
He has developed into a very nice horse because he wasn't easy to deal with when first arriving from France. Free in his races over hurdles, he has started to settle since switching to fences and enjoys making the running. A three times winner last season, including the Grade 2 Wayward Lad and Pendil Novice Chases at Kempton, he is better racing right-handed. The Haldon Gold Cup at Exeter (6th November) is a possible starting point followed by the Grade 2 chase at Ascot (24th November) over two miles five.

DAN MCGRUE (IRE) 6 b g Dansant - Aahsaypasty (IRE)
A three times winning English pointer, he won twice over hurdles at Taunton last season but hasn't raced since January due to an injury. He won't be in action until after Christmas when he will probably go novice chasing.

DANNY KIRWAN (IRE) 5 b g Scorpion (IRE) - Sainte Baronne (FR)
He is an exciting prospect and I love him. An eleven lengths winner of his Irish point in October for Pat Doyle, we bought him soon afterwards and he was an impressive winner of a bumper at Kempton in February. I then made a mistake by running him at Aintree in the Grade 2 bumper at the Grand National meeting. He looked light in the paddock beforehand and was over the top and is much better than he showed that day. We have given him lots of time since and he now looks twice the horse he was. He jumps well and will run in two mile novice hurdles.

DANNY WHIZZBANG (IRE) 5 b g Getaway (GER) - Lakil Princess (IRE)
A big horse, he won the second of his two Irish points for Colin Bowe in the spring and we purchased him at the Punchestown Festival Sale at the end of April. A staying chaser in the making, he will go novice hurdling this season.

DANSE IDOL (IRE) 5 b m Dansant - Screen Idol (IRE)
She is a nice mare we acquired at the Cheltenham Sale in February. Successful in her only point-to-point in Ireland, she finished runner-up behind the subsequent Cheltenham Festival bumper winner Relegate at Punchestown in January. We may run her in another mares' bumper before going hurdling over two and a half miles.

DENSFIRTH (IRE) 5 b g Flemensfirth (USA) - Denwoman (IRE)
Big and backward last year, he ran well first time out in a bumper at Exeter but was too free next time at Chepstow. A stronger horse now, he will want a trip over hurdles this season.

DIAMOND GUY (FR) 5 b g Konig Turf (GER) - Unique Chance (FR)
A lovely young horse who appreciates good ground. Still a novice until the end of October, he won over hurdles at Wincanton and Ludlow in the spring. He could run in a Listed novices' hurdle at Kempton (21st October) before going chasing.

DIEGO DU CHARMIL (FR) 6 b g Ballingarry (IRE) - Daramour (FR)
He is a smart horse who did very well over fences last season coming back from injury. A winner on his chasing debut at Newton Abbot early on, he ran well in the Grade 2 Kingmaker Novice Chase at Warwick in February. Unlucky not to win next time at Ascot when falling three out, he then produced a very good performance to win the Grade 1 Maghull Novices' Chase at Aintree.

He jumped and travelled beautifully. I would put a line through his last run at Sandown because it came too soon. Good fresh, I think he will progress again and is another who may start off in the Haldon Gold Cup at Exeter (6th November) before continuing to contest the good two mile chases.

DIVIN BERE (FR) 5 b g Della Francesca (USA) - Mofa Bere (FR)
He struggled with his breathing last season and we have therefore operated on his wind since his last run in the County Hurdle at Cheltenham. Even though he isn't over big, he will go novice chasing on better ground.

DJINGLE (FR) 5 b g Voix Du Nord (FR) - Jourie (FR)
Twice a winner over hurdles at Auteuil last Autumn, we shouldn't have run him at Exeter in February. He looked light and raced too freely. We have therefore given him the summer off and the plan is to send him novice chasing.

DOLOS (FR) 5 b g Kapgarde (FR) - Redowa (FR)
Kept improving and had a good season over fences winning at Ascot and finishing runner-up in a Listed chase at Ayr's Scottish National meeting. He ran against some good horses and it won't be easy this year off a mark of 152. We will aim him at the decent two mile handicap chases, although he is another possible for the Intermediate chase at Newton Abbot (12th October) over two miles five. I am keen to try him over further.

DR SANDERSON (IRE) 4 b g Jeremy (USA) - Guydus (IRE)
Another new arrival, he won his only bumper at Carlisle for Stuart Crawford in the spring. Subsequently bought by the Million in Mind partnership, he will go novice hurdling and I think he will provide its members with a lot of fun.

EARTH PRINCE (FR) 4 rg g Al Namix (FR) - Quarline De L'Ecu (FR)
Made an encouraging start to his career when finishing runner-up in a bumper at Newton Abbot in May. He may run in a similar event before going hurdling.

EASYRUN DE VASSY (FR) 4 b g Muhtathir - Royale The Best (FR)
A winner and runner-up in three Irish point-to-points for Colin Bowe, we bought him at the Cheltenham May Sale. He looks another nice type for novice hurdles this season.

ECCO 3 b c Maxios - Enjoy The Life
A very nice three year old who was trained on the Flat in Germany by Peter Schiergen. He has only raced four times finishing sixth in a Group 2 at Cologne in June before taking his chance in the German Derby last time. We bought him soon afterwards and he arrived in July. He will be going juvenile hurdling.

EL BANDIT (IRE) 7 bb g Milan - Bonnie Parker (IRE)
An easy winner on his chasing debut at Warwick in the spring of last year, he missed the whole of last winter due to an injury. However, he is back in work now and his first target is the Badger Ales Chase at Wincanton (10th November).

ENVOYE SPECIAL (FR) 4 b g Coastal Path - Santa Bamba (FR)
A half-brother to French Champion Hurdle winner De Bon Coeur, he won over hurdles in France before finishing runner-up twice over fences. He was inclined to race quite freely but is a good jumper and, following a summer break, we are going to send him novice chasing.

ERITAGE (FR) 4 b g Martaline - Sauves La Reine (FR)
He won his only start in a French bumper in July by three and a half lengths. Only four, he is likely to go straight over hurdles.

FLIC OU VOYOU (FR) 4 b g Kapgarde (FR) – Hillflower (FR)
He is a nice horse who has always shown us plenty at home. We usually take our bumper horses to Wincanton for a racecourse gallop but were unable to do so last winter because it was so wet. I therefore expect those we ran in bumpers last spring to improve enormously this season, including this horse who finished fourth at Fontwell. He has also had a wind operation since his run.

FRODON (FR) 6 b g Nickname (FR) – Miss Country (FR)
He has been a grand horse for us winning seven times over fences, including a Grade 3 handicap chase at Cheltenham's Trials meeting in January. Effective on any ground, he is in the grip of the handicapper off his mark of 158 but I am sure he will continue to pick up plenty of prize money. I am keen to try him over the National fences at Aintree and feel he is ideal for the Grand Sefton Chase (8th December).

GIVE ME A COPPER (IRE) 8 ch g Presenting – Copper Supreme (IRE)
I love him and I think there is a big race in him. He won over fences at Kempton in November but then, unfortunately, suffered a minor injury which was enough to keep him off for the rest of the season. I want to aim him at the Ladbroke Trophy at Newbury (1st December) with the intention of running him in a Graduation chase beforehand. He jumps and travels and I view him as a Grand National horse one day.

GRAND SANCY (FR) 4 b g Diamond Boy (FR) – La Courtille (FR)
Runner-up three times last season, including twice over hurdles, I don't know how he is still a maiden. We have operated on his wind since his run in the Fred Winter Juvenile Hurdle at Cheltenham because he wasn't finishing his races off. His mark looks fair because I think he will improve and may have needed a bit of time.

GREANETEEN (FR) 4 b g Great Pretender (IRE) – Manson Teene (FR)
Third on his only run over hurdles in France when trained by Guillaume Macaire, he is a very nice horse who we have purposely given plenty of time. I think his owner's patience will pay off because he is a lovely horse for novice hurdles this season.

HUGOS OTHER HORSE 4 b g Gold Well – Wicked Crack (IRE)
A half-brother to Cue Card, he is a nice unraced horse who I like. He will start off in a bumper.

IBIS DU RHEU (FR) 7 b g Blue Bresil (FR) – Dona Du Rheu (FR)
Still a maiden over fences, we set him some tough tasks at Cheltenham and Aintree and he is rated 139. The first aim is to find a suitable beginners' chase and get a win under his belt.

IF YOU SAY RUN (IRE) 6 b m Mahler – De Lissa (IRE)
A lovely mare who won over hurdles at Chepstow and Wincanton before finishing runner-up in a Grade 2 mares' hurdle at Sandown in February. It was heavy ground that day and I think it left its mark. She appreciates better ground and we have cauterized her palate since her last run. We may give her one more run over hurdles before switching to mares' novice chases.

KAPCORSE (FR) 5 br g Kapgarde (FR) – Angesse (FR)
I hope he is an improving horse because he surprised us when winning on his chasing debut at Bangor in April, having shown little in three runs over hurdles beforehand. Ex-French, he has been backward and, while the handicapper has raised him twelve pounds for his win, he is still only five and lightly raced.

LE PREZIEN (FR) 7 br g Blue Bresil (FR) - Abu Dhabi (FR)
Placed at Cheltenham a couple of times in the first half of the season, including in the BetVictor Gold Cup, he came good at the Festival winning the Grand Annual Chase. He likes a strongly run two miles and, while life won't be easy off 156, he could run in the Haldon Gold Cup (6th November) at Exeter and we have the option of taking him to Ireland at some stage. He is rated ten pounds lower over hurdles and that is another possibility.

LISA DE VASSY (FR) 3 b f Cokoriko (FR) - Mona Vassy (FR)
An interesting juvenile hurdler, she won her first two starts on the Flat in France before finishing third in a Listed race at Saint-Cloud over ten furlongs in March.

MAGIC SAINT (FR) 4 b g Saint Des Saints (FR) - Magic Poline (FR)
Owned by John Cotton, he had a very good level of form in France for Guillaume Macaire winning two out of two over hurdles at Auteuil and two out of four over fences at the same track. He could be interesting in something like the BetVictor Gold Cup at Cheltenham (17th November).

MAGOO (IRE) 6 gr g Martaline (FR) - Noche (IRE)
A winner on the Flat and over hurdles in France, he had been off the track for nearly two years when winning on his first start for us at Fontwell in March. He will go chasing this season.

MALAYA (FR) 4 b f Martaline (FR) - Clarte D'Or (FR)
She is a nice filly who won the Listed Wensleydale Hurdle at Wetherby and a handicap hurdle at Ascot last season. Runner-up in the Grade 2 Adonis Hurdle at Kempton, she is rated 141. We may give her one more run over hurdles before going novice chasing and receive age and sex allowances.

MASTER TOMMYTUCKER 7 b g Kayf Tara - No Need For Alarm
Unbeaten in two starts, he is a smart horse and an exciting prospect. A late maturing horse, he didn't join us until he was six. He produced two impressive performances at Exeter last season and is rated 143. The plan is to send him novice chasing, although he could have another run over hurdles in something like the Silver Trophy at Chepstow (13th October).

MODUS 8 ch g Motivator - Alessandra
He won three times over fences last season, including the Grade 2 Rising Stars Novice Chase at Wincanton in November. He struggled on soft ground at Cheltenham and Aintree because he prefers better ground. Good fresh, he is rated 146 over fences and I hope he will improve.

MONT DES AVALOIRS (FR) 5 b g Blue Bresil (FR) - Abu Dhabi (FR)
A full brother to Le Prezien, he developed into a smart horse last season winning a bumper at Chepstow and twice over hurdles at Aintree and Market Rasen. Third in the Grade 1 Tolworth Hurdle and fourth in the Grade 2 Dovecote Novices' Hurdle at Kempton, I was pleased with his last run at Sandown on the final day of the season. I think he will make a very nice novice chaser and he ought to stay two and a half miles.

MOVEWITHTHETIMES (IRE) 7 ch g Presenting - Dare To Venture (IRE)
We know he is a very good horse but he endured a frustrating first season over fences. Runner-up behind the ill-fated Finian's Oscar at Cheltenham in November, he pulled up at the Festival last time. Suited by two and a half miles, we will try and find a suitable beginners' chase and go from there.

MY WAY (FR) 4 gr g Martaline (FR) – Royale Majesty (FR)
A very nice horse who had some good form over hurdles and fences in France, I am delighted to be training him. Placed twice over hurdles, he was also placed in all four runs over fences at Auteuil, including twice in Grade 3 company. Only four, I like him a lot and I would think he will go novice hurdling this season and chasing next year. We will probably find a maiden hurdle over two miles, although we could consider the Grade 2 Persian War Novices' Hurdle at Chepstow (14th October) over two and a half miles.

OLD GUARD 7 b g Notnowcato – Dolma (FR)
He has been a fantastic horse for us winning three times last season, including the Grade 2 National Spirit Hurdle at Fontwell. The runner-up Lil Rockerfeller won easily at Goodwood during the summer and there is a possibility we might run him on the Flat, too. Rated 81 on the Flat and 153 over hurdles, I am tempted to try him over fences again at some stage. We ran him twice a couple of years ago and he won at Exeter before reverting back to hurdles. A two and a half miles Graduation chase would suit him.

OSTUNI (FR) 5 b g Great Pretender (IRE) – Mamassita (FR)
Big and backward last season, he only ran once in a bumper at Sandown in November. Given time, I think he will leave that run behind over hurdles this year.

PEAK TO PEAK (IRE) 6 br g Authorized (IRE) – Bayourida (USA)
A three times winner over hurdles, he ran well on his reappearance finishing third in the Silver Trophy at Chepstow in October. Unfortunately, he suffered a setback and missed the remainder of the campaign. He is OK now though and will go novice chasing over two and a half miles.

POLITOLOGUE (FR) 7 gr g Poliglote – Scarlet Row (FR)
He enjoyed a very good season winning the Grade 2 Haldon Gold Cup at Exeter, Grade 1 Tingle Creek at Sandown, Grade 2 Desert Orchid Chase at Kempton and then successfully stepped up to two and a half miles in the Grade 1 Melling Chase in the spring. We fitted him with a tongue tie and hood at Aintree and I think the longer trip suited him. Good fresh, we may start him off in the Old Roan Chase at Aintree (28th October) and then, all being well, run him over three miles in the *Betfair* Chase at Haydock (24th November), which is what we did with Kauto Star. The plan is to give him an entry in the King George at Kempton on Boxing Day. For some reason, he doesn't seem to finish his races off at Cheltenham and is happier on a flatter track.

POSH TRISH (IRE) 5 b m Stowaway – Moscow Demon (IRE)
A nice filly who ran well in mares' bumper last season winning a Listed event at Cheltenham's November meeting. She won a point-to-point in Ireland before we bought her and we will run her in mares' novice hurdles over two and a half miles.

PRESENT MAN (IRE) 8 b g Presenting – Glen's Gale (IRE)
He won the Badgers Ales Chase at Wincanton (10th November) last year and the plan is to go back there and defend his title. A winner over hurdles at Kempton, too, last season, I thought he ran well in the Bet365 Gold Cup at Sandown finishing third. He is good fresh.

QUEL DESTIN (FR) 3 ch g Muhtathir – High Destiny (FR)
Placed on the Flat, he has already raced four times over hurdles for Guy Cherel in France winning his latest start at Auteuil in May. He will run in juvenile hurdles.

RHYTHM IS A DANCER 5 b g Norse Dancer (IRE) – Fascinatin Rhythm
He had a couple of runs in bumpers on soft ground finishing second and fourth at Kempton but appreciated better ground when winning easily at Exeter in the spring. A nice horse to go novice hurdling with.

RISK AND ROLL (FR) No Risk At All (FR) - Rolie De Vindecy (FR)
Fourth over hurdles in France, he won twice last season at Kempton and Taunton. We are likely to send him novice chasing and receive a four year old allowance.

ROMAIN DE SENAM (FR) 6 b g Saint Des Saints (FR) - Salvatrixe (FR)
Decent ground is important to him and he started the season very well by winning at Chepstow and Stratford. Despite finishing fifth in the BetVictor Gold Cup at Cheltenham, he never really got his ground thereafter. We have cauterized his palate since his last run and I think he may stay three miles this year.

SAINT DE REVE (FR) 4 b g Saint Des Saints (FR) - Ty Mat (FR)
Another of our young horses who will improve hugely on what he showed in his only bumper at Wincanton during the spring. He is likely to go straight over hurdles.

SAN BENEDETO (FR) 7 ch g Layman (USA) - Cinco Baidy (FR)
Although he didn't win last season, he ran some good races in defeat, including when runner-up in the Haldon Gold Cup at Exeter and also the Celebration Chase at Sandown. He therefore accumulated plenty of prize-money. Not easy to place off 155, he will follow a similar programme, although he prefers better ground.

SAO (FR) 4 bb g Great Pretender (IRE) - Miss Country (FR)
A half-brother to Frodon, he won over hurdles in France but raced too keenly in his three starts for us last season. Runner-up at Wincanton and Newton Abbot, he needs to learn to relax. We will probably send him over fences and aim him at a novices' handicap chase off his mark of 124.

SECRET INVESTOR 6 b g Kayf Tara - Silver Charmer
He won over hurdles at Stratford and Kempton in the spring and is a horse I have always liked. We have cauterized his palate during the summer and the intention is to send him novice chasing. A winning Irish pointer, he prefers better ground.

SOME MAN (IRE) 5 b g Beat Hollow - Miss Denman (IRE)
Another winning Irish pointer, he was fourth at Worcester on his hurdles debut but then picked up an injury after finishing fifth at Cheltenham in November. Absent since, he is OK now and will continue in novice hurdles, although his future lies in staying chases.

SOUTHFIELD STONE 5 gr g Fair Mix (IRE) - Laureldean Belle (IRE)
Third on his debut in a bumper at Exeter in February, I thought he ran OK. He will go novice hurdling and will appreciate a step up in trip.

SOUTHFIELD TORR 5 rg g Fair Mix (IRE) - Chamoss Royale (FR)
From a family we know well, he is a half-brother to Southfield Theatre and Southfield Vic. Third in a bumper at Fontwell on his first start, he then finished fourth at Taunton. He will go straight over hurdles.

STORM ARISING (IRE) 4 b g Yeats (IRE) - Ceol Rua (IRE)
A nice horse who finished third in his only Irish point-to-point for Denis Murphy in February. We bought him shortly afterwards at the Cheltenham Sales. I watched the video of his run and he did well to finish third considering he didn't jump very well. He may have a run in a bumper before going novice hurdling.

TAMAROC DU MATHAN (FR) 3 b g Poliglote - Thisbee Du Mathan (FR)
Another French recruit who won his only start over hurdles at Angers in April for Arnaud Chaille-Chaille. He is one to look out for in juvenile hurdles.

THE DELLERCHECKOUT (IRE) 5 b g Getaway (GER) – Loreley (IRE)
We have operated on his wind since last season and I think there will be more to come from him. He had four runs over hurdles finishing second at Bangor. The handicapper has given him a mark of 122 and he is capable of winning a novices' handicap hurdle off that.

TOMMY SILVER (FR) 6 b g Silver Cross (FR) – Sainte Mante (FR)
Despite winning at Leicester, he had a frustrating season over fences. He should have won at Kempton and was disappointing in the spring. We have given him a nice break and hopefully he will show what he's capable of. He likes good ground and I think two and a half miles may prove to be his trip this season.

TOMORROW MYSTERY 4 b f Nathaniel (IRE) – Retake
Yet to run for us, she won over a mile and a half on the Flat and is rated 83. We gave her time last year and the plan is to run her in mares' novice hurdles. She is a nice filly.

TOPOFTHEGAME (IRE) 6 ch g Flemensfirth (USA) – Derry Vale (IRE)
An exciting prospect, he fell on his chasing debut at Newbury so we decided to revert back to hurdles. Having finished fourth in the Lanzarote Hurdle at Kempton in January, he won a good prize over nearly three miles at Sandown before producing a very good performance in the Coral Cup at Cheltenham. Beaten a neck, he won an Irish point and will go back over fences and I think he will make a smart staying novice chaser.

TREVELYN'S CORN (IRE) 5 b g Oscar (IRE) – Present Venture (IRE)
A seven lengths winner of his only point-to-point in Ireland for Colin Bowe in December, he was an expensive buy a few days later at the Cheltenham Sales. A big scopey horse, he wants time to mature and won't be over raced in novice hurdles this season.

TRUCKERS LODGE (IRE) 6 b g Westerner – Galeacord (IRE)
He joined us during the summer having won a maiden hurdle at Southwell in May. Still eligible for novice events, he had some useful bumper form beating Mont Des Avaloirs at Chepstow. Having won an Irish point his future lies over fences but he will continue over hurdles for the time being.

VICENTE (FR) 9 b g Dom Alco (FR) – Ireland (FR)
A dual Scottish Grand National winner, he ran very well on his reappearance at Cheltenham in November finishing a neck second in another valuable staying handicap chase. Fifth at Ayr in the Scottish National last time, he will follow a similar programme although he doesn't want it too soft.

WARRIOR'S TALE 9 b g Midnight Legend – Samandara (FR)
Ran two very good races last year finishing a neck second at Newbury in December before being beaten a head in the Skybet Chase at Doncaster the following month. Pulled up in the Grand National, he didn't stay the trip but I am keen to aim him at the Grand Sefton Chase over the same fences (8th December).

WORTHY FARM (IRE) 5 b g Beneficial – Muckle Flugga (IRE)
A half-brother to Mister Miyagi, he won his only English point-to-point for Jack Barber by thirty lengths before joining us. He ran very well on his hurdles debut at Bangor in April finishing a close third. Staying novice hurdles are on his agenda.

ZYON 4 gr g Martaline – Temptation (FR)
Yet another of our bumper horses who will improve a lot for his debut run at Wincanton last April. Only four, he will go hurdling this Autumn.

TRAINER'S HORSE TO FOLLOW: MONT DES AVALOIRS

Fergal O'BRIEN

Stables: Grange Hill Farm, Naunton, Gloucestershire.
2017/2018: 60 Winners / 338 Runners 18% Prize-Money £711,945
www.fergalobrienracing.co.uk

AGENT VALDEZ 5 b m Arvico (FR) - Soleil Sauvage
A super looking mare, she ran in two Irish points for Ross O'Sullivan winning on her latest start in May. We bought her at the Cheltenham Sale later in the same month and I like her a lot. She has had a summer break and will be running in a mares' bumper in the Autumn.

ASK DILLON (IRE) 5 b g Ask - Mum's Miracle (IRE)
He is a lovely horse who won his second point-to-point in Ireland in January before we acquired him at the Cheltenham Sales the following month. We gave him some time off when he first arrived and then ran him in a bumper at Towcester in the spring. I was very pleased with his run in second because the winner looks useful and the third has won twice since. We may give him another run in a bumper before going hurdling.

AYE AYE CHARLIE 6 b g Midnight Legend - Trial Trip
He must be one of, if not, the highest rated maiden hurdler in Britain with a mark of 145. Seventh in the Ballymore Novices' Hurdle at the Cheltenham Festival, he produced a cracking performance at Aintree finishing fourth in the Grade 1 two and a half miles novice hurdle. He will reappear in the same two and a half miles maiden hurdle at Aintree (28th October), in which he finished third last season. Effective on any ground, he will step up in trip later on but, if it came up heavy at Newbury in late December (29th), he could be the sort for the Grade 1 Challow Hurdle.

BARNEY DWAN (IRE) 8 b g Vinnie Roe (IRE) - Kapricia Speed (FR)
Twice a winner over fences at Market Rasen and Musselburgh, he finished fourth in the novices' handicap chase at the Cheltenham Festival. A faller at Ayr last time, he has enjoyed a great summer with Jason Maguire and looks tremendous. He is the nicest horse anyone could hope to train. It won't be easy for him off a mark of 143 and we haven't nominated any targets but I am sure he will do us proud once again. In terms of trip, I think around two miles six is ideal because he lacks a gear over two and a half miles and a truly run three miles stretches him a bit.

BENECHENKO (IRE) 6 br g Beneficial - Beann Ard (IRE)
He is a lovely horse but he endured a frustrating season last year. Runner-up over hurdles a couple of times at Wincanton and Fakenham, we got the tactics wrong on occasions. Still a novice, he will continue over hurdles but it won't be long before he is jumping fences. I think two and a half miles is probably his trip at the moment.

BENNY'S BRIDGE (IRE) 5 b g Beneficial - Wattle Bridge (IRE)
A very nice horse who I thought would run well on his debut in a bumper at Market Rasen. The fact he won by two and a half lengths, I couldn't have been happier. He then ran a cracker to finish third in the Goffs UK Spring Sales bumper at Newbury in March. He will go novice hurdling over two and a half miles and is a lovely prospect.

BLUE MONDAY (IRE) 5 b g Beneficial - Bradbury Baby (IRE)
Ran in four Irish points for Tom Keating finishing second last time. We haven't done a great with him but he appears to be a nice straightforward horse who is likely to run in a bumper before jumping hurdles.

CAGE OF FEAR (IRE) 4 b g Milan - Baile An Droichid (IRE)
Runner-up in his sole Irish point-to-point for Donnchadh Doyle in April, I loved him at the sales the following month. We bought him for Neville Statham and he spent the summer with Paddy Brennan. He looks great and we will aim him at a bumper.

CAP SOLEIL (FR) 5 b m Kapgarde (FR) - Move Again (FR)
Unbeaten in mares' bumpers the previous season, she enjoyed a very good novice hurdle campaign winning twice at Newbury and Haydock, including a Listed event at the latter track. Runner-up in another Listed hurdle at Newbury in between, she was beaten by a better mare on the day. I thought Paddy (Brennan) gave her a very good ride at the Cheltenham Festival finishing second behind Laurina in the mares' novices' hurdle. It's fair to say she bumped into one. We will start her off in a two miles Listed hurdle at Wetherby (3rd November) before stepping her up in trip later on. Two and a half miles is ideal at the moment but I think she will want three miles eventually.

CHAMPAGNE WELL (IRE) 5 b g Gold Well - Perkanod (IRE)
We acquired him at the Punchestown Festival Sale in late April having won the third of his three Irish points for Roisin Hickey. He has settled in well and is another who will run in a bumper before going hurdling. I have been pleased with him and he looks a lovely horse.

CHASE THE SPUD 10 b g Alflora (IRE) - Trial Trip
A former Midlands National winner, he won a valuable staying handicap chase at Haydock in November but the wheels fell off thereafter. We aimed him at the Welsh National but that didn't go to plan and we won't be doing that again. All being well, he will reappear in the same race at Haydock (24th November) before we consider the various National type races.

COOLANLY (IRE) 6 b g Flemensfirth (USA) - La Fisarmonica (IRE)
Another very nice horse who won a bumper at Chepstow in October on his first run for us. He then finished second behind the unbeaten Vinndication on his hurdles debut at Leicester in December. Unfortunately, he picked up an injury to a hind leg which meant he needed time off. Too free in the Ballymore Novices' Hurdle at Cheltenham, we dropped him back to two miles at Aintree and he ran very well in fifth in Grade 1 company. The Grade 2 Persian War Novices' Hurdle at Chepstow (14th October) is his first target.

CROSSGALESFAMEGAME (IRE) 4 b f Mahler - Fame Forever (IRE)
Third in both her starts in Irish points, she looks a nice filly who we purchased at the Doncaster May Sales. She will run in a mares' bumper in the Autumn.

CUDDLES MCGRAW (IRE) 5 b g Court Cave (IRE) - Stefphonic (IRE)
He has taken a long time to come to hand but I am fortunate to have a lot of patient owners, including Graham and Alison Jelley. We operated on his wind last year and he has improved with experience and I think he will develop into a lovely chaser one day. Unlucky at Perth last time, he is still a novice over hurdles and, with a rating of 99, we will have a look for a suitable novices' handicap hurdle.

DE NAME EVADES ME (IRE) 6 b g Vinnie Roe (IRE) - Sound of The Crowd (IRE)
A cracking horse who gained plenty of experience in Irish points for Tom Keating. He won one and was placed in the other five before we bought him for an affordable price. I was pleased with his two runs over hurdles at Kempton for us in the spring and he remains a novice for this season. He is a three miles chaser in the making though.

GOLDEN TAIPAN (IRE) 4 b g Golden Lariat (USA) - Rose of Taipan (IRE)
Bought for the Loose Chips syndicate, Barrels of Courage, he is a smashing horse who was placed in his second Irish point for Sean Doyle. We acquired him at the Cheltenham May Sale and he is a nice sized individual and I love him. He doesn't really strike me as a bumper horse so he will probably go straight over hurdles.

GOOD AND HARDY (IRE) 5 b g Westerner - Kilganey Maid (IRE)
We bought him on the same day as Ask Dillon at the Cheltenham February Sales. A winning pointer, we ran him in a bumper at Chepstow in the spring but the race came too soon and it didn't pan out as we had hoped. Another who is likely to go hurdling straight away, I think he will want a trip.

GRAGEELAGH GIRL (IRE) 7 b m Craigsteel - Smiths Lady (IRE)
She is a good mare who did well in bumpers winning at Perth before being harshly disqualified after finishing first at Aintree in October. She was then runner-up in a Listed bumper at Cheltenham in testing conditions. Seventh at Huntingdon on Boxing Day, we then decided to give her a break. Returning over hurdles in the summer, she won at Newton Abbot and Stratford and should have made it three out of three at Perth last time. We intend running her in a two miles five novices' hurdle at Cheltenham (26th October). She is versatile in terms of ground.

HERECOMESTHEBOOM (IRE) 6 b g Darsi (FR) - Dympnajane
Runner-up in his only Irish point-to-point for Denis Murphy, we were delighted when he won first time out for us in a bumper at Cheltenham last Autumn. Paddy (Brennan) was raving about him afterwards and we therefore aimed him at a Listed bumper at Ascot before Christmas. A few of ours were not running well at the time though and he was disappointing. Given a break, we brought him back at Ludlow in the spring and, while he ran respectably in third, the track didn't really suit him, plus he was conceding weight. He will go novice hurdling over two and a half miles.

I'M WISER NOW (IRE) 4 b g Presenting - Reine Angevine (FR)
He is a lovely unraced four year old who belongs to Paul and Clare Rooney. Bought at the Land Rover Sale in Ireland last year, he is 16.2hh and we nearly ran him in a bumper last spring but the ground dried out. He is a very nice horse who will contest a bumper in the Autumn. I like him a lot.

JARVEYS PLATE (IRE) 5 ch g Getaway (GER) - She's Got To Go (IRE)
Another lovely horse who Sally (Randell) found. She goes through all the point-to-points every Sunday/Monday. He was placed in both his runs and ridden by Derek O'Connor on each occasion. I therefore rang Derek who recommended him and Chris Coley loved him so we bought him. We took him to Perth in the spring for a competitive bumper and he won in good style. There were plenty of fancied horses in behind and I think the form will work out. An out and out chaser in the making, he could run in another bumper before going novice hurdling.

JENNYS SURPRISE (IRE) 10 b m Hawk Wing (USA) - Winning Jenny (IRE)
A winner at Ffos Las, she also finished runner-up in the West Wales National at the same track in February. Second in a Listed chase at Perth last time, she loves the mud and will contest those long distance handicap chases. She will be running at the likes of Haydock and Chepstow and we may give her an entry in the Welsh National (27th December).

LILY OF LEYSBOURNE 5 b m Shirocco (GER) - Alegralil
A well bred mare who her owner Cedric Brookes sent to Jimmy Mangan in Ireland to run in bumpers and over hurdles. She joined us in the spring and, being quite a keen going mare, we fitted her with a hood at both Ffos Las and Market Rasen. I thought she was unlucky last time finding the track too sharp. Provided she learns to settle, she should have no trouble winning races. Still a maiden, we have the option of running her in a handicap off her mark of 108.

LIOSDUIN BHEARNA (IRE) 5 b g Beneficial - Cloth Fair (IRE)
Bought for the FOB Racing Partnership, he was placed in two of his three Irish points. A nice straightforward horse, we are still learning about him but I would imagine he will start in a bumper.

LOVELY JOB (IRE) 8 ch g Touch of Land (FR) - Wyckoff Queen (IRE)
Enjoyed a good season over fences winning three times at Uttoxeter, Hexham and Taunton before finishing fourth at Cheltenham in April. Rated 138, it isn't going to be easy for him but hopefully he will improve again. He stays well and appreciates better ground.

MASTER DEE (IRE) 9 b g King's Theatre (IRE) – Miss Lauren Dee (IRE)
He has done very well and has been so consistent throughout his career. Yet to finish out of the first three in twenty three career starts, he was rated 119 when joining the yard a couple of years ago. Now rated 151, he won the Grade 3 Betdaq Handicap Chase at Kempton in February. Barry (Geraghty) gave him a fantastic ride holding him up during the early stages before producing him at the last. He is a very solid horse who always tries his best and is suited by flat tracks. We will aim him at the good staying handicaps.

MERCY MERCY ME 6 b g Shirocco (GER) – Monsignorita (IRE)
We were delighted with him when winning on his debut in a bumper at Sandown in November. Forced to miss the Listed bumper at Ascot before Christmas, he had been off a while before contesting the Cheltenham Festival bumper but I was very pleased with his performance. Staying on well in eighth, he is very much one for the future and hopefully one day he will make a lovely chaser. A bit disappointing last time at Aintree, he will go hurdling and I think he will make a very nice staying novice.

MOUNT BATUR (IRE) 5 ch g Mahler – Massini's Daughter (IRE)
He was fourth in a bumper at Uttoxeter in November but hung badly. We sent him to Louise Cabble who does some pre training and we discovered he was suffering with a kissing spine. He has therefore had an operation and hopefully that will make a difference because he is a nice horse who works well at home.

OCEAN COVE (IRE) 6 ch g Ask – Sand Eel (IRE)
Third in his only point-to-point, he was very consistent last season with his only disappointing run at Uttoxeter in a small field. We fitted him with a tongue tie that day and he may have resented it. Unlucky not to win at Warwick in March, he appreciated the step up to three miles at Ayr last time and won a nice pot. Effective on any ground, he could have another run over hurdles but I think he is ready to go chasing. I love him.

OSCAR ROSE (IRE) 6 b m Oscar (IRE) – Ben Roseler (IRE)
I am not quite sure how she is still a maiden over hurdles. She kept bumping into one last year and deserves a change of luck. Third in a Listed mares' handicap hurdle at Cheltenham in the spring, she has plenty of experience for a second season novice. The plan is to start her off in a two miles three mares' novice hurdle at Chepstow (13th October), a race in which she finished fourth last season.

PAULS HILL (IRE) 6 b g Marienbard (IRE) – Lunar Star (IRE)
Bought for £10,000 having run in a couple of Irish points, he has a great attitude and wants to win. He has improved with racing and needed a couple of runs last season before he produced a very game effort to win at Towcester before Christmas. Third at Chepstow last time, he stays well and will go chasing.

POETIC RHYTHM (IRE) 7 ch g Flemensfirth (USA) – Sommer Sonnet (IRE)
He enjoyed a very good first half of last season winning the Grade 2 Persian War Novices' Hurdle at Chepstow and the Grade 1 Challow Hurdle at Newbury. We freshened him up after

that and kept him for the Albert Bartlett Novice Hurdle at Cheltenham in March but he was disappointing and was never at the races. I fear he left his race behind at Newbury because it was such a game effort in very testing conditions. We intended running him at Aintree but the ground dried out and then he had had enough by the time he went back to Cheltenham in April. We have given him a good holiday and he will go chasing this Autumn. I hope he will make a very nice staying novice chaser and he will reappear in a three miles novice at Chepstow (14th October).

PRIDE OF LECALE 7 b g Multiplex – Rock Gossip (IRE)
He has had some time off due to injury but is a lovely horse and I am lucky to have him. A smart bumper horse a couple of seasons ago, he was in training last season but I was under no pressure to run him so we gave him all the time he needed. He looks well at the moment and I am very pleased with him. He will go novice hurdling and, judged on his homework, he retains all of his ability.

RISKY GOLD (IRE) 5 b g Gold Well – Ask Me Sister (IRE)
Ran in four Irish points for Colin Bowe who recommended him to us. We therefore acquired him at the Cheltenham November Sales and he won a point-to-point at Andoversford in April. We then ran him in a point-to-point bumper at Aintree the following month but the ground dried out and he came back jarred up. He is OK now though and we will send him novice hurdling.

ROBYNDZONE (IRE) 4 br g Frammassone (IRE) – Rebecca Susan
By an unknown sire, he won his only point-to-point in Ireland in the spring. He went to the sales but was unsold so we managed to buy him privately. An unknown quantity, he is unbeaten and we will see what he is capable of in a bumper in the Autumn.

SOLDIER OF LOVE 5 b g Yeats (IRE) – Monsignorita (IRE)
A half-brother to Mercy Mercy Me, he finished second in a bumper at Ascot for Mark Pitman and then Malcolm (Denmark) kindly sent him to us when Mark stopped training. Seventh at Kempton in March, he is a lovely horse to go novice hurdling with.

STRONG GLANCE 5 bl g Passing Glance – Strong Westerner (IRE)
A very nice horse from the family of the Hennessy Gold Cup winner Strong Flow, he won first time out at Southwell in November. We then sent him to Ascot for a Listed bumper the following month and he ran very well in fifth and wasn't beaten far. The Cheltenham Festival bumper was the plan thereafter but he, unfortunately, cut a leg while out in the field and missed the rest of the season. Back in work now, I hope he will make a useful novice hurdler.

TASHUNKA (IRE) 5 b m Flemensfirth (USA) – Las Palmlas (IRE)
She did nothing wrong in two starts in bumpers for us in the spring and I like her. Runner-up at Market Rasen, she was beaten by a nice mare of Harry Fry's (Definitelyanoscar) and then she finished well at Cheltenham last time. A keen going filly, she is quite gassy and still green and we have been educating her. She will run in mares' novice hurdles over two and a half miles.

TIME TO MOVE ON (IRE) 5 ch g Flemensfirth (USA) – Kapricia Speed (FR)
Unbeaten in two starts, he is a half-brother to Barney Dwan and I hope he is very good. We were expecting him to run well on his debut in a bumper at Exeter in December and he produced a very impressive performance to beat the subsequent Newbury Sales bumper winner Caribert by ten lengths. He went back there a couple of months later and, while he wasn't as impressive, it was still a good performance because they went no pace and he took it up quite early. Still green, he is a lovely horse for the future. He will stay further but we will start him over two miles over hurdles because he can be quite gassy. He is one to look forward to.

TRAINER'S HORSE TO FOLLOW: BARNEY DWAN

David PIPE

Stables: Pond House, Nicholashayne, Wellington, Somerset.
2017/2018: 33 Winners / 361 Runners 9% Prize-Money £497,554
www.davidpipe.com

ACKER BILK (IRE) 4 ch g Rip Van Winkle (IRE) – Portentous
Twice a winner at Southwell and Wolverhampton over a mile and a half earlier this year for Keith Dalgleish, he has plenty of size about him and his schooling had gone well prior to him winning on his hurdles debut at Worcester in late August. He may not want it too soft and we will aim him at a two miles novices' hurdle under a penalty.

CHAMPERS ON ICE (IRE) 8 gr g Robin Des Champs (FR) – Miss Nova
Fifth in the valuable Grade 3 handicap hurdle at Haydock in November, he then suffered an injury after his next run at Cheltenham the following month. Forced to miss the rest of the season, he won't return until the second half of the campaign. We have the option of continuing over hurdles or going back over fences, although he isn't the most natural of chasers. He endured a hard first season for us as a novice hurdler and has never really recaptured that level of form.

DAKLONDIKE (IRE) 6 b g Gold Well – Strong Irish (IRE)
Took well to fences last season winning three times at Wetherby, Wincanton and Newbury with his rating rising from 114 to 140. He was beginning to creep into contention at Punchestown last time, too, when making a mistake at the third last. Still only six, he jumps and stays well but can race lazily on occasions during his races. He needs to improve again off his current mark but it is possible having progressed so much for the switch to hurdles from fences. We will be aiming him at the decent long distance chases and we may give him an entry in the Welsh National at Chepstow.

DAUPHINE EREINE (FR) 6 b m Saint Des Saints (FR) – Bellissima De Mai (FR)
A half-sister to Dynaste, she won three times over fences in France and, while she hasn't won for us yet, she remains lightly raced and has more to offer. A consistent mare who likes the mud, she is a strong traveller who jumps well. Two and a half miles plus on soft ground is ideal.

DELIRANT (FR) 5 b g Khalkevi (IRE) – Kusea (FR)
Unbeaten in two APQS bumpers in France, including a Grade 1 event at Saint-Cloud a couple of years ago, he hasn't been the easiest to train hence he didn't make his debut for us until the summer. A free going sort, he was quite keen following a lengthy absence eventually finishing fourth at Bangor. He improved for that run and being fitted with a hood when winning next time at Newton Abbot in August. It was good ground on that occasion but we know he handles easier surfaces. We will keep him to trips around two miles for the time being until he learns to settle.

DRUIDE PREMIER (FR) 5 b g Martaline (FR) – Bellissima De Mai (FR)
A full-brother to Dynaste, he has finished third in both his bumpers at Newton Abbot and Uttoxeter during the summer. Still a weak horse, he is different to his brother in that he has taken time to come to hand. We will send him hurdling sooner rather than later over a trip.

DUC DE BEAUCHENE (FR) 5 b g Saddler Maker (IRE) – Quatia D'Angron (FR)
Back in having missed the whole of last season, he is a heavy horse who ran well on his debut finishing runner-up in a bumper at Ffos Las before finding the ground too quick next time at Wetherby. Two miles on soft ground over hurdles will be OK but he will be suited by a step up in trip in time.

DUSKY HERCULES (IRE) 4 b g Shantou (USA) - Annalecky (IRE)
A half-brother to Cheltenham Festival winner Black Hercules, he ran OK on his first start in a bumper at Wincanton in the spring when the penny started to drop in the latter stages. Initially, I thought he was going to be one of our most forward bumper horses but he has taken time and is now starting to strengthen up. He will want a trip over jumps but we may give him another run in a bumper beforehand.

EAMON AN CNOIC (IRE) 7 b g Westerner - Nutmeg Tune (IRE)
Had a good first season over fences winning at Haydock and Plumpton before travelling strongly for a long way in the three miles handicap chase at the Cheltenham Festival. David (Noonan) didn't think he quite stayed the trip so we decided to drop him back to two and a half miles over hurdles at Aintree but it proved one run too many by that stage of the season. Despite having a somewhat in and out profile, he is a decent horse who I think is capable of winning a big prize. We will give him an entry in the BetVictor Gold Cup at Cheltenham (17th November) with two and a half miles appearing to be his trip at present.

EASTER ERIC 4 b g Martaline - Easter Comet
He is a half-brother to Easter Legend and Easter Meteor and I was pleased with his debut in a bumper at Southwell finishing third. I don't think it was a bad race either and he wouldn't have been suited by the way the race was run because they went no pace and then sprinted. That experience will stand him in good stead and, having schooled well, he will go jumping this season.

EDEN DU HOUX (FR) 4 b g Irish Wells (FR) - Maralypha (FR)
A four lengths winner of his only Irish point-to-point in late April, we bought him privately and I hope he has a bright future. We have given him a holiday since arriving and we may start him off in a bumper before going hurdling.

EKAYBURG (FR) 4 b g Sageburg (FR) - Kayseri (FR)
Owned by Cheveley Park Stud, he is a nice big horse who won two of his four races in APQS Flat races in France, including a Grade 2 at Maisons-Laffitte last October. We planned to run him last season but the ground dried up in the spring. He schools nicely and will go hurdling over two miles.

FIRST LORD DE CUET (FR) 4 gr g Lord Du Sud (FR) - Alyce (FR)
Bought at the Cheltenham May Sales five days after winning his only point-to-point by a head for Donnchadh Doyle. The front pair were ten lengths clear of the third and the time was good. I like the sire and he was still weak when he first arrived. Only four, we will take our time with him and probably aim him at a bumper to begin with.

FRIDAY NIGHT LIGHT (FR) 5 b g Air Chief Marshall (IRE) - Peninsula (FR)
A winner at Newbury in January, he was placed on another four occasions before his form tailed off during the spring. However, he had been on the go for a long time and was ready for a holiday. I am not sure he stayed two miles seven at Exeter on his final run and will benefit from dropping back in trip. Indeed, I think he would cope with two miles on soft ground with two and a half miles being ideal. He is open to further improvement and we will give him another run on the Flat at some stage.

GARRAN CITY (IRE) 7 ch g City Honours (USA) - Native Orchid (IRE)
A winning Irish pointer, he was off for nearly two years due to a tendon injury. Placed a couple of times over hurdles at Chepstow, he disappointed last time at Ffos Las. We have operated on his wind since, which will hopefully make a difference. An out and out galloper, he will continue over hurdles. He wants two and a half miles plus in the mud.

GLEN VINE 4 ch g Robin Des Champs (FR) - Gaspara (FR)
Out of Gaspara who completed the Imperial Cup and Cheltenham Festival double for us in 2007, he shows traits of his mother but has more size than her. In training last season, he was ready to run but the ground dried out. We will run him in a bumper and go from there.

JASMIN DES BORDES (FR) 4 b g Great Pretender (IRE) - Queen Des Bordes (FR)
By a good sire, he was runner-up in his sole Irish point for Donnchadh Doyle in May before we bought him at the Cheltenham Sales later the same month. He looks a staying chaser in the making but we may run him in a bumper before going hurdling this season. It is early days because we have done very little with him so far but he looks a nice horse.

KING'S SOCKS (FR) 6 b g King's Best (USA) - Alexandrina (GER)
Third in a Graduation chase at Kempton in February on his first run for us, he then ran well in the Brown Advisory & Merriebelle Stable Plate Handicap Chase at the Cheltenham Festival finishing fifth. Tom (Scudamore) didn't think he quite got home though hence we dropped him back to two miles at Aintree next time. However, it proved one run too many and he was pulled up. He has undergone surgery on his wind since and we may have a look at the Haldon Gold Cup at Exeter (6th November) for him and the BetVictor Gold Cup at Cheltenham (17th November).

KNOW THE SCORE (IRE) 5 b g Flemensfirth (USA) - Prairie Bell (IRE)
He was bought at the Cheltenham November Sales, having won his only Irish point by six lengths a few days earlier for Sean Doyle. He won nicely on his first run for us in a bumper at Towcester in February scoring by thirteen lengths. We then ran him in the Festival bumper at Cheltenham and I was surprised by the speed he showed. He arguably did too much during the first half of the race and paid for it late on. I have been pleased with him since because he has summered well and is an exciting prospect for novice hurdles. A horse with a lot of ability, he is built for fences long-term but will spend this season over hurdles starting off over two miles.

MISS TYNTE (IRE) 6 b m Mahler - Top Quality
She has always worked well at home but it has taken a while for her to get her head in front winning at Ludlow in April. Although she isn't easy to catch right, I hope she will improve this season with two and a half miles and some cut in the ground being ideal.

MOON RACER (IRE) 9 b g Saffron Walden (FR) - Angel's Folly
We were always on the back foot with him last season having undergone surgery following a bout of colic during the summer. He found the ground too soft in both the *Betfair* and County Hurdles at Newbury and Cheltenham respectively, but was back to form when winning at Ayr's Scottish National meeting. Appreciating the better ground and step up to two and a half miles, he won well and has only been raised three pounds. Still on a decent mark over hurdles, we will school him over fences at some stage. It is difficult to make plans because he has been fragile over the years but we know he is a very talented horse. He will be worth a try over three miles at some point.

MR BIG SHOT (IRE) 7 br g Flemensfirth (USA) - Une Etoile (IRE)
Despite being a seven year old, he has only raced five times because he is such a big horse. We didn't get the smoothest runs with him last season either hence he didn't reappear until the Cheltenham Festival. I thought he ran well in my father's race but he appreciated the step up to three miles for the first time at Aintree. He showed a very good attitude and the form looks strong. He has got a tremendous amount of ability but is still a playboy and he doesn't know he's a racehorse yet. In all likelihood, we will send him over fences this season but may give him a run or two over hurdles beforehand. He could be entered at Haydock (24th November) for the race which was previously known as the fixed brush handicap hurdle. We have won it in the past with Grands Crus, Dynaste and Gevrey Chambertin.

MR CLARKSON (IRE) 6 b g Jeremy (USA) - Wynsleydale (USA)
He did us proud the previous season winning a bumper and three times over hurdles. Unfortunately, he picked up a leg injury at Cheltenham on his final run and missed the whole of last term. Not over big, he is very tough and has proved a good buy having finished second in a point-to-point for Stuart Crawford. He will jump fences in time but will resume over hurdles.

NEW AGE DAWNING (IRE) 4 ch g Stowaway - Captain Supreme (IRE)
An old fashioned chaser in the making, he will come into his own over fences in time. Runner-up in his point for Colin Bowe in February, the winner has subsequently finished second in a bumper for Evan Williams. A galloper, we did a bit of work with him during the spring but he was still backward and will only improve.

POKER PLAY (FR) 5 ch g Martaline (FR) - Becquarette (FR)
Placed in a couple of Pertemps qualifiers at Exeter and Chepstow last season, he has dropped a bit in the ratings and hopefully we can take advantage. He has summered very well and, while I need to discuss plans with his owners, there is every chance he will go over fences and be aimed at a novices' handicap chase over two and a half miles plus. He's a galloper.

QUEENS CAVE (IRE) 5 b m Court Cave (IRE) - Shuilan (IRE)
A lovely mare who won an Irish point for Aidan Fitzgerald by ten lengths in November before we bought her at the Cheltenham Sales five days later. An easy winner of a mares' bumper at Uttoxeter on New Year's Eve, she then produced a very good performance when narrowly denied in a Listed mares' bumper at Sandown in March. Only beaten a neck, she looked like winning and the form is solid. She has summered well and there is no doubt she has an engine. We will aim her at mares' novice hurdles starting off over a stiff two miles at somewhere like Exeter.

RAMSES DE TEILLEE (FR) 6 gr g Martaline (FR) - Princesse D'Orton (FR)
A horse I have always liked, he won twice over fences at Chepstow and is another who will probably get an entry in the BetVictor Gold Cup at Cheltenham (17th November). A very good jumper, he possesses a lot of ability but he has had wind issues. We have therefore operated on his breathing since his last run and, while it won't be easy off a mark of 141, he tries hard and is still only six. The jury is still out whether two and a half or three miles is his optimum trip.

RATHLIN ROSE (IRE) 10 b g Bonbon Rose (FR) - A Plus Ma Puce (FR)
He won the Royal Artillery Gold Cup at Sandown in February for a second consecutive year before winning again at Ascot the following month. Although high enough off his mark of 132, I am sure he will continue to pay his way. He loves soft ground and it will be no surprise to see him turn up in the Veterans' chase final at Sandown (5th January).

REMASTERED 5 ch g Network (GER) - Cathodine Cayras (FR)
A big horse who showed a good level of form in bumpers for Liz Doyle finishing runner-up a couple of times at Punchestown and Fairyhouse. I thought he produced a good performance to win a bumper at Chepstow in February on his first start for us and the form looks strong with the runner-up finishing second again in the Grade 2 bumper at Aintree. He is not really a bumper horse which bodes well for the future and I have been very pleased with him during the summer. He will make a lovely chaser eventually but I think he will be an exciting novice hurdler this winter. We will start him off over two or two and a half miles but he will stay three miles in time. He loves soft ground.

SHAAMA GRISE (FR) 6 gr m Montmartre (FR) - Shaama Rose (FR)
Things didn't quite go to plan over fences last season. Even though she finished runner-up at Plumpton and Exeter, I don't think she was at her best. We were preparing her for my father's race at Cheltenham but she suffered an injury, which means she won't be back in action until the second half of this season. Depending on when she returns, we may shelve chasing until the following season because there is no point losing her novice status so late in the year. I hope there is more to come from her.

STORY OF FRIENDS (FR) 4 b g Kingsalsa (USA) – Royale Malinelle (FR)
Pulled up on his debut in a point-to-point, he showed a good turn of foot to win next time in May and we purchased him at the Cheltenham Sale later the same month. We did a bit with him at home and I have been pleased with his progress since arriving. I would think he will have a run in a bumper before going jumping.

STREAM LADY (IRE) 5 b m Curtain Time (IRE) – Victory Queen (IRE)
A twelve lengths winner of her only Irish point in May, she won impressively and the second, third and fourth have scored since. By an unfashionable sire, we bought her privately afterwards and she may contest a mares' only bumper.

UMBRIGADO (IRE) 4 br g Stowaway – Dame O'Neill (IRE)
He looks a nice horse who was well thought of by Aidan Fitzgerald, prior to finishing second in a point-to-point in March. We acquired him five days later at the Cheltenham Festival Sale and Paul Nicholls bought the winner (Brewers Project) at the same sale. We like what we see at home and he is another who may contest a bumper before jumping hurdles.

UN TEMPS POUR TOUT (IRE) 9 b g Robin Des Champs (FR) – Rougedespoir (FR)
Missed last season having incurred a leg injury following his second victory in the Ultima Handicap Chase at the Cheltenham Festival. He is back now though and we are looking forward to seeing him in action. His first target is the Ladbroke Trophy at Newbury (1st December) before being aimed at Cheltenham and Aintree once again. We will probably enter him in the Grand National. He has been a very good horse for us winning the French Champion Hurdle and twice at the Cheltenham Festival but I still don't think we have seen the best of him.

VIEUX LION ROUGE (FR) 9 ch g Sabiango (GER) – Indecise (FR)
Ran in the Grand National for a third time in April finishing ninth. There is every chance he will get an entry once again this season but we intend running him more often this time around and will mix and match hurdling with chasing. His first target will be the Becher Chase (8th December), a race he won two years ago but wasn't at his best in it last year. He will have a run beforehand.

WARTHOG (FR) 6 gr g Martaline (FR) – Shekira (FR)
Proved frustrating last season having worked well at home. He was placed over hurdles at Exeter and Wetherby and finished third at Ascot but wasn't finishing off his races. A big strong horse who won an Irish point before we bought him, he will go over fences and hopefully make a better chaser because we know he has an engine. He wants two and a half miles plus.

WHAT A MOMENT (IRE) 8 b g Milan – Cuiloge Lady (IRE)
He won the amateur riders' handicap chase at Cheltenham's November meeting (16th) last year but wasn't right afterwards and hasn't raced since. The plan is for him to go back there for the same race and defend his title.

WHITLEY NEILL (IRE) 6 b g Shantou (USA) – Maidrin Rua (IRE)
Following a couple of runs in bumpers, he came good on his hurdles debut at Exeter in April after a lengthy absence. Fourth next time at Worcester, he didn't travel as well that day. He then finished third at Newton Abbot in August. He is quirky but talented and I hope there is more to come from him. Still a novice for this season over hurdles, he will jump fences in due course.

YOU SAY WHAT (IRE) 8 b g Milan – Wave Back (IRE)
A winner at Exeter in November, he is a long distance chaser who likes soft ground, although he doesn't want it bottomless. I think his mark is fair and I will be disappointed if he isn't open to more improvement.

TRAINER'S HORSE TO FOLLOW: KNOW THE SCORE

BROMLEY'S BEST BUYS

The 2017/2018 National Hunt Season broke all records for the Highflyer Bloodstock buying team of Anthony Bromley, David Minton and Tessie Greatrex. **ALTIOR**'s victory in the Celebration Chase at Sandown on the last day of the season was the 26th Grade 1 winner purchased by them and comfortably beat the Company's previous-best score of 19 Grade 1 victories (in the 2008/2009 season). Along with **ALTIOR**, both **BUVEUR D'AIR** and **FOOTPAD** were other purchases to remain unbeaten throughout the season and the Aintree Festival saw 7 of their buys win over the three days, including **MIGHT BITE** and **POLITOLOGUE**, plus the Simon Munir/Isaac Souede trio of **L'AMI SERGE**, **TERREFORT** and **WE HAVE A DREAM**.

Bromley's Best Buys produced **29 winners** in last year's *One Jump Ahead* at a strike-rate of **27%.** They included smart novice hurdlers **MR WHIPPED (3 wins), ON THE BLIND SIDE (3 wins)** and **WE HAVE A DREAM (5 out of 5).** For the **NINETEENTH** consecutive year, Anthony Bromley has kindly put together a list of names he has bought in France and Ireland, who are set to make an impact in their new surroundings in the UK this winter.

ADJALI (GER) 3 b g Kamsin (GER) - Anabasis (GER)
Trainer: Nicky HENDERSON
A good-looking, athletic youngster, he showed very useful form in the Parisian juvenile hurdles this spring for Guillaume Macaire who has been a great source for us over the years. He won easily at Compiegne on the 26th April, prior to a decent third in the prestigious Prix Stanley Hurdle over the Grand Steeplechase weekend. He should be up to carrying his penalty over here initially and then we will see how he shapes up after that.

BEYONDTHESTORM (IRE) 5 b g Flemensfirth (USA) - Blue Gale (IRE)
Trainer: Nicky HENDERSON
He did not run for Nicky (Henderson) in the spring but showed plenty at home before the ground dried up in April. Owned by the Thompson's of **Cheveley Park Stud**, he is a typical Irish stamp of chaser for the future who handled the heavy conditions well on his only career start in a point-to-point last December for Denis Murphy.

CARIBEAN BOY (FR) 4 gr g Myboycharlie (IRE) - Caribena (FR)
Trainer: Nicky HENDERSON
Purchased at the Auteuil Sale during the Grand Steeplechase Weekend, he is a really tall four year old grey gelding who showed quite a high level of form over hurdles at Auteuil last season as a juvenile. He won in October and posted a career-best effort on his latest outing when a close second to the smart Lou Bucks in a Listed hurdle in late April. Given his physique, Nicky (Henderson) might be tempted to go straight novice chasing with him despite his young age.

CHAMPAGNE MYSTERY (IRE) 4 b g Shantou (USA) - Spanker
Trainer: Nicky HENDERSON
From the same vendors who sold us the likes of River Wylde, Peddlers Cross and Kilcooley, this medium-sized four year old pointer showed plenty of promise in a couple of starts in soft ground this spring, finishing a close second to Espoir De Loire (since joined Ben Pauling) on his last run. He will run in **Trevor Hemmings'** colours.

CHECKITOUT (IRE) 4 b g Salutino (GER) - Akasha (IRE)
Trainer: Charlie LONGSDON
Showed plenty of promise in a really hot-looking four year old point in Northern Ireland finishing third to The Very Man (sold for £210,000) and Jasmin Des Bordes (£145,000). This fellow was

bought outside the ring for £37,000 after he did not sell initially and I think he looks a good value buy for some rather lucky owners in **Fred Mills** and **Dave Mason** as he was far from the finished article this May and will improve.

CHINENSIS (IRE) 5 b g Well Chosen - Emily Vard (IRE)
Trainer: Nigel TWISTON-DAVIES
David Minton purchased this tough Irish five year old pointer for **Trevor Hemmings** at the Goffs UK May Sale. He won all three of his Irish points last season, having been placed on his only start in his first season. He acts on soft and made most of the running to win going away on his last outing in May which certainly marked him out as above-average.

CONSTANCIO (IRE) 5 b g Authorized (IRE) - Senora Galilei (IRE)
Trainer: Donald McCAIN
A useful 86-rated Flat performer for Jim Bolger, he has been an improved horse for being gelded this year and appears to act on any ground. I like his sire as a dual-purpose one and I think he could prove a real fun horse for the **Elite Racing Club** under both codes.

DIAMOND BRIG 6 b g Black Sam Bellamy (IRE) - Lady Brig
Trainer: Rose DOBBIN
The success of former British pointers under Rules has really improved in recent years and it is definitely a market we are looking at very seriously now. One of the best youngsters around last season was this Scottish-trained six year old. He has only been beaten once in five career starts and that was when he encountered quick ground. He relished the heavy conditions when winning his maiden hunter chase at Kelso (The Buccleuch Cup) by twenty one lengths in April and looked a real out and out stayer who could be a Welsh/Midlands National type in the future. He was bought for **Trevor Hemmings**.

DOWNTOWN GETAWAY (IRE) 5 b g Getaway (GER) - Shang A Lang (IRE)
Trainer: Nicky HENDERSON
A very impressive winner of his only bumper in Ireland last December for Mags Mullins, he did not make the track for new connections last spring but hopes are high that he can pick things up again this time around. He easily beat some good subsequent winners at Fairyhouse that day, including Remastered (now with David Pipe) and Lone Wolf (Punchestown Festival winner for Joseph O'Brien) and I hope he can take high rank over hurdles.

DRAGON D'ESTRUVAL (FR) 5 b g Enrique - Rose D'Estruval (FR)
Trainer: Nicky HENDERSON
This grand stamp of horse was a useful chaser as a four year old last year for Guillaume Macaire and only arrived at Nicky's (Henderson) late this spring. He had not won a hurdle in France so he easily rectified that at Ffos Las at the end of May. He will stay novice hurdling this winter and will appreciate softer conditions. Chasing can wait until the following season.

DREAM DU GRAND VAL (FR) 5 b g Puit D'Or (IRE) - Apple Mille (FR)
Trainer: Nicky HENDERSON
This maiden five year old is the **Million In Mind**'s inmate at Seven Barrows this season. He was an improved horse last winter, placing twice at Auteuil and once at Pau over hurdles on his last three starts, including a good third in a decent two miles two handicap hurdle in Paris on his latest run in March. He should hopefully pay his way over both hurdles and fences.

DR SANDERSON (IRE) 4 b g Jeremy (USA) - Guydus (IRE)
Trainer: Paul NICHOLLS
A likeable type by a hot stallion in Jeremy, he was a decisive winner of his only UK bumper for the Crawford Brothers at the end of March. Very little has run subsequently from the race, although the well-beaten fifth has actually won over hurdles this summer at Perth for Nicky

Richards. He was purchased privately for the **Million In Mind** Partnership and I am hoping their good record with ex-Crawford horses continues (the last four have all won, with the best being The Organist).

DRUMLEE WATAR (IRE) 5 ch g Watar (IRE) - Dolly of Dublin (IRE)
Trainer: Warren GREATREX
Tessie Greatrex bought this unbeaten five year old pointer for her husband Warren to train from the McParlan Family in Northern Ireland after he had absolutely bolted up in his five year old point in May. Winning jockey Noel McParlan had ridden Warren's Cheltenham Festival victor Missed Approach and was very upbeat about this youngster's prospects. To be fair at £65,000 he did not look an expensive buy given how many pointers were making six figures plus this season. He should be one to follow.

ESPOIR DE LOIRE (FR) 4 b g Anabaa Blue - Grischa (FR)
Trainer: Ben PAULING
Tessie and Ben Pauling bought a number of Irish pointers at the Goffs UK May Sales as trade did not feel quite so mad and, on reflection, it may have been a good plan. This £60,000 buy won his only four year old point in a fast time from the aforementioned Champagne Mystery (now Trevor Hemmings/Nicky Henderson) at the end of April and it looked a really solid performance.

FAITHFULNESS (IRE) 5 b m Robin Des Champs (FR) - Ballycowan Lady (IRE)
Trainer: Charlie LONGSDON
A typical rangy daughter of Robin Des Champs, this five year old won her only career start in an Irish maiden point at the end of April in testing ground. Trained by Sean Doyle of Monbeg fame, she galloped her rivals into submission that day and comes from an excellent jumping family, being out of a half-sister to Harbour Pilot. Tessie (Greatrex) looks to have picked up a very interesting sort for the next couple of seasons.

FALCO BLITZ (FR) 4 b g Falco (USA) - Ignited
Trainer: Nicky HENDERSON
An attractive son of Falco (also sire of Peace And Co, amongst others), he showed distinct promise in his only four year old point at the end of May for the Monbeg Doyle Brothers, going down narrowly to Port Stanley (sold to Jessie Harrington at the same sale), who had the benefit of running previously. Bought for a syndicate, he looks like he could have enough pace to perhaps start off in a bumper before going over hurdles.

FULL GLASS (FR) 5 b g Diamond Green (FR) - Full Tune (FR)
Trainer: Alan KING
I only got this chap over from Guillaume Macaire's in mid-March and it was a bonus that Alan (King) decided to give him a run before the end of the season. He ran with plenty of promise to be third in a Listed handicap chase at Ayr and I am more than hopeful that he can be competitive in some of the big middle-distance chases this coming winter.

HILL SIXTEEN 5 b g Court Cave (IRE) - Chasers Chic
Trainer: Sue SMITH
David (Minton) bought this good-moving son of Court Cave at the Aintree Sale for **Trevor Hemmings** after he had prevailed at Dromahane in his only point-to-point on the 8th April in soft ground. A late-maturing type of horse, he may be even better with another winter under his belt.

INTERCONNECTED 4 br g Network (GER) - R De Rien Sivola (FR)
Trainer: Nicky HENDERSON
One of two new purchases I have made this year for the **Grech and Parkin** team, the four year old was an extremely impressive winner of his only English point-to-point at Larkhill for Tom

Lacey in February by a long-looking twenty lengths. A great big horse, we had to outbid the Gigginstown team to secure him at the Cheltenham Festival Sale. Realistically this season will probably be more of a learning one over hurdles, preparing him for the following one when he can get over a fence as a five and six-year-old.

JILLYTHEJET (IRE) 4 bl f Jeremy (USA) – Listen Up
Trainer: Nicky HENDERSON
An attractive black filly by Jeremy, David Minton bought her at the Aintree Festival Sale for **Lady Tennant** to join Nicky Henderson after winning her only four year old point in desperately heavy conditions in mid-March. She jumped beautifully out in front and, whilst the winning margin was not all that big at the end, it was only greenness and her inexperience late on which caused that. She had a great way of going throughout the race and certainly did not look a filly who needed such testing conditions. She might prove to be a really good racemare, particularly when she encounters better ground.

LAKE VIEW LAD (IRE) 8 gr g Oscar (IRE) – Missy O'Brien (IRE)
Trainer: Nick ALEXANDER
David (Minton) purchased this useful handicapper privately over the summer to stay at Nick Alexander's and he will now run in **Trevor Hemmings'** colours. A smart northern novice chaser last winter in soft/heavy ground, he showed on his last outing at Kelso in April that he also stays beyond three miles and he can develop into a cracking long-distance handicapper this season, particularly when the ground is deep. I suspect he will have a few more targets at Haydock this time around as he runs well there and it is one of the owner's favourite tracks.

LECALE'S ARTICLE (IRE) 4 b g Malinas (GER) – Brookville (IRE)
Trainer: Nicky HENDERSON
Nicky Henderson and David Minton fell in love with this youngster at the Punchestown Festival Sale and he ended up topping the sale, with them outbidding the Willie Mullins' team. He had been very impressive the week before the sale, winning his only four year old point-to-point by an easy eight lengths. A real athlete with plenty of scope, he probably won't come fully into his own until he is chasing but he should certainly be competitive over hurdles beforehand.

MILLARVILLE (IRE) 5 b m Court Cave (IRE) – Portavoe (IRE)
Trainer: Oliver SHERWOOD
We are hoping lightning can strike again as Oliver's good mare The Organist was originally bought from the Crawford Brothers for the **Million In Mind** Partnership. This athletic five-year-old won her only point-to-point for youngest brother, Ben Crawford, in January and the form of the race looks rock-solid. The well-beaten third and fourth placed mares both came out and won their very next starts and she may have enough pace to start off in a mares' bumper before novice hurdling.

MILVALE (IRE) 4 b g Ask – House-of-Hearts (IRE)
Trainer: Sandy THOMSON
The first horse I have purchased for Sandy Thomson, he is particularly well-related, being a half-brother to Welsh National winner Emperor's Choice out of a half-sister to Our Vic. He was narrowly beaten in his only four year old point in May and, interestingly, the close-up third Eagle De Guye sold for £66,000 to Rose Dobbin at Doncaster whilst this chap cost £40,000 at Cheltenham a week later. He looks a horse who should improve physically for a bit more time and is hopefully one to follow in the North over the next couple of seasons.

MY WAY (FR) 4 ch g Martaline – Royale Majesty (FR)
Trainer: Paul NICHOLLS
This is a horse I did not buy but rather wished I had. Unfortunately, I could not find a client willing to match the bid that connections had received for him in March. He is a gorgeous-looking horse whom I knew well and I am sure he will be a well-known name by the season's end. Nicely positioned for the UK, being a maiden, he was a leading juvenile in France last season, placing

in all six of his starts over hurdles and fences at Auteuil, including two seconds in a couple of Graded steeplechases in November and March on his last two outings. It will be interesting to see which route Paul (Nicholls) decides to go with him, novice hurdling or novice chasing first.

NORTHERN BOUND (IRE) 4 b g Fruits of Love (USA) - Noble Choice
Trainer: Ben PAULING
A half-brother to Lord Scoundrel and Balnaslow, he was bought from the latter's trainer Graham McKeever at the Goffs UK May Sale by Tessie to join Ben Pauling. He was only narrowly beaten when second in his only four year old point in Northern Ireland in mid-May on yielding ground, keeping on really gamely to the line. He looked the sort that Ben usually does well with, although his pedigree is a late-maturing chasing one so any bumpers or hurdles he wins will be a bonus.

NOTACHANCE (IRE) 4 b g Mahler - Ballybrowney Hall (IRE)
Trainer: Alan KING
Alan King and I only buy a few pointers each year but we generally have a good record and I think this is a horse to follow, although he is probably more of a horse for next season. A great big four-year-old, it was a surprise he was ready to run in the first four-year-old point-to-point of the year in Ireland, let alone almost make all the running, going down narrowly at the line to Some Operator. By the same sire as a horse Alan and I both like for this season in Canelo, he is from the family of Over The Deel.

SHANNON HILL 4 b g Kayf Tara - Shannon Native (IRE)
Trainer: Alan KING
The second of the two buys this spring for the **Grech and Parkin** team, this neat, active son of Champion British sire Kayf Tara, absolutely annihilated his opposition when winning a twelve runner open maiden point-to-point at Brampton Bryan for English trainer Francesca Nimmo. He did so unchallenged by 40 lengths and we think he could be anything. He looked to have enough toe in his point to be competitive in a bumper first.

SHE MITE BITE (IRE) 5 b m Scorpion (IRE) - That's Moyne (IRE)
Trainer: Nicky HENDERSON
Not a dear buy at £28,000, David Minton and Nicky Henderson rather liked her at the end of the session of Irish pointers at this year's Goffs UK May Sale. Whilst her name and sire appealed quite a bit to them, her actual winning points performance was very eye-catching as she sluiced up by twelve lengths on yielding ground on the 12th May. Owned by a partnership which has many of the same faces in it as Might Bite, she is a great big deep-chested mare who should certainly pay her way.

THE GLANCING QUEEN (IRE) 4 b f Jeremy (USA) - Glancing (IRE)
Trainer: Alan KING
This unbeaten four year old winning Irish pointer excites me and I felt at the time that we had done some decent business to secure her for £80,000 when she was sold early on (Lot 3) in the Cheltenham Festival Sale. She had the measure of the faller at the last, Little Light, on the day and it was interesting to see that the latter went on to finished a close second next time out and sell for £200,000 at the Aintree Sale just a few weeks later. I really like her sire Jeremy and I think she might turn out to be one of our best buys from this spring. Time will tell.

TRIO FOR RIO (IRE) 5 br g Getaway (GER) - Rio Trio (IRE)
Trainer: Warren GREATREX
The stallion Getaway, along with the much missed Jeremy, are two of my favourite Irish jumps sires currently and this five-year-old is yet another flashy, attractive, good-moving product of his father. A progressive pointer last season for Jimmy Mangan, he won two of his last three starts in really good fashion in yielding/soft ground and he also ran well to be second in between his two victories to subsequent hunter chase winner Oscar Contender. A hardy type, I think the members of the **Million In Mind** Partnership should get a lot of action from this fellow over the coming months.

YOUNG LIEUTENANT (IRE) 4 b g Robin Des Champs (FR) – Be My Gesture (IRE)
Trainer: Warren GREATREX
This relation of Rhinestone Cowboy did all the right things in his only point-to-point except actually win it. It was a cracking debut in what looked a decent end-of-season maiden as he injected a great turn of speed from two out only to get collared in the shadows of the post by Easyrun De Vassy (£105,000 to join Paul Nicholls). At £60,000, I would have to say that Warren and Tessie Greatrex appear to have got some good value and he is one to keep on the right side of in the seasons to come.

THE TOP CHASES

It will be exciting to see some of our buys clashing in the top races this winter, with **ALTIOR** and **FOOTPAD** possibly clashing in the Tingle Creek at Sandown before Christmas, although Simon Munir and Isaac Souede do have the option of sending **SCEAU ROYAL** instead for that assignment. The staying division will once again see **MIGHT BITE** and **BRISTOL DE MAI** renew rivalry and I suspect the *Betfair* Chase at Haydock will be their first showdown. Of last year's novices, it will be interesting to see how the five-year-old **TERREFORT** fares against the big boys this time around. I know Nicky (Henderson) favours a tilt at the Ladbroke Trophy, although he hardly looks thrown in off a mark of 158 but we shall see. I am also intrigued to see whether **TOP NOTCH** and **POLITOLOGUE** try three miles at some stage this winter as both could be serious King George contenders, in my opinion.

THE TOP HURDLES

BUVEUR D'AIR reigned supreme again last year but was not as impressive as one might have expected him to be when taking his second successive Champion Hurdle in March. I suspect there will be a few pretenders out there fancying to take his crown. Whether last year's top English juvenile **WE HAVE A DREAM** is yet in his class only time will tell but his rating of 156 does mean that handicaps are out of the equation, at this stage anyway. Over the longer trips it is a shame that **L'AMI SERGE** tweaked his leg in trying to defend his French Champion Hurdle victory in May, which has resulted in him missing this season. In his absence, the likes of **THE NEW ONE**, **WHOLESTONE** and **CALL ME LORD** all look to have the credentials to win some of the big staying hurdles and I am keen to see if Nicky can bring **ON THE BLINDSIDE** back to his best as he looked a real talent early last season.

HIGHFLYER BLOODSTOCK'S HORSE TO FOLLOW: THE GLANCING QUEEN

CHANGING CODES

The following feature highlights a selection of Flat horses set to go jumping for the first time this winter who will, hopefully, prove profitable to follow.

BRONAGH'S BELLE has proved a different proposition since stepped up to middle distances this year. Willie Mullins' three year old raced exclusively over six and seven furlongs as a two year old earning a mark of 59 in the process. However, the daughter of High Chaparral hasn't looked back since recording a two and three quarters of a length win at Leopardstown (1m 5f : Good/ Firm) in June. Raised sixteen pounds, she was then a running on second in a two miles handicap at the Galway Festival (Soft/Heavy) in August. Runner-up once again at Tramore (1m 4f : Good) less than three weeks later, she may not have been suited by the drop back in trip behind Fiesole. Rated 83, she looks tailormade for juvenile hurdles.

Gordon Elliott has won the Triumph Hurdle twice (Tiger Roll (2014) and Farclas (2018)) and he will be hoping expensive purchase **LETHAL STEPS** develops into a contender next March. A dual winner on the Flat as a juvenile for Ger Lyons at Leopardstown (6f) and Killarney (1m), he was also Listed placed. The son of Lethal Force was transferred to Andrew Balding this summer finishing fourth in another Listed contest at Newmarket's July meeting (1m : Good/Firm). Twenty four hours later, he was bought by Cheveley Park Stud for 300,000gns and sent back to Ireland for a dual purpose career. Gelded since joining Elliott, he hasn't raced beyond ten furlongs and both his wins on the level were gained on decent ground. Perhaps he will be more of an Aintree type next spring.

I am hoping Ian Williams has juvenile hurdles on the agenda for his progressive three year old **MATEWAN**. Bought as a yearling for €95,000, the gelded son of Epaulette is a half-brother to stablemate Richie McCaw. Unplaced in three races over seven furlongs as a two year old, he is another who has improved markedly since talking longer distance this year. Placed at Wolverhampton and Newmarket over nine and ten furlongs respectively, he then stayed on well to beat dual winner Black Lotus by a length and a half on the July course in August off a mark of 61 (now rated 68). He could develop into a decent dual purpose horse.

Owner Henry Ponsonby has sent useful Flat horses First Mohican, Scarlet Dragon and Who Dares Wins over hurdles in recent seasons. It would therefore be no surprise to see him doing likewise with **ON TO VICTORY**. A four year old gelded son of Rock of Gibraltar, he is rated 103 having won 3 of his 17 races on the level. All three of those victories were gained last year, including an eight lengths win in the Bibury Cup at Salisbury (1m 4f : Good/Soft) in June 2017. Fourth in the Melrose Stakes at York, he was beaten a neck by Mount Moriah in the Listed Further Flight Stakes at Nottingham (1m 6f : Good/Soft) in April. If sent down the jumping route, he promises to be an exciting recruit.

Tadcaster based Tom Tate paid 36,000gns for the former Mark Johnston trained **RIVER GLADES** at the Newmarket July Sales. A big strong powerful gelding by Cape Cross, he didn't race as a two year old but had nine races between February and July this season. A six lengths winner at Wetherby (1m 6f : Soft), he was beaten three parts of a length on his final run for his previous connections at Hamilton (1m 5f : Good/Firm). Rated 76 on the Flat, he stays well and looks ideal juvenile hurdle material for his new connections. It would be no surprise to see him return to the A1 track on Wednesday 17th October for the Globe-Trotting Joe Browns Juvenile Hurdle at 2.10.

In addition to Face The Facts, Willie Mullins also bought **ZENON** out of John Gosden's yard. Purchased for 120,000gns at the Tattersalls February Sale, the four year old son of Galileo won 2 of his 8 races on the Flat earning an official mark of 96. Successful at Chepstow (1m 4f : Soft) and Haydock (1m 6f : Good/Firm) during the summer of last year, he was well held in two Listed events at Goodwood and Ascot but has been given a long break since joining Ireland's champion trainer. A full-brother and former stablemate of three times hurdles winner Lord Napier, he ought to make a smart novice this season.

ENGLISH POINTERS

Following the overwhelming success of last year's article, my *Racing UK* colleague and English point expert **Jonathan Neesom** is back for more of the same in 2018. His selections in the 2017/2018 edition yielded a £10 level stakes **PROFIT** of £93.80 with a strike-rate of **40%**. They included **CAPTAIN CATTISTOCK (3 wins), DAN MCGRUE (2 wins)** and Grade 1 winning novice hurdler **SANTINI (3 wins)**. The *Talking Trainers* section of *One Jump Ahead* contains a number of horses who plied their trade 'between the flags' on this side of the Irish Sea last winter and are set to race under Rules for the first time this season. Therefore I have consulted Jonathan regarding many of them and he has kindly offered his thoughts on their prospects for the weeks and months ahead, plus some extra names who caught his eye last winter.

DEFINITELYANOSCAR (Harry Fry): "Landed quite a gamble when winning on her debut at Barbury Castle in January. This five year old then won a Market Rasen bumper before finishing second in another at Cheltenham, where she gave the impression that she was still a horse to follow despite that defeat."

EGGARDON HILL (Paul Nicholls): "Narrowly beaten on his debut, he made very light work of twelve rivals at Upcott Cross (Devon) at the end of May, winning impressively. Among his owners is Paul Nicholls, so a career under rules is likely to arrive sooner rather than later."

ENERGUMENE (Willie Mullins): "Early season Larkhill form is always worth noting closely and he was one of two winners at the track at the start of the year for Sophie Lacey. Despite not jumping with great fluency, he quickened up smartly to win. The placed horses have not exactly advertised the form but this looked star quality in the making. He's since joined Willie Mullins."

FINANCIER (Kerry Lee): "Beat modest rivals in a very slow time on his only appearance, for Nicky Tinkler at Witton Castle (Durham) in May. There was something quite taking about the performance, however, certainly enough for Kerry Lee to spend £115,000 on him later that month. He's a five year old by Dubawi out of a Rainbow Quest mare!!"

INTERCONNECTED (Nicky Henderson): "Another from the Lacey academy to win at Larkhill, this time in February. Having fallen on his debut, he made no mistake here, winning with plenty in hand. Another that looks bound for success under Rules, he really looks the part - as he should as he has since been sold for £220,000 and will be trained by Nicky Henderson."

KING ROLAND (Harry Fry): "Yet another from the Lacey yard to make a winning debut at Larkhill, this time in March. He too won very easily and has since joined Harry Fry. Another to note closely when appearing under Rules."

FOXWORTHY (Nicky Henderson): "When King Roland won at Larkhill, his task was made easier when his main rival, Foxworthy, lost all momentum with a blunder three out, when travelling as well as the winner. This six year old was having his debut and made amends when winning back at Larkhill in April. Rather like Santini, he is owned by Richard Kelvin-Hughes and was trained in his points by Ed Walker but has subsequently joined Nicky Henderson."

NINTH WAVE (Philip Hobbs): "This one won a point-to-point bumper on soft ground at Bitterley in April. What the form is worth is open to question but he won with plenty in hand for top pointing trainer Philip Rowley. Has since been sold to Trevor Hemmings for £40,000 and has joined Philip Hobbs."

ONE TOUCH (Michael Scudamore): "From the yard of Francesca Nimmo, he made a taking debut at Badbury Rings (Dorset) in April. Patiently ridden, he swept by several rivals over the last three fences and won cosily, despite showing signs of inexperience. Only a four year old, he is likely to appear next under Rules for Michael Scudamore, I believe."

PORT OF MARS (Olly Murphy): "This one recorded a fair time when winning at Brocklesby Park, in Lincolnshire, in February. Related to several winners, he has been bought for £60,000 and will next appear from Olly Murphy's yard."

SEBASTOPOL (Tom Lacey): "Later on that same Larkhill card which featured Energumene, this son of Fame And Glory made a winning debut in fine style, scoring with ease. He's since landed an Ayr bumper for Tom Lacey, who described the horse after that as "gorgeous". Clearly one to note when sent jumping."

SHANNON HILL (Alan King): "As with the case of One Touch, Francesca Nimmo is adept at producing racecourse debutants to win and this son of Kayf Tara did likewise at Brampton Bryan in April. This four year old took the last race of the day by which time conditions were attritional and only two of the twelve starters completed. He left a distinct impression that he could be useful, however, and was subsequently sold for £85,000 to race out of Alan King's yard."

JONATHAN'S HORSES TO FOLLOW: ENERGUMENE & INTERCONNECTED

Please see pages 162-170
for details of the
One Jump Ahead Updates

FRENCH REVOLUTION

Last year's article produced **31 winners** from 112 runners (28%), including smart novices **ESPOIR D'ALLEN (4 wins), MITCHOUKA (4 wins), SAGLAWY (Grade 2 winner), SAINT CALVADOS (3 wins)** and **SHARJAH (2 wins). ANTEY (9/1), CHEF D'EQUIPE (7/1), DAME DE COMPAGNIE (2 wins), DUCA DE THAIX (4/1), REAL STEEL** and **STORMY IRELAND** were also featured twelve months ago. The following will hopefully prove exciting recruits for their new connections, the majority of which have yet raced in either Britain or Ireland. Largely unknown, some of them may develop into household names in years to come.

WILLIE MULLINS

Owner: RICH & SUSANNAH RICCI

ECLAT DES MOTTES (FR) 4 b g Poliglote - Sun Des Mottes (FR)
Narrowly beaten in a three way photograph in an APQS bumper at Argentan (1m 6f : Good/Soft) in October last year for Yannick Fouin, he was purchased in early November. The gelded son of Poliglote had his first run over hurdles at Downpatrick (2m 6f : Yielding) in August and ran out a comfortable three and a quarter lengths winner from Present In Court (won since). Highly regarded, he is very much one to follow in staying novice hurdles.

EDEN FLIGHT (FR) 4 b g Great Pretender (IRE) - Traviata (FR)
He was bought for €140,000 at the Arqana Deauville Autumn Mixed Sale last November having won his only APQS bumper at Saumur (2 miles) by three lengths on the 15th October for Patrice Quinton. Harold Kirk, who bid alongside Pierre Boulard, said at the Arqana Sales: **"We've been lucky with Great Pretender before, buying horses such as Great Field."** Boulard added: **"This one looks a proper horse who showed pace and stamina when winning his bumper very easily."** Given time to mature since joining Mullins, he looks an exciting novice hurdle prospect for his new connections.

ELEONORE D'APSIS (FR) 4 b f Apsis - Teedouna (FR)
A three and a half lengths winner of an APQS bumper at Durtal (1m 7f : Good) in April for Laure Cordonnier, she was bought the following month and has the option of running in a bumper in Ireland or more likely going mares' novice hurdling.

ELITE CHARBONIERE (FR) 4 b g Gris De Gris (IRE) - Star Folle Prail (FR)
Trained by Patrice Quinton, he was beaten eight and a half lengths on his debut when only finishing fifth behind Éclair De Beaufeau (joined Gordon Elliott) in a French bumper at Seiches-Sur-Le-Loir (1m 5f) in early December. Reappearing two and a half months later over the same course and distance, the son of Gris De Gris ran out a two and a half lengths winner. Subsequently bought for £155,000 at the Cheltenham Festival Sale, he will go novice hurdling.

JON SNOW (FR) 3 b c Le Havre (IRE) - Saroushka (FR)
A well regarded three year old who showed progressive form on the Flat in France for Fabrice Chappet. The son of Le Havre didn't race as a two year old and was only eighth on his debut at Chantilly (1m 2f : Heavy) in late March. However, he was then stepped up to a mile and a half and tackled better ground at Compiegne (Good/Soft) less than a month later and finished an encouraging fourth behind Andre Fabre's Lindberg. He confirmed the promise with a length and a quarter win from Haloul in another maiden over a mile and a half at Maisons-Laffitte (Good). He is considered a very nice prospect for juvenile hurdles.

KARL DER GROSSE (GER) 4 gr g Jukebox Jury (IRE) – Karsawina (GER)
Bought as a yearling for €17,000, the German bred gelding was owned by Walter Connors and trained by Emmanuel Clayeux in France. Third on his hurdles debut at Vichy (2m 1f : Soft) in September last year, he was beaten five lengths by Rosemarie Has. The runner-up, Sayo, subsequently finished third in the Triumph Hurdle for Willie Mullins. Bought the following month, the grey son of Jukebox Jury was given time by his new trainer and he made a winning Irish debut at Tramore (2m : Good) in August. A four lengths winner from stablemate Sweet Flight, he is held in high regard by his new connections.

TIGER TAP TAP (GER) 3 g Jukebox Jury (IRE) – Tomato Finish (GER)
Twice raced on the level for Henk Grewe, the Jukebox Jury gelding was beaten a length and a half on his debut at Le Pin Au Haras (1m 2f) in May. Confirming the promise he had shown first time out, he beat the Pascal Bary trained Lennox by the same margin at Compiegne (1m 2f : Soft) a month later. Purchased in July, he is another one to look out for in juvenile hurdles.

Others with Mullins

ALLAHO (FR) 4 b g No Risk At All (FR) – Idaho Falls (FR)
Three lengths runner-up behind Melchief (won again since) in the Listed Prix Rohan at Auteuil (2m 2f : Very Soft) in early March. Trained by Guy Cherel, the form looks sound with the third also scoring subsequently. Bought by **Cheveley Park Stud** since, he looks a smart addition to Mullins' ranks and will take some stopping in a maiden hurdle.

CONCERTISTA (FR) 3 ch f Nathaniel (IRE) – Zagzig
Acquired for €75,000 at the Arqana Sale in July last year, the Nathaniel filly was bought on behalf of **Simon Munir** and **Isaac Suede**. She won one of her six races on the Flat for Christophe Ferland taking a ten furlongs handicap at La Teste Buch (Good) in May. Placed at Fontainebleau (1m 2f) and Nantes (1m 4f), she was fourth on her final start at Saint-Cloud four days before her sale. By the same sire as the brilliant four times Group 1 and dual Classic winning filly Enable, she is one for novice hurdles.

EARTH DAY (FR) 4 b g My Risk (FR) – Sirani (FR)
Bought as a three year old for €26,000 at the Arqana Autumn Sale in November 2016, he finished seventh in a twelve furlongs maiden at Moulins in August last year for Patricia Butel. A month later, the My Risk gelding made his hurdling debut in the second division of the Prix Pride of Kildare at Auteuil (2m 2f : Very Soft) and he was beaten less than three lengths in third behind Espion Du Chenet. The runner-up Valcroix was subsequently placed in two Listed hurdles at the same track. Purchased on behalf of **Simon Munir** and **Isaac Suede**, his novice status was purposely protected for this season and he could be an exciting recruit.

ELFILE (FR) 4 b f Saint Des Saints (FR) – Rapide
Very consistent in APQS bumpers, the daughter of Saint Des Saints finished 22121 in her five starts for Thomas Fourcy before being acquired in December. Runner-up at Royan and Moulins, she gained a four lengths win at Angouleme (1m 5f) in September. A neck second in a Grade 3 bumper at Moulins (1m 4f) the following month, she was back in the winners' enclosure at Angers (1m 7f : Soft) when beating Easy Time by a length and a half. Bought on behalf of **Kenny Alexander** (CEO of GVC Holdings), she is one for mares' novice hurdles.

ELIMAY (FR) 4 gr f Montmartre (FR) – Hyde (FR)
The daughter of Montmartre was purchased by **J.P.McManus** at the Arqana Sale last November (€310,000). Handled by Carlos Lerner, she won one of her six races over hurdles. A five lengths winner at Auteuil (2m 1f : Very Soft) in May last year, she was subsequently placed in two Grade 3 hurdles at the same track and was also runner-up twice in Listed hurdles at the Parisian venue. Very consistent, she has yet to race beyond two and a quarter miles but is open to further improvement over longer distances. She is a smart filly.

EL MERANO (FR) 4 b g Saddex - Violaska (FR)
Acquired for £120,000 at the Cheltenham December Sale for **Cheveley Park Stud**, he raced in two APQS Flat races for Alain Couetil. Three and a half lengths third at Fontainebleau (1m 5f : Soft) in early October, he was then beaten a neck by Elixir D'Ainay (subsequently bought by J.P.McManus) at Lyon (1m 4f : Soft) six weeks later. The pair pulled nine lengths clear of the third.

EN BETON (FR) 4 b g Network (GER) - Nee A Saint Voir (FR)
Trained by Nicolas de Lageneste, he was a length runner-up behind Audacieux D'Alin (only sixth next time) in a conditions hurdle at Auteuil (2m 2f : Very Soft) in April. The form hasn't worked out particularly well but he is once raced and was bought on behalf of **Cheveley Park Stud** in May and will be running in novice hurdles this winter.

FARID (FR) 3 b g Diamond Boy (FR) - Querrana De Sivola (FR)
Espoir D'Allen developed into a high-class juvenile hurdler for J.P.McManus and Gavin Cromwell winning four of his five starts, including a Grade 2 at Leopardstown on St Stephen's day. This Diamond Boy gelding won the same twelve furlongs APQS Flat race at Lignieres (Soft) in April as Espoir D'Allen the previous year by a neck for the same connections, namely owner Walter Connors and trainer Mlle Anne-Sophie Pacault. The runner-up has won since. Snapped up by **J.P.McManus**, he is believed to be very useful and is considered Triumph Hurdle material. He is reportedly more of a hurdling type than an embryonic chaser.

FENTA DES OBEAUX (FR) 3 b f Denham Red (FR) - Quenta Des Obeaux (FR)
An exciting prospect who made all to win the Prix de La Jaille-Yvon (a coveted newcomers event) at Le Lion D'Angers (1m 4f : Good) in late April by two lengths. Owned/trained and bred by Nicolas Devilder, she built up a big advantage early on and maintained a strong gallop to defeat French Made (bought by J.P.McManus since). By the same sire as new stablemate Un De Sceaux, she could be a very smart juvenile hurdler.

FOVEROS (FR) 3 b g Authorized (IRE) - Fanurio's Angel (FR)
Epsom Derby winner Authorized has produced some top-class jumpers including the ill-fated Stayers' Hurdle winner Nichols Canyon and Grand National winner Tiger Roll. He is also responsible for this lightly raced three year old who is now owned by **Luke McMahon**, who enjoyed Grade 1 glory courtesy of Whiskey Sour last winter. Trained on the Flat by Francis-Henri Graffard, he was third on his only start as a juvenile at Deauville (AW) last December. Placed a couple of times at Pornichet (1m 1f) in January, the white faced three year old got off the mark at the sixth attempt in a nine furlongs handicap at Longchamp (Heavy) in April. Gelded since joining Mullins, he is one for juvenile hurdles.

FRERE TUCK (FR) 3 g Secret Singer (FR) - Tete Et Corde (FR)
Bought for €120,000 at the Arqana Summer Sale in July, he won his only APQS Flat race by a nose at Argentan (1m 5f : Good/Soft) the previous month for Philippe Chemin. Harold Kirk, who purchased the son of Secret Singer, commented at Deauville: "**He's only a baby of a horse but he's shown potential. The man that trained him likes him and he knows what good horses are. He'll be a long-term project for us and hopefully he'll make a nice jumping horse.**" Only three, it will be interesting to see if he is sent juvenile hurdling or saved for next season.

KLASSICAL DREAM (FR) 4 b g Dream Well (FR) - Klassical Way (FR)
Trained by Isabelle Gallorini, he won on the Flat at Sable-Sur-Sarthe (1m 6f) in September last year. Still a maiden over hurdles, his form figures are P324P. Placed a couple of times at Auteuil in October, the Dream Well gelding produced a career best when four and a half lengths fourth behind Master Dino and Tunis in the Grade 1 Prix Cambaceres (2m 2f : Very Soft) at the same track in early November.

LAMARCKISE (FR) 3 ch f Martaline – Shannongold (FR)
She made her debut in a conditions hurdle for unraced three year old fillies at Auteuil (1m 7f : Very Soft) in April for Francois Nicolle. Beaten four and a quarter lengths by Shahina Du Berlais (won again since), the runner-up Thrilling has also scored subsequently to give the form a solid look. Bought a month later to join Mullins, she looks a smashing prospect for three year old hurdles in Ireland.

LORD ROYAL (FR) 3 gr g Lord Du Sud (FR) – Tinoroyale
Owners **Twenty Seven Black Partnership** were responsible for Listowel maiden hurdle winner Makitorix and they have purchased another ex-French gelding during the summer. Unraced over hurdles, he finished three parts of a length runner-up at Durtal (1m 3f : Good) in early May on his sole Flat outing. Bought the following month, he will presumably go juvenile hurdling.

RUNRIZED (FR) 3 b g Authorized (IRE) – Courseulles (FR)
Draconien provided **Clipper Logistics Group Ltd** with Grade 1 success at the Punchestown Festival last spring. Steve Parkin has returned to France for another potentially useful novice hurdler in this thrice raced son of Authorized. Runner-up over ten furlongs at Angers in November last year, he then won on his reappearance by four lengths at Durtal (1m 2f : Heavy) in early April. Fifth at Chantilly (1m 2f : Good) last time, he is stoutly bred being out of a Monsun mare and is effective in testing ground. Gelded since joining Mullins, **he is described as a 'beautiful horse' who will be trained as a Triumph Hurdle horse. He could be a very smart juvenile hurdler this season.**

STAKING (FR) 3 gr g Stormy River (FR) – Shaking
Like Frere Tuck, this three year old was recruited at the Arqana Sale in July (€140,000). Unraced at two, he ran with credit at Chantilly (4th over 1m 2f), Strasbourg (5th) and Granville (4th over 1m 1f) on his first three starts. However, the son of Stormy River improved upon those performances when winning a mile handicap by three lengths at Longchamp (Good) at the end of June – only six days before he was sold. Bloodstock agent Harold Kirk remarked at the sale: **"He's been bought to run over hurdles first and then he'll go back on the Flat. We've been very lucky with horses we've bought out of Nicolas Clement's yard and he recommended him highly. He's a gorgeous-looking horse and looks like a jumping type. Even though he's only won over a mile we think he'll stay well, but he's got lots of speed and gears too."**

GORDON ELLIOTT

AUTHORIZO (FR) 3 b g Authorized (IRE) – Street Lightning (FR)
By the same sire as their Grand National winner Tiger Roll, he raced four times on the Flat for Sachiaki Kobayashi. Third and fourth at Angers (1m 2f : Soft) and Deauville (1m 1f) respectively as a two year old, he won by a length on his reappearance at Cagnes-sur-Mer (1m 3f : Very Soft) in January. Third last time over the same course and distance, he has been gelded since being bought by **Gigginstown House Stud** and is set to embark on a juvenile hurdle career.

ÉCLAIR DE BEAUFEU (FR) 4 b g Monitor Closely (IRE) – Tenebreuse Gemm (FR)
Unbeaten in two starts, he scored by a length and a half on his debut at Seiches-Sur-Le-Loir (1m 5f) in December last year. The four year old then followed up by a length at Pornichet (1m 4f : Standard) in early March. Bought during the summer, he is a smart novice hurdle prospect for **Gigginstown House Stud**.

ELWOOD (FR) 4 gr g Martaline – Robbe (FR)
A half-brother to the same connections' Pertemps Final winner Delta Work, he was acquired for €170,000 at the Arqana Grand Steeple Auteuil Sale in May. Previously trained by Emmanuel Clayeux, he raced twice in APQS bumpers finishing sixth and fourth at Cluny (1m 4f) and Paray-Le-Monial (1m 4f) respectively. Sent hurdling in April, the grey gelding was fourth at Strasbourg (2m 1f : Soft) behind Guillaume Macaire's dual Grade 1 winner On The Go. Reappearing a fortnight later at Moulins (2m 2f : Soft), he bolted up by a dozen lengths under Felix De Giles. Significantly, that win was gained on the 29th April, which means he is a novice for this season and is very much one to follow for **Gigginstown House Stud**.

HENRY DE BROMHEAD

A PLUS TARD (FR) 4 b g Kapgarde (FR) – Turboka (FR)
Owned by **Cheveley Park Stud**, the gelded son of Kapgarde won twice over hurdles for Dominique Bressou last season and was placed in his other three starts. A fourteen lengths winner on his debut at Saint-Brieuc (2m 2f : Good/Soft) in October, he was then runner-up twice at Angers and Pau before finishing six and a quarter lengths third in a Listed hurdle at Auteuil (2m 2f : Heavy) in March. He then won a similar event over the same course and distance on the 1st April by three and a half lengths and was bought soon afterwards. Gelded since joining Henry De Bromhead, it will be interesting to see if he is sent novice chasing with a four year old allowance.

EMBRUN MITJA (FR) 4 b g Anzillero (GER) – Italique De Cotte (FR)
Gigginstown House Stud own this unbeaten four year old who was bought during the summer having won his only APQS Flat race for Gab Leenders. A four lengths scorer at Angouleme (2m 1f : Very Soft), the runner-up City Korri has won over hurdles at St Malo since. Watch out for him in a maiden hurdle in the Autumn.

J.P.McMANUS

DALILA DU SEUIL (FR) 5 gr m Bachir (IRE) – Misery (FR)
Trained in France by Mickael Seror, she was bought for €210,000 at the Arqana Sale in November. A winner of three of her ten starts over hurdles, it took her six races to get off the mark but she showed improved form last year. Following a two lengths win at Compiegne (2m 2f : Very Soft) in April 2017, she won a Listed hurdle at Auteuil (2m 2f : Heavy) in September by a dozen lengths. The winning margin was the same in another Listed contest at Compiegne the following month before she finished fourth in a Grade 1 hurdle at Auteuil in November last year. Sold eight days later, she has joined **Harry Fry**. Either the mares' hurdle at the Cheltenham Festival or a novice chase campaign could be on the five year old's agenda this season.

ELIXIR D'AINAY (FR) 4 g Muhtathir – Perle Du Bocage (FR)
The four year old raced in two APQS Flat races for owner Walter Connors and trainer Emmanuel Clayeux. Sixth on his debut at Lyon (1m 4f : Good) in April last year, he improved on that effort next time when winning over the same course and distance (Soft) nearly seven months later. Partnered by Ronan Thomas, he beat the aforementioned El Merano by a neck before being acquired by the legendary owner. He is set to go novice hurdling this winter.

ENJOY OF SIVOLA (FR) 4 b g Anzillero (GER) – Loachapoka (GER)
He, too, was handled by Emmanuel Clayeux and was bought in the summer. Beaten two lengths in third on his hurdles debut at Aix-Le-Bains (2m 1f : Soft), the winner Ecole D'Estruval has won again since. Open to plenty of improvement, he should be a real force in novice hurdles this season.

EVIDENCE DE THAIX (FR) 4 b f Network (GER) – Nacre de Thaix (FR)
Purchased last Autumn, the daughter of Network has yet to race for **Philip Hobbs**. A winner of two of her three races in APQS Flat races for Guy Cherel, she was beaten a couple of lengths on her debut at Corlay (1m 3f : Good/Soft) in June 2017. A four lengths winner the following month at Brehal, she then beat stablemate Extra Noire by the same margin at Les Sables-D'Olonne (1m 5f : Good/Soft) in August last year. She looks a useful addition to the mares' novice hurdling ranks.

FREE (FR) 4 bb f Mr Sidney (USA) – Funny Feerie (FR)
Mares' novice hurdles are also the plan for this well bred daughter of Mr Sidney. A half-sister to Group 1 winner Full of Gold, she cost €125,000 at the Arqana November Sale last year. Trained on the Flat by the recently retired Criquette Head-Maarek, she won one of her five starts. A three parts of a length winner at Chantilly (1m 4f : Good) in May 2017, she finished fifth in Listed company at Saint-Cloud before being narrowly beaten at Deauville over twelve furlongs. Placed on soft ground, she has been given plenty of time since being bought last Autumn and has joined **Anthony Honeyball**.

FRENCH MADE (FR) 3 b f Dream Well (FR) – Sempiternelle (FR)
Set to carry the silks of **Mrs Margaret McManus**, she was trained in France by Jean-Francois Doucet. A highly promising two lengths runner-up in a newcomers event at Le Lion D'Angers (1m 4f : Good) in April behind the aforementioned Fenta Des Obeaux, she was acquired soon afterwards and is a nice prospect for juvenile hurdles.

ROBCOUR

TIGER VOICE (FR) 3 b g Poet's Voice – Tarsia (GER)
The big spending owners, who have the majority of their jumping string with either **Henry De Bromhead** or **Jessica Harrington**, have purchased this potentially exciting juvenile hurdler. Trained across the English Channel by Fabrice Chappet, he has only raced four times. Eighth and fifth at Deauville (1m 1f) and Lyon (1m 2f) respectively in two starts last year, he has shown improved form in 2018. A narrow margin winner on his reappearance at Fontainebleau (1m 3f : Very Soft) in March, he beat Ziyad who has won four times since, including at Listed level. His final run came in the Listed Prix Francois Mathet at Saint-Cloud (1m 2f : Heavy) nineteen days later and the son of Poet's Voice finished a length and a half runner-up behind Andre Fabre's Gyllen. The winner has subsequently landed the Group 2 Prix Eugene Adam at Maisons-Laffitte. Gelded since, he could be top-class if taking to jumping.

TOM GEORGE

FARO DE KERSER (FR) 3 b g Ungaro (GER) – Nuit De Kerser (FR)
Owned by **The Twenty One Club**, he was an eight lengths winner on his hurdles debut at Sable-Sur-Sarthe over two miles in May for Patrice Quinton. He joined the Cheltenham Festival winning trainer during the summer and will be aimed at juvenile hurdles with one penalty.

NOEL MEADE

LIGNOU (FR) 3 b g Rajsaman (FR) – Lady Meydan (FR)
A €120,000 purchase at the Arqana Sale in July, he won two of his three races on the Flat this year for Jean Claude-Rouget. Unraced as a juvenile, he finished fourth on his debut at Chantilly (1m 1f : Standard) in March. A half length winner at Tarbes (1m 2f : Very Soft) a month later, he then followed up by a length from stablemate Ionic at Dax (1m 2f : Good). The son of Rajsaman is owned by **Gigginstown House Stud** and he looks one to follow in three year old hurdles in the Autumn.

NICK WILLIAMS

The South Molton based handler has done particularly well with his juvenile hurdlers in recent years with the likes of Flying Tiger, Le Rocher, the ill-fated Me Voici and Reve De Sivola all being above average. Once again, he appears to have assembled a strong team of three year olds for the 2018/2019 campaign. I suggest keeping an eye on this trio:

FAIRE PART SIVOLA (FR) 3 b g Noroit (GER) – Lettre D'Estruval (FR)
Bought for **€42,000** as a two year old at the Arqana Summer Sale last year. Owned by **K.Alexander** & **R.Watts.**

FAVORI DE SIVOLA (FR) 3 b g Noroit (GER) – Suave de Sivola (FR)
He was also acquired as a two year old at the same sale in July 2017 for **€30,000**. Owned by **John White** & **Anne Underhill**.

FELICIDAD (FR) 3 b f Racinger (FR) – Sacade (FR)
Owned by **Mr K.Alexander**, she is a half-sister to Nicky Henderson's Bloody Mary, who finished third in the Grade 2 Dawn Run Mares' Novice Hurdle in 2016. She finished six lengths fourth on her debut at Le Lion D'Angers (1m 4f : Soft) in a fillies' conditions event in late August.

VENETIA WILLIAMS

ECEPARTI (FR) 4 b g Enrique – La Pommeraie (FR)
A winner on his chasing debut at Mont-De-Marsan (2m 3f : Good/Firm) in November last year, the former Guillaume Macaire trained four year old remains a maiden over hurdles. Placed on three occasions, he looked set for victory at Fontainebleau (2m 2f : Very Soft) when unseating his rider at the penultimate hurdle. Still lightly raced, the Enrique gelding looks one to follow in novice hurdles for the Herefordshire based handler.

ESPOIR DE GUYE (FR) 4 bl g Khalkevi (IRE) – Penelope De Guye (FR)
Purchased for €70,000 at the Arqana Summer Sale in July, he raced twice over hurdles for Gaetan Taupin finishing nearly eight lengths fifth at Compiegne (2m 2f : Heavy) in May on his debut. The gelded son of Khalkevi stepped up on that performance next time when winning by a length at Les Sables-D'Olonne (2m 3f : Good/Soft) a month later. Still a novice for this season, he looks a good long-term prospect for his new owner **Mrs J.Hitchings**.

Please see pages 162-170
for details of the
One Jump Ahead Updates

IRISH POINTERS

As in previous editions, point-to-point expert **Declan Phelan** has written his invaluable article regarding those horses who caught his eye 'between the flags' in the Emerald Isle last winter/ spring. Last year's feature yielded **37 winners** at an impressive **strike-rate of 30%** and they included **CHOOSEYOURWEAPON (9/1, 5/6), GLOBAL CITIZEN (3 wins including the Grade 2 Dovecote NH), MR WHIPPED (3 wins), ON THE BLIND SIDE (3 wins including two Grade 2 victories), RAPID ESCAPE (3 wins)** and **SPEAK EASY (10/1)**.

ALNADAM (FR) 5 b g Poliglote – Rosadame (FR)
Trainer: Dan SKELTON **Form Figures: 1**

Sharp athletic bay gelding: from a French jumps family packed with winners. Derek O'Connor partnered him on his one start at Dromahane (Yielding): the horse was owned by Derek and other family members and trained for the race by Robert Tyner. In a ten runner maiden, Derek elected to tuck in close to the pace setters: he made a move for glory jumping three out and, with the horse illustrating the capacity to quicken, the race was soon put to bed and Alnadam scorched away for an eight lengths success. The way he won signalled that he could be at home racing at any trip from two and a quarter to three miles and his optimum could prove to be in the two and a half miles zone. Bought by team Skelton at Doncaster Sales for £130,000, I think this five year old will make an impact as a novice hurdler, and have sound aspirations of knocking on the door of winning a Graded novice hurdle. Later, I think he could easily develop into a Grade 2/3 novice chaser and he has a bright future. He has been hobdayed, so heavy ground may not be his cup of tea.

ANDY DUFRESNE (IRE) 4 b g Doyen (IRE) – Daytona Lily (IRE)
Trainer: Gordon ELLIOTT **Form Figures: 1**

The joint sales topper at the Cheltenham March Sales, where a price of £330,000 saw him change ownership, though he remains in the Elliott stable, who had successfully pointed him six days before the auction. Obviously well prepared for his debut at Borris (Yielding/Soft), he was confidently ridden by Jamie Codd. Electing to wait at the rear for the opening two miles, the partnership progressed to a close fifth at the fourth last. Nudged to the front after three out, this bay gelding accelerated into a four lengths lead on the run to two out and comfortably held his nearest pursuer Faustinovick to record a cosy six lengths win. On face value, one of the smartest four year old maiden performances of the campaign. At the sales J.P. McManus paid top dollar to add this youngster into his ownership. A well built individual, I would imagine he should win a soft ground bumper and can be borderline Graded class over hurdles. One spot of concern is that there are few talented horses in his family tree: his half-brother, Clondaw Rigger is an honest low level handicap chaser in the UK, and the dam of Andy Dufresne managed one bottom of the barrel, fast ground two miles maiden hurdle win when trained by Jessica Harrington.

APPRECIATE IT (IRE) 4 b g Jeremy (USA) – Sainte Baronne (FR)
Trainer: Willie MULLINS **Form Figures: 31**

A half-brother to Danny Kirwan: well touted prior to his debut at Ballinaboola (Yielding/Soft : 2m 4f), he came unstuck in that race: he tried to make all, when challenged by Envoi Allen at the second last, he folded tamely and was a well beaten third at the finish. He did atone at Dromahane (Soft/Heavy) in a three mile event in March: it was a bit of a mickey mouse affair as the race was run on a snow covered surface and there was little or no gallop with only four runners. Derek O'Connor rode him, and they shared the lead for most of the journey and, although headed on the run to the last, Appreciate It picked up for a few nudges and regained the advantage for a snug length and a half success. Assessed on his two starts 'between the flags', he cannot be rated more than a 120 track horse. I do respect the view of Pat Doyle who opined that this bay gelding was naturally talented: secured by Willie Mullins in a private deal, perhaps his new handler can translate the fine homework into track results. It is possible that this horse has a decent cruising speed, but lacks those extra gears that are prevalent in top class horses.

ASK FOR GLORY (IRE) 4 b g Fame And Glory – Ask Helen (IRE)
Trainer: Paul NICHOLLS Form Figures: 1

The point to point sales topper at the Doncaster Goffs UK sale in May. At the start of that month, he delivered a commanding, stout staying effort when posting a clear cut ten lengths win at Bartlemy (Soft). He raced smoothly during the race, for the first half anchored in midfield: he made his move to close on the long run to the third last. In front soon after that obstacle, he simply asserted at his leisure to win with plenty in hand from a fair selection of rivals. Veteran Cork point handler Donal Coffey has past history with talented pointers, the "Copper" line is his equine family (Give Me A Copper, Presenting Copper etc): he is a very good trainer catering for generally a small string and, even though Paul Nicholls paid £280,000 to add this four year old to his squad, there is no guarantee that the former champion trainer will improve upon the Coffey handling. Ask For Glory is a tall, lanky bay gelding and, on the evidence from Bartlemy, he jumps cleanly, relaxes and should have no bother winning from two and a half miles and upwards. The damline of this horse fails to set the pulses racing, and my gut feeling is that he will become more of a 125-140 staying chaser as opposed to a top graded jumper.

AXIOMATIC (IRE) 4 b g Milan – Thegoodwans Sister (IRE)
Owner: GIGGINSTOWN HOUSE STUD Form Figures: F1

Recruited by Gigginstown House Stud for €60,000 at the 2017 Land Rover store sale, he is a sibling of 130+ winning pointer Beyond The Law and his grand dam was the mother of Grade 1 winning mare Cailin Alainn. Pat Doyle raced this strapping bay gelding in two points during the spring. He was close to the leaders when falling five from home on his debut at Tinahely. Derek O'Connor took over in the saddle next time and he came home alone to win on testing ground at Ballynoe (Soft/Heavy). Always travelling smoothly, he was set to pounce when the leader (and only realistic danger) fell three out and from there to the finish, he enjoyed a solo as the rest pulled up. He was certainly different gravy to the opposition. Examining his family, one characteristic pops up: they all appreciate deep winter ground and that ingredient may be the key to successfully latching onto this four year old in the future. On evidence to hand, he will be a 130+ stayer, more will be revealed when he is pressurised in a finish.

BEAKSTOWN (IRE) 5 b g Stowaway – Midnight Reel (IRE)
Trainer: Dan SKELTON Form Figures: 12

A chestnut son of Stowaway: trainer Andy Slattery kept things local as he travelled a few miles down the road from his home base to debut this four-year-old in November. Punters well wise to his homework were willing to take any price as he was gambled from 4/1 to 4/5 to the exclusion of everything else. He made the running in that race at Turtulla (Yielding/Soft): with three fences in the homerun, he had challengers queueing behind him as he climbed for home. He pinged the last three fences and hit the line three lengths clear with running left. It was an impressive effort and proved he could jump slickly, stay a stiff three miles and was prepared to battle when tested. A private bidding war between Dan Skelton and Willie Mullins ensued with an apparent successful bid of a staggering £440,000 resulting in victory for Skelton. Raced for new connections in an above average bumper at Kempton (Good/Soft) in February. Harry Skelton kicked for home five furlongs out and put most of his rivals in bother. Commanche Red latched onto him and claimed his scalp in the final hundred yards, Beakstown having to settle for second, I suspect a stiffer track could have produced a result in favour of Beakstown. He will win his maiden and novice hurdles from two and a half miles and upwards and he will be competitive in UK mid winter Graded novice hurdles. A race such as the Grade 1 Challow Hurdle at Newbury in December could be within his scope, depending on the calibre of opposition.

BEYONDAPPROACH (IRE) 4 b f Jeremy (USA) - Gonebeyondajoke (IRE)
Trainer: Donnchadh DOYLE **Form Figures: 21**

Racy bay mare with a white face: recorded a commendable debut second at Tinahely (Yielding) in February, as she made very good late progress to in the end be denied by two lengths in a fair maiden: as the only mare mixing with geldings, there was plenty to admire about her application (beaten by The Hollow Chap). Next up, she faced two rivals in a mares' only maiden at the Bellurgan (Good/Soft) circuit just outside the town of Dundalk. A hot favourite, ridden by Barry O'Neill, she controlled matters from the outset and coasted home by an untroubled two lengths: with the runner up, Gipsy Lee Rose, scoring on her next run, the form received a boost. In terms of ratings, the combination of her two runs entitles Beyondapproach to be regarded the equal of any other four year old mare from the 2018 academy this spring. Between her two pointing performances, she did travel to Cheltenham March Sales and was led out unsold at £75,000. Her dam is a daughter of a Footstepsinthesand mare, and on pedigree, Beyondapproach inherits speed and she will function to effect at trips from two miles to three miles over hurdles/fences and, an extra bonus with her, is that she can operate on soft and good ground and such versatility can result in plenty of opportunities for her to win track races: she can aim at a mark of 120, and could be on the cusp of Graded level as a hurdler.

BEYONDTHESTORM (IRE) 5 b g Flemensfirth (USA) - Blue Gale (IRE)
Trainer: Nicky HENDERSON **Form Figures: 1**

Produced a gutsy effort to prevail in a head bobbing finish at Moira (Heavy) in hock deep ground in December: looked like an old fashioned staying chaser on this evidence and was sharper than his main rivals for the job at hand that day. Another from the Denis Murphy academy, purchased by Nicky Henderson on behalf of Cheveley Park Stud for £150,000. My hunch was that he was gunned to win this point and there was not too much meat left on the bone for the rest of the season at least. Hence Henderson may have parked him up and that decision may reap long term rewards. Will figure in staying novice hurdles this season, especially on soft/heavy, the Albert Bartlett could be a seasonal target, whether he may get his desired ground at Cheltenham in March is down to the weather gods. Long term, a 130-140 staying handicap chaser, if he can be kept sound.

BIRCHDALE (IRE) 4 br g Jeremy (USA) - Onewayortheother (IRE)
Trainer: Colin McKEEVER **Form Figures: 1**

Tall, unfurnished bay gelding, supplied owner Wilson Dennison with his only four year old winner this spring. Birchdale coped with the tight track at Tyrella (Good) and enjoyed the sound surface: coaxed into contention (in a six runner race) by Derek O'Connor upon jumping the second last, he was upsides jumping the last and, once given a squeeze, he extended to win by a length. It was a master class of riding a raw horse, allowing the horse to learn on the job and winning without punishing. He is fertile material and, if he develops and strengthens, he will make an impact in track races. His optimum performances could happen in two and a half miles handicap chases on good ground, and he has a realistic chance of scaling a chase rating of 125+.

BLAZER'S MILL (IRE) 4 b g Westerner - Creation (IRE)
Trainer: Olly MURPHY **Form Figures: 2**

Lost no honour in defeat when a close second at Tyrella (Good) in March: one of three horses who locked in combat as the tempo increased from the third last: there was no quarter given, and approaching the final fence he was then slugging it out with the aforementioned Birchdale. Both jumped the last cleanly, and on the short run in, Birchdale found that bit extra to land the spoils by a length. The concluding stages had the sense of a proper race, and the first two home emerged with credit. A fine big bay gelding, and having top class horses such as Coneygree, Destriero and Palette in his extended family, the future as a two and a half miles hurdler and chaser is bright for Blazer's Mill. Pointed by Warren Ewing, two of his siblings,

Taniokey and War Creation, have won bumpers in the UK on their first track starts, and the prospects would be bright on this younger family member also lifting a bumper. Long term, he can mature into a 130+ handicap chaser and could be likely to contest Grade A & B handicaps. Changed hands for £160,000 at Aintree April Sales.

BOLD PLAN (IRE) 4 b g Jeremy (USA) – Kings Orchid (IRE)
Trainer: Evan WILLIAMS Form Figures: 12
Ran out an easy eight lengths winner of a five runner maiden at Kirkistown (Heavy) in February when in the care of Warren Ewing. He led from halfway, jumped neatly, and asserted control from the second last. Medium sized, a potential lack of physical scope could be an issue. He changed hands for £195,000 at Cheltenham February sales. Past winners in his pedigree include the ex-Hobbs pair Crack On and Captain Khedive: those two horses were primarily good ground performers, so it may be an added feather in the cap of Bold Plan that he coped with the heavy conditions in his point win. Evan Williams pitched the horse into a late spring bumper at Wincanton and he ran a cracker, foiled by a neck in a driving finish. That bumper was on good to soft ground and on a tight circuit over 1m 7f. This bay gelding is clearly versatile and, as a middle tier (120-135) horse, will pay his way. He may struggle to climb to the upper rungs of the ratings scale.

BREWERS PROJECT (IRE) 4 b g Aizavoski (IRE) – Shaylee Wilde (IRE)
Trainer: Paul NICHOLLS Form Figures: 1
One of two four year old point winners by an emerging stallion this spring (from a tiny crop): received a confident front running ride from Rob James, jumping crisply, injecting pace on the run towards the penultimate fence at Ballyarthur (Heavy), he gained a three lengths cushion and was not troubled to see off the threat posed by Umbrigado. Medium sized, his dam pulled up twice in points and was useless: she was a full-sister to Cheltenham Festival winner Andytown, which would offer more in the way of encouragement. Paul Nicholls successfully bid £185,000 for him at the Cheltenham March Sales. To my eye he will not be a top class horse, rather a 120-140 above average handicapper. He handled the heavy terrain with aplomb, watching his style of movement, I fancy a sounder surface would not be an issue and he may be as effective at two and a half miles as three miles during his future track career.

BUSTER VALENTINE (IRE) 5 b g Ask – Femme Du Noir (IRE)
Trainer: Ruth JEFFERSON Form Figures: 1
Looked a sharp sort when he made all under Derek O'Connor to register a debut win at Stowlin (Yielding) in April. He jumped accurately and kept on stoutly to fend off a pair of fair opponents (the 3rd Alfie Corbitt won his next race). With Captain Khedive and Crack On populating his family tree, it is possible that this five year old may enjoy a drop in trip and could be an effective two to two and a half miles chaser, as opposed to the normal three miles you associate with ex-pointers. Joins Ruth Jefferson at a price of £100,000 via Doncaster Sales, and he can become a 115-120 hurdler and should win a maiden event this season. He will be a more exciting chaser and I have visions of him winging around the tight bends of Catterick and bolting up in a novice chase at a future date. I am told he prefers safe middle terrain (good to soft), not so keen on the extremes (heavy or fast).

CHAMPAGNE MYSTERY (IRE) 4 b g Shantou (USA) – Spanker
Trainer: Nicky HENDERSON Form Figures: F2
Racy bay gelding, has a sprinkling of decent Flat and jump winners in his pedigree, including Oaks winner Talent and the dual purpose performer Thomas Hobson. Pointed by the husband/wife partnership of Roisin Hickey/Thomond O Mara: was starting to feel the pinch as the tempo increased at the third last and fell two out (when held) on his debut at Ballyarthur (Heavy) in testing ground. Saved for a sounder surface, he returned to action at Lisronagh in late April. The ground was officially described that afternoon as soft/heavy, though it was nearer to good

ground in reality. Champagne Mystery led the field along at an even gallop, keeping up the revs, he had most of his rivals in trouble with three to jump. Unfortunately, Espoir De Loire managed to keep in touch, and he attacked at the last and took the measure of Champagne Mystery on the short run in. Assessed on this performance, Champagne Mystery will be suited to two and a half miles track races and he made a price of £68,000 at the Cheltenham May Sales, and could be a money spinner in middle of the road (110-130) hurdles and chases.

CHINENSIS (IRE) 5 b g Well Chosen - Emily Vard (IRE)
Owner: Nigel TWISTON-DAVIES Form Figures: 411 - 1

Running for the county Waterford based handler, Vinnie Halley, this strapping bay gelding with a white blaze on his face, hinted at better to come, when a promising fourth in a backend maiden at Dromahane in May 2017. He duly delivered the goods when returning to action in November as he led most of the way and then repelled a few late challengers to score at Dromahane (Soft), landing his maiden victory. He then ventured to the Cheltenham Sales, but returned home having failed to make his reserve price. Up until ten years ago, owners/trainers of Irish pointers were more than happy to test maiden winners in point winners' races, as the view back then was, that an extra victory would add value to the stock. Nowadays that notion is frowned upon, and once a four/five year old shows a piece of form in a maiden, then that horse is straight to the sales, because to run in a winners' point is currently viewed as a risk of exposing such a young horse: given that the market is all about selling the dream, and the potential, anything likely to diminish a positive vision is avoided. Hence, very few four year old maiden winners continue racing in points. Due to the non sale at Cheltenham, connections of Chinensis almost had their hand forced: to command a sales price of their desire, they had to further demonstrate the ability of the horse. Chinensis to his credit did not let the side down. He ran in a brace of winners' races (against older stock) in the spring of 2018 and won both races. He was successful at Dromahane (Soft) again in late April, and Dawstown (Yielding/Soft) in the first week of May. Each time, he moved confidently during the races and always foot perfect, he was able to take control inside the final half mile. He completed his hat trick in the manner of a progressive young jumper. He found favour at Doncaster Sales as he was secured by Highflyer Bloodstock for £82,000 on behalf of Trevor Hemmings. I think he is a very safe purchase at that price: likely to be an average novice hurdler, he is destined to comfortably mould into a 125+ staying chaser and, given that he has illustrated that he can take relatively quick races, he will be a good consistent earner as a chaser.

DANNY KIRWAN (IRE) 5 b g Scorpion (IRE) - Sainte Baronne (FR)
Trainer: Paul NICHOLLS Form Figures: 110

Pat Doyle had this son of Scorpion primed and readied for his debut point win at Lisronagh (Soft/Heavy) in October: he swotted aside his rivals with contempt, as Jamie Codd enjoyed an armchair steer on a rare ride for the stable. He won eased down by eleven lengths, in a different league to ordinary rivals. I did note that like other progeny by his sire, he carried his head a little awkwardly...I question what his temperament will be like when he comes under pressure. Purchased privately by Paul Nicholls for a price north of £300,000, he posted a silky smooth win on his UK debut in a Kempton (Good) bumper in February. He closed his season in timid fashion as he faded out of the picture inside the final three furlongs of the Grade 2 bumper at Aintree. He has size and class and will win loads of races: he may be a horse who will look special dominating inferiors, when pitted against top notch rivals he may not appreciate being pressured.

DANSE IDOL (IRE) 5 b m Dansant - Screen Idol (IRE)
Trainer: Paul NICHOLLS Form Figures: 12

One of the classier mares to have been seen pointing in the 2017/18 campaign. She came with a power packed finish to win a highly competitive sixteen runner four year old mares' maiden at Boulta (Soft/Heavy) in November. Only sixth at the third last, she showed raw speed in the final quarter mile to secure a two lengths win. In January, she placed a highly creditable second to subsequent Cheltenham Festival bumper winner Relegate in a mares' bumper at Punchestown (Soft/Heavy). There have been some crazily high prices paid for winning female pointers this past twelve months: Paul Nicholls paid a more than reasonable (and justifiable) £110,000 for this lady at Cheltenham February Sales given the substance of her accumulated point and bumper form. She was bred to be a Flat horse, as her dam is a progeny of Sadler's Wells: possessing a pleasing mix of speed and stamina, Danse Idol looks fertile material for winning Graded novice hurdles this coming winter. She handles soft/heavy, I have no idea how she will operate on a drier sod. A robust and athletic mare, she will be one to keep on your side when racing in mares' novice races.

DEISE ABA (IRE) 5 b g Mahler - Kit Massini (IRE)
Trainer: Philip HOBBS **Form Figures: 1**

A middle sized bay gelding with a white strip on his face: he has very little in his immediate pedigree, though if you trace back four generations you do find the Gold Cup winner Bregawn nesting in the family tree. Raced out of the Kieran Purcell yard for a hotly contested five year old maiden at Dromahane (Yielding) in May, he tracked the leader for two and a half miles: leaving the backstraight on the trek to the third last, he was being niggled along, one of a group of five in contention, and did not look a likely winner. Landing over that third last fence in a share of third place, he found generously for the urgings of rider Declan Queally and upon reaching the final fence had surged to the lead and extended away to record a four lengths success. Judged on this performance, he strikes me as a horse who will enjoy running in races with a fast gallop and it is a positive that he can apply himself willingly under pressure. Secured by Highflyer Bloodstock on behalf of Trevor Hemmings for £66,000 at Doncaster Sales, he will be a competitive 110-120 novice hurdler and may advance on a rating of 125 when he switches to chasing in due course.

DEJA VUE (IRE) 4 b f Fame And Glory - Westgrove Berry (IRE)
Trainer: Anthony HONEYBALL **Form Figures: 1**

Tall, athletic bay mare with some class: she jumped smartly as she easily outflanked her five rivals with a commanding front running win at Inch (Yielding/Soft) in March when under the tutelage of Aidan Fitzgerald. She was picked up for €15,000 at the 2017 Derby Store Sale and following this success a spin through the Cheltenham April Sales resulted in her value rising to £82,000 as she moves to Anthony Honeyball. I note her dam won a bumper on her debut for Nicky Richards, and I would imagine this mare could replicate history. Definitely one of the better class mares from the four year old spring crop of 2018, a hurdles mark north of 120 is within her talent range and she could achieve Listed/Graded class black type in the jumping game. She travelled with such ease for the three miles at Inch and on that basis she could be as potent at two and a quarter miles as three miles in track races.

DIOL KER (FR) 4 b g Martaline - Stiren Bleue (FR)
Owner: Noel MEADE **Form Figures: 2F1**

A French bred bay gelding, and son of a battle hardened jumps mare (5 times winner and 20 places in her Gallic career). A €75,000 Derby Store buy in 2017, he was handled by Pat Doyle for his spring time points. He ran three times. On his debut at Cragmore (Soft/Heavy), I think he found the two and a a half miles trip too sharp, as he failed to reel in the front running winner Sams Profile, losing by two lengths. On his second run, at Horse & Jockey (Yielding/Soft), he was looking a threat to all when he fell three from home. It was third time lucky for this sizeable bay gelding. Venturing to Curraghmore (Soft) on Easter Sunday. Patiently ridden in midfield, he crept into second place rounding the home turn, leading at the second last, for a squeeze he extended away for a silky eight lengths triumph. Many of the four year olds featured in this article have raced once between the flags, and some could well be one hit wonders. With Diol Ker having raced three times, he has shown that he is consistent, can take his racing (ran in three points in the space of six weeks) and he is progressive, and based on his win, he learned from his Horse & Jockey fall. Even though he may not become a top of the ladder chaser, he has the hallmarks of past Gigginstown pointers who have emerged as winners of premium handicaps.

DUNDRUM WOOD (IRE) 4 b g Flemensfirth (USA) – Ruby Isabel (IRE)
Trainer: Sam CURLING **Form Figures: 3**
Fine big bay son of a former Tim Vaughan trained track winning mare: raced in the colours of Timmy Hyde when trained by Sam Curling for his only point run at Dromahane (Good) in May. As can be the way, there were some positive vibes for this four year old pre-race and he certainly impressed from a physical perspective in the parade ring. In the race itself, in what was one of the classiest four year old maidens of the spring, he sat off the pace, was clumsy at times in the jumping department: with three to jump, he was looking in trouble and well held. To his credit, although well adrift of the main players at the finish (Fury Road & El Barra), his racing brain clicked into action from the second last and he picked up from seventh to finish purposefully and claim third place with a determined late effort (beaten eleven lengths). If retained for pointing, he is a dead cert to bag a maiden win: should he be sold on, then I would advise that you pay respect to him as one of the better maidens to emerge from the spring of 2018: with time and the scope to blossom, he could very easily become a 130+, even Graded class track performer, probably at trips beyond two and a half miles.

EGALITY MANS (FR) 4 bl g Network (GER) – Quissisia Mans (FR)
Trainer: Willie MULLINS **Form Figures: 1**
Medium sized black gelding he finished alone to win his point at Liscarroll (Soft/Heavy) in March. At the time representing Pat Doyle and owner Walter Connors, he faced three modest opponents and it is difficult to quantify what he achieved in victory. With the small field, there was no early pace, and Egality Mans was ponderous at his jumps, especially the second (nearly refused): I did like the fact that he then warmed to the jumping task as the race developed and taking control of the race from three out, he pinged the last two fences and was enjoying the adventure at the finish. He maintained a steady gallop in testing terrain in the last mile and his three rivals pulled up exhausted. From a French jumps family (half brother to Coquin Mans), he was privately acquired by Willie Mullins for a six figure sum on behalf of owner Joe Donnelly. By the same sire as the great Sprinter Sacre, he does not have the same physical presence as that former champion. For now, I would peg him as a 125-135 horse and Mullins will hope to unlock extra from him in time.

ENVIOUS EDITOR (IRE) 4 b g Aizavoski (IRE) – Moll The Rol (IRE)
Trainer: Jessica HARRINGTON **Form Figures: 15**
Despite boiling over in the parade ring pre-race, this athletic bay gelding still managed to secure a debut point win at Belharbour (Yielding/Soft) in February for Nicky Stokes. There were five runners in the picture leaving the backstraight and entering the concluding three furlongs, he produced a fair turn of foot to move clear from the final fence and win by four lengths from Famous Saying (subsequent bumper winner). He supplied his sire with his first point winner: delving into the family tree, there is little to excite. He was secured by the Harrington team for £195,000 at the Cheltenham Tattersalls February sale. New connections dipped their toes into track action by running him in a bumper at the Punchestown Festival. Sporting a hood (to try and becalm him), he was far from disgraced, finishing fifth of thirteen, beaten a dozen lengths, and doing best of the four year olds in that 4 to 7 year olds bumper. He was sited towards the rear of midfield most of the way until closing a little with three furlongs to cover. Ultimately, he was not subjected to a hard ride and the experience gained may translate to wins in time. He has talent and some temperament: Jessica Harrington can develop him into a 130+ hurdler/ chaser if she fosters the first trait and tames the second.

FAUSTINOVICK 4 b g Black Sam Bellamy (IRE) – Cormorant Cove
Trainer: Colin TIZZARD **Form Figures: 2**

A really attractive bay gelding with a distinctive grey tail and prominent rear white sock and white star on his face. A beautiful walker, he posted an excellent debut second at Borris (Yielding/Soft) in March. Nursed around out the back for two miles by Derek O'Connor, he gradually improved his position and entered the picture as a close third jumping the third last. He was unable to match Andy Dufresne when that rival kicked on between the last two fences, and Derek elected to coast home to finish a clear second. He travelled very smoothly for much of the journey and could be a horse as comfortable at two and a half miles as three miles. Ellie Marie Holden purchased him at a cost of €26,000 at the 2017 Land Rover Sale and garnered an excellent profit by selling for £170,000 at Aintree Sales. Colin Tizzard has already demonstrated that he can upgrade a promising Irish point maiden into a top class track horse (Native River for example), and I would be very positive on the prospects of Faustinovick making a proper impact on the track in high end races. I have him amongst a select band of "very exciting" recruits from the 2018 spring campaign.

FULL TIME SCORE (IRE) 4 ch g Flemensfirth (USA) – Is It Here (IRE)
Owner: Chris JONES **Form Figures: 2**

A chestnut gelding with a distinctive feature of four white socks. Bred by Jimmy Mangan, the Monbeg boys purchased him for €47,000 at the 2017 Derby Sale and the horse returned to his birth county to debut at Knockanard (Soft/Heavy) in February in a two and a half miles maiden. On the basis of some excellent schooling reports, he went to post a well supported favourite. A horse with a fine big stride, he was never too far away from the leaders in that six runner race: produced to challenge on the climb away from the second last, he failed to match the striking speed of Shadow Rider and a creditable six lengths second place was his lot, it was his misfortune to run into a very good opponent. A son of an unraced Arctic Lord mare, down her page you locate many long distance chasers. That may be the clue to where this youngster's long term prospects rest. He was secured following this run in a private transaction by owner Chris Jones (he is likely to be trained by either Gordon Elliott or Henry De Bromhead) for a six figure sum. When he reaches physical maturity, he will be a powerful unit and one that could figure in those Grade A & B style staying handicap chases (130-145). I think he will function on most ground surfaces and can win from two and a half miles and upwards over hurdles this season.

HILL SIXTEEN 5 b g Court Cave (IRE) – Chasers Chic
Trainer: Sue SMITH **Form Figures: 1**

A well proportioned bay gelding: very little to recommend in terms of his immediate family, however, he may be about to boost the "page". Colin Bowe travelled to Dromahane (Soft/Heavy) in April for what was a very competitive maiden. A race run at a proper gallop, Hill Sixteen was one of four in contention heading to the third last: the first of the quartet off the bridle, he responded to the urgings of Barry O'Neill and a swift jump at the last allowed him to draw alongside Spyglass Hill, and he found most in the final hundred yards to win by a length. This victory had the hallmarks of an old fashioned staying chaser: slowly run, tactical races over trips beneath two and a half miles may compromise him. He has a hunger to please and placed appropriately he has the capacity to mature into a "Saturday" 120+ staying handicap chaser. He fetched a price of £100,000 at the Aintree April Sale and should give his new connections plenty of fun in the coming years. Whilst the win was on tacky ground, I noted him as a fluid walker in the parade ring and he may be active on a sounder surface, a true run race rather than ground may be the key to him.

HONEYSUCKLE 4 b f Sulamani (IRE) – First Royal (GER)
Owner: PEARL BLOODSTOCK **Form Figures: 1**

Athletic racy mare from a German family stocked with mixed winners (Flat and jumps). Travelled a long way south from her County Down base to run in a mares' maiden at Dromahane (Soft) in April. I spoke with her then owner/jockey Mark O'Hare, before the race and he was merely hoping for a good educational outing. The mare certainly proved a surprise package to Mark and his wife Sara. Restrained in mid pack for two miles, Mark produced her to get involved on the downhill run to three out (first of three fences in the homestraight). She jumped to the lead at the third last and, once over the penultimate fence, she showed an extra gear instantly extending her advantage and scorched up the run in to record a fifteen lengths win: certainly one of the more taking four year old mares' maiden wins of the season. That the performance stunned connections may lead to one of two conclusions, (1) that it was a poor race and the effort could have been a flash in the pan, or (2) she is a mare who saves her best for race day. If the latter is the verdict then it is conceivable she can win a bumper and may have valid aspirations to earn Graded success as a hurdler/chaser in the two and a half to three miles range within her own sex on the track proper. Given the strength of the market for four year olds, the price of €110,000 paid to secure her at Punchestown Goffs Sale looked more justified than other such six figure transactions.

IFICUDIWUD (IRE) 5 b g Trans Island – Manucrin
Trainer: Noel MEADE **Form Figures: 0 - 1**

Tipperary trainer Harry Kelly, who works in association with renowned vet John Halley, produced this chunky bay gelding fit and ready to win on his point debut at Dromahane (Good) in a five year old maiden at the tail end of the season in late May. An athlete who relished the prevailing fast conditions, he came to challenge at the third last and, once he gained the lead at the second last, the race was settled and he won by a comfortable three lengths. He has a nice relaxed way of travelling and that should serve him well overtime. He had run in a bumper at the 2017 Punchestown Festival (tailed off): the extra year has helped him mature. Purchased at the Cheltenham May Sales for £100,000 assessed on the promise of this success, I would fancy him to make an impact in a bumper in the autumn and he will win a maiden/novice hurdle and could be on the fringes of Grade 3 as a hurdler/chaser. His pedigree is all about Flat racers, hence my inclination would be to regard him as more of a summer style jumps horse than a winter one.

JILLYTHEJET (IRE) 4 bl f Jeremy (USA) – Listen Up
Trainer: Nicky HENDERSON **Form Figures: 1**

Gets her name from her jet black coat, and she does have a white face and, as a result. she has a very distinctive physical presence: if she was a human, she would be one of those tall dark attractive South American Miss World candidates. She has talent and class to match her looks. She contributed to a relentless gallop from the start of a Ballyarthur (Heavy) mares' maiden and always jumping slickly, she found generously in the final uphill furlongs to fend off the persistent challenge of the aforementioned Another Annie. Jillythejet is a tall mare who will enjoy jumping fences: before embarking on a chase career, she can win a bumper and become a 120+ novice hurdler. I think her style of racing could lend itself to her becoming versatile from a trip perspective as she could win from two to three miles. On the fourth page of her pedigree you locate the treble champion hurdle winner See You Then, and I was a little surprised that the Monbeg Doyles only realised £100,000 when they parted with her at Aintree Sales, as lesser four year old mares have made bigger prices this spring.

KNOW THE SCORE (IRE) 5 b g Flemensfirth (USA) – Prairie Bell (IRE)
Trainer: David PIPE **Form Figures: 110**

Touted as the best of the Monbeg Doyles autumn squad of four years olds, this Flemensfirth gelding picked his way from mid pack to lead approaching the final fence and coasted clear for a six lengths win at Ballinaboola (Yielding/Soft) in November. A relatively expensive store purchase, team Monbeg cashed in at the Cheltenham Sales with David Pipe paying £380,000 for his services. Although he won a five runner bumper at Towcester by thirteen lengths, he did make hard work of asserting his superiority. It came as a surprise that Pipe pitched this mudlark into the Cheltenham Festival bumper: as expected he found his rivals going a gear too high for him and, in the circumstances, was not disgraced as he finished fourteenth of twenty three runners. My initial impression is that this strapping bay gelding will become more of a high end handicapper than a premium Graded chaser. If the trainer concocts a two or three years plan of attack for a race like the Welsh National, then there could be a beautiful ending to a dream.

LARQUEBUSE (FR) 4 b f Saddler Maker (IRE) – Sirene Du Rheu (FR)
Trainer: Gordon ELLIOTT **Form Figures: 1**

One of the best four year old mares of 2018. A bay mare with a commanding physical presence, she trounced her five rivals when recording a smooth eight lengths win at Durrow (Soft) in March. Ridden with confidence by Barry O'Neill, the then Colin Bowe trained mare jumped crisply, and when given a squeeze away from the second last, she instantly put the race to bed. Purchased as a three year old store at the 2017 Derby Sale for a fee of €50,000, I gather in a private transaction, she was bought by Cheveley Park Stud and given to Gordon Elliott to develop. Gordon turned a similar ex-point winning mare, Shattered Love, into a Cheltenham Festival winning chaser: I would rate Larquebuse in the same league as Shattered Love, and fully anticipate she will win a bumper and win Listed jump races at her leisure. There is an extensive list of winners in her French jumps dam line. Whilst the victory at Durrow was recorded on testing ground, I would have no fears for her functioning on a sounder surface as she is such a fluent mover in her paces.

LECALE'S ARTICLE (IRE) 4 b g Malinas (GER) – Brookville (IRE)
Trainer: Nicky HENDERSON **Form Figures: 1**

The sales topper at the Punchestown Goffs sale in April, fetching his vendor (Pat Turley) a big cheque of €320,000. Five days before the sale he managed to win on his debut at Largy on good ground. A maiden won previously by Getabird, and keeping with past trends it seemed to have a competitive field for the 2018 version. He raced at the head of affairs from the start and was comfortable handling some tight bends on the Largy circuit. Jockey Declan Lavery stepped on the gas after the second last and kicked into a clear lead and a clean jump at the last sealed the verdict, ultimately posting an eight lengths win, with the next three home all representatives from the leading Wexford pointing establishments. A medium sized bay gelding, certainly no oil painting, lurking in his family tree are the likes of Wahiba Sands and Medaille Militaire, talented horses who tended to flatter to deceive at the highest altar of jump racing. There was one alarming aspect to his success, on the flat in the final 150 yards when he was clear, the jockey touched him twice with the whip, and the horse flashed his tail in response. Another negative, is that County Down based handler Turley has had impressive point winners in the past, which failed to enhance their careers on the track. One such example was Lecale Lad in 2012 who clocked a super time in a freak like win at Loughanmore, then was sold for a six figure sum and never won a track race in his career with Tim Vaughan. I do expect Henderson to manage to win a two and a half miles style maiden/novice hurdle with this new recruit, I would fancy a 130-140 ceiling may be the limit of his ability and therefore despite his lofty price tag, aspirations for Cheltenham Festival glory may be fanciful.

LISNAGAR OSCAR (IRE) 5 b g Oscar (IRE) – Asta Belle (FR)
Trainer: Rebecca CURTIS **Form Figures: 1**

Award winning North Cork based butcher Dinny Fitzgerald is a long time point supporter and generally keeps a couple of pointers on the go running under the "Lisnagar" moniker. A patient man, he resisted the temptation to run Lisnagar Oscar as a four year old, instead he decided to give the youngster an extra year to improve physically. That decision paid off because this tall lanky bay gelding rocked up at Liscarroll in March for the five year old maiden (a race won by Denman in 2003), and obliged on his debut, landing a pleasing touch in the betting ring for connections in the process. Amateur jockey Ciaran Fennessy does most of the work with the Fitzgerald pointers, and he was in the plate at Liscarroll (Soft/Heavy): he was sympathetic to Lisnagar in the first half of the race, held up at the rear, giving him plenty of daylight at his fences and time to warm to the task. When the race heated up on the downhill run to the third last, Lisnagar Oscar picked up the bit, arrived with his challenge and with a swift jump at the second last he readily settled the contest. Eventually drawing away for an eight lengths success. There may have been a lack of quality in the opposition, nonetheless this gelding stamped his authority and hinted that he would be all the better for the experience, particularly as he has the scope to physically mature into a stronger model. His dam is a full sister to Whisper and this lad secured a sales price of £105,000 in a private transaction during Aintree auctions. I would describe him as promising raw material and believe he will achieve more as a chaser than as a hurdler. For now, I think he has bright prospects of becoming a 130 rated chaser, he enjoyed the easy surface in his point, it is impossible to recommend if soft/heavy will always be his preferred underfoot terrain.

LOCK'S CORNER (IRE) 4 b g Gold Well – Last Century (IRE)
Trainer: Jonjo O'NEILL **Form Figures: 1**

A powerful bay gelding from an average jumps family: cost Colin Bowe €39,000 at the 2017 Derby Sale. Lined up for his debut as the Bowe first string with Barry O'Neill riding in a division of the four year old maiden run at Dawstown (Yielding/Soft) in May. It was a twelve runner race with all the leading point yards represented. Barry O'Neill bided his time towards mid pack. He produced Lock's Corner to lead as they climbed to the third last fence: leading at the obstacle, he soon surged clear to win untroubled by twelve lengths from stablemate Bbold. My instant impression was that we were at least watching a 130+ prospect and he had the top buyers interested when he appeared at Cheltenham Sales ring in May. Team McManus paid a sizeable £215,000 as they fended off Gigginstown House Stud and Paul Nicholls in the bidding war. This is a proper good, good to soft three miler, and his vocation should rest in top echelon staying handicap chases, his career pattern may be one of a 115-125 hurdler and 135-145 chaser, possibly a borderline Grade 3 or Grade 2 chaser at peak.

LORD SPRINGFIELD (IRE) 5 ch g Well Chosen – Super Thyne (IRE)
Trainer: Donald McCain **Form Figures: 1**

Tall unfurnished chestnut gelding who sports a white face: won on his pointing debut for local trainer James Fahey at the Stradbally (Yielding/Soft) fixture in April. Never far from the pace, jumping aggressively, he disputed the lead inside the final mile and kept galloping along resolutely and fended off all his rivals to record a narrow half length win. There is nothing much in his near at hand pedigree, yet as an individual he has size and scope. Bought by Donald McCain for €42,000 at Punchestown Goffs Sale, I rate this transaction as an ideal marriage as he has been acquired at a competitive price, and he is certain to win hurdle and chase races in the coming seasons for McCain on the northern circuit. He will be a tough nut to crack around Carlisle and the likes, and he can run to a rating of at least 120 and more as a hurdler and chaser. The ground at Stradbally was officially described as yielding, it was soft in places and good on certain sections of the course and, having handled the mixed terrain, Lord Springfield may be versatile on the count of going preference.

MANOFTHEMOMENT (IRE) 4 br g Jeremy (USA) – Endless Ambition (IRE)
Trainer: Tom GEORGE **Form Figures: 1**

Compact bay gelding: winner of his only point start: the success coming at Loughrea (Yielding/Soft): he was travelling with poise and sitting two lengths off the favourite (Pistol Whipped), when that jolly slipped up before the home turn: left in front, Manofthemoment galloped on powerfully to win snugly by over three lengths. It was a neat professional debut display. From the family of Lord of the River, Moorcroft Boy and No Hassle Hoff, he was secured by Tom George for £58,000 at Doncaster Sales, in that price bracket, this youngster represents a fair risk reward investment. He should be competitive in middle tier maiden/novice hurdles and may go close to winning a bumper, if that route is selected as his track career commencement arena. If he develops positively, he may one day be a player in competitive 130-145 handicap chases at the bigger tracks. Noting the way he carried himself, I reckon he may be versatile from a ground preference angle, though, winter heavy could be his least favoured terrain.

MEGA YEATS (IRE) 4 br f Yeats (IRE) – Mega Mum (IRE)
Trainer: Ruth JEFFERSON **Form Figures: 1**

Won a muddling five runner mares' maiden at Monksgrange (Soft/Heavy) in April: with the favourite in that race slipping up (when under pressure) and her nearest threat falling two out, Mega Yeats coasted home for an eased down win: she beat two home and those two have since failed to frank the form. On the credit side, Mega Yeats is a bay mare with a physical presence: she jumped efficiently and gave the instant impression that she enjoys the jumping code. Changed hands for £60,000 at Doncaster Sales and I do expect her to make an impact in mares' novice hurdles in the north for Ruth Jefferson: she could be difficult to beat on home turf, and she could progress to earning a crack at the bigger mares' races down south. One to keep on the right side of this winter.

MINELLA INDO (IRE) 5 b g Beat Hollow – Carrigeen Lily (IRE)
Trainer: Henry DE BROMHEAD **Form Figures: 13**

A rangy bay gelding with scope, hailing from an Irish jumps family rich in a heritage of proven stayers, he is a half brother to Benatar. Representing John Nallen, he turned up on a snowy afternoon at Dromahane (Soft/Heavy) and made light work of winning a five year old maiden. Leading from the start, he controlled the tempo, and a slick jump two from home placed his rivals in trouble. He was clumsy at the last, it did not matter, as he coasted clear for a six lengths success. Purchased a few days later for a six figure sum, he now carries the colours of Barry Maloney of Monalee fame. He ran for his new connections at the Punchestown Festival and recorded a commendable third in the concluding bumper at that fixture. I believe he will be seen at his best racing at two and a half miles and beyond and some dig in the ground will aid his prospects. I fancy he can be competitive to at least Grade 3 level when he goes down the chasing route, hurdling this coming season will be about education and garnering extra race experience.

MONKFISH (IRE) 4 ch g Stowaway – Martovic (IRE)
Trainer: Willie MULLINS **Form Figures: P1**

A rather plain chestnut gelding: the Monbeg boys got a decent payoff with this lad: having bought him for €36,000 at the 2017 Derby Sale, after winning a point, they succeeded in selling him at Cheltenham May Sales for £235,000. Monkfish started his career in a two and a half miles maiden at Cragmore (Heavy) in February, and it was either the tacky ground or the trip which was an issue as he was well beaten with three to jump, soon pulling up: on that performance he was not worth ten grand. His second run produced the lottery outcome for the Monbeg boys: on a drier sod at Stowlin (Yielding) and this time racing over three miles, he was mostly stationed close to the leaders: inheriting the lead three out, he looked a sitting duck as dangers loomed up onto his quarters. However, in commendable fashion he kept finding and eventually toughed it out to defeat Gameface by half a length in the fastest time of the day. His grand-dam was Martomick, an eight times track winner who gained most of her wins in the care of Kim Bailey. To date none of her offspring, first or second generation (like Monkfish) have set the track alight. It was Willie Mullins who paid the £235,000 at Cheltenham Sale on behalf of Rich and Susannah Ricci to add this horse to the Closutton squad: this gelding does not make an instant impact on me as one with top class potential: his game spirit and his battling appetite are qualities that Mullins has a great record in harnessing to much effect. He reminds me of another horse Mullins recruited from pointing, Cooldine, and like that past star, Monkfish has a very good chance of becoming a Grade 2 or 3 hurdler/chaser at staying trips.

NEEDHAMS GAP (IRE) 4 br g Flemensfirth (USA) – Blue Maxi (IRE)
Trainer: Gary MOORE **Form Figures: 1**

Justified heavy support when winning on his debut at Courtown (Soft) in April. Ridden with confidence by Rob James, he picked his way from the rear to lead at the third last. From there to the finish he was forced to deal with a serious challenge laid down by Southern Sam. Pulling clear from the rest, a cleaner jump by Needhams Gap settled the issue as he prevailed by three lengths. A well constructed almost black son of a leading sire, he has an excellent racing attitude and may be a horse with a powerful gallop and not necessarily one with gears. Secured by Moore for €120,000 at Punchestown Sale, this recruit from the Monbeg team will have no trouble winning over hurdles this coming winter and his prospects of becoming a 130+ rated chaser are more than bright. There are Graded chase winners in his pedigree (Frickley, Ottowa, Calling Brave), and he may add to the family collection. The ground was officially soft at Courtown, as a coastal track, the terrain was bordering on good to soft, and this four year old may be versatile when it comes to acting in different surfaces.

NORTHERN BOUND (IRE) 4 b g Fruits of Love (USA) – Noble Choice
Trainer: Ben PAULING **Form Figures: 2**

A sibling of the classy chasers Balnaslow and Lord Scoundrel: contested a competitive late season maiden at Loughanmore (Yielding): held up in last place for two miles: in the final half mile, he made a tremendous amount of ground on the leaders: fourth at the second last, he jumped his way into second place over the last and was pegging back Tribesman Glory with every stride, save for the winning post coming too soon, as he lost out by half a length: he powered home like a horse with real ability at the death, and for me was easily the best horse in that race. I expected him to fetch a higher price than the £55,000 which Ben Pauling paid at Doncaster Sales. If he remains sound, I think he has a bright future and he could easily scale a mark of 130 over hurdles/fences and, having joined a canny handler, he is one I am keen to remain loyal to this winter as he may reward the pocket.

ONTHEROPES (IRE) 4 b g Presenting – Dushion (IRE)
Trainer: Willie MULLINS **Form Figures: 2**

An athletic loose moving bay gelding with two front white socks: he contested the two and a half miles maiden staged by Punchestown (Soft/Heavy) in February. It was a race which lacked a proper gallop and consequently all eight runners were tightly packed approaching the third last, with this fellow towards the rear. With the tempo rising after the second last, Harley Dunne produced his mount to challenge on the run to the final fence and he looked to have momentum. A bad mistake at the last cost him a few valuable lengths: despite rallying deep inside the final furlong, the post came too soon, he was failed by a rapidly diminishing head to reel in the winner (Madiba Passion). What we learned from this outing is that his jumping technique requires attention, the major positive is the gallant way he battled when under pressure, he has a very likeable attitude and this alone will lend itself to track success. Harley Dunne apart from riding the horse also had some share in the ownership, and with Willie Mullins forking out £240,000 on behalf of Cheveley Park Stud at Cheltenham March sales, a healthy profit materialised for the sellers. In terms of pedigree, there is little to excite from either dam or grand dam. I am sure Willie Mullins can win a winter bumper with this horse and he can prosper into a Graded staying novice hurdler.

PASSAGEWAY (IRE) 5 ch g Stowaway - Lusty Beg (IRE)
Trainer: Willie MULLINS **Form Figures: 421**

A nicely put together liver chestnut gelding with a solid frame to him. Raced twice for Pat Doyle when pointing: did disappoint connections when only managing fourth in a four year old maiden at Belclare (Yielding) in April 2017: he returned to action at Loughrea (Soft/Heavy) and failed by a short head to Rath An Iuir: he travelled beautifully throughout the race and looked the winner all the way: he got in tight to the final fence, an error which slowed his momentum and, on the short run in, he did not have time to retrieve the situation as the winner blindsided him. Acquired by Willie Mullins in a private deal, he posted a stylish bumper debut win at the Punchestown Festival (Yielding/Soft): settled in midfield, he made smooth headway and in the final quarter mile coasted home for a comprehensive three and a half lengths victory. For the long term outlook, he may be a little beneath Cheltenham Festival standard, and he may slot in as a Grade 3 2m 4f - 3 miles hurdler and chaser. He appears to prefer mid range ground such as good to soft: heavy terrain he may find troublesome.

PRAGMATIC (FR) 5 gr g High Rock (IRE) - Electrostatique (FR)
Trainer: Willie MULLINS **Form Figures: F1**

The most impressive winner on Dungarvan's card in January (Soft) was this five year old grey gelding Pragmatic: handled by Donnacha Duggan, he was racing for the second time. Four weeks earlier, he fell at the halfway point when in rear at Templenacarriga (Heavy). At Dungarvan different tactics were deployed: he led the field from the start, racing with a controlled zeal: he had an appetite for attacking his fences and outjumped his rivals for a large part of the race. Heading to the second last, four rivals were ready to tackle him: he kept up the revs, and once over the last, found a final telling gear to assert to the tune of eight lengths, much the best horse on show. Three of those in behind (Stung For Cash, Ballybreen and Champagne Mystery) won afterwards, lending substance to the merit of the winner. He is by a relatively unknown stallion, High Rock (a son of Rock Of Gibraltar) and his pedigree page contains some fair French jump winners. In a season when prices reached new heights for pointers, I think Willie Mullins got value when securing this five year old for £82,000 at Cheltenham February Sales on behalf of Cheveley Park Stud. With a good racing attitude and high cruising speed, he has realistic aspirations to developing into a Grade 2/3 chaser.

RATHHILL (IRE) 5 b g Getaway (GER) - Bella Venezia (IRE)
Trainer: Nicky HENDERSON **Form Figures: 2**

Derek O'Connor has for several years had a retainer to ride for leading Northern point owner Wilson Dennison. In the last two years, he has added a retainer to ride for J.P. McManus in amateur races as well as guiding said owner regarding pointing talent. Rathhill raced in the Dennison silks once during the autumn, at Loughbrickland (Heavy) in November. He moved best for the majority of the race, until he began to struggle on the climb to the final fence and was eased to finish a twelve lengths second to Derby. Viewing the race, I think the horse gave Derek a very good feel, and he looked after him when the horse found the testing conditions too taxing in that last quarter mile. Derek encouraged J.P. McManus to buy the horse and he has dispatched the five year old to Nicky Henderson. In 2016/17, O'Connor advised McManus to purchase the talented Jerrysback from the same pointing source, so the top amateur's judgement may be that Rathhill has a bright future and has shown him enough to recommend that he is a young horse of 120 + track potential.

REDZOR (IRE) 5 b g Shantou (USA) - Knockara One (IRE)
Trainer: Dan SKELTON **Form Figures: P31**

County Wexford based jumps owner Pat Redmond of Big Zeb fame normally invests in store stock with appealing pedigrees: Redzor is a case in point, as Pat forked out €55,000 when securing him at the 2016 Derby Sale. The unraced dam of this five year old is a half sister to former RSA winner One Knight and such a pedigree is attractive from an investment angle. Redzor did not race in the spring of 2017 and made no impact when pulling up on his belated debut at Tinahely (Yielding/Soft) in October. His career has perked up in 2018: a fair third at Ballinaboola (Yiedling/Soft) in February (forced the pace until weakening two out) was followed by a gold medal display at Ballyraggett (Soft) in late March. He moved with poise in midfield until asked to get into the picture rounding the hometurn and onwards to the second last fence. He galloped on resolutely to pass the long time leader Crio Cuervos and assert on the run in for a three lengths success. Purchased for Dan Skelton at Cheltenham April Sales at a price of £80,000, this is a five year old who could improve on his pointing exploits and may climb to be a 120+ handicap chaser.

RUN WILD FRED (IRE) 4 ch g Shantou (USA) – Talkin Madam (IRE)
Owner: GIGGINSTOWN HOUSE STUD Form Figures: 1

Tall chestnut son of a modest point winning mare: racing out of the James Doyle barn, he lined up for his only point start at Dawstown (Yielding/Soft) and was supported into favouritism in the betting ring. He moved comfortably through the first two miles and then picked his way into contention racing uphill to three out. There were four with a shot at victory taking off at the second last: he fought his way to the front and then, despite hanging to his left, he stuck his head out in a dash to the line and defeated Easyrun De Vassy in a photo finish. The performance hinted that he had plenty of raw talent, though you would like to see him curb the tendency to hang under pressure. The runner up franked the form by winning his next start and when Run Wild Fred featured at Cheltenham May Sales, he moved to one of the biggest owners in the jumping game at a sales price of £225,000. He could be Graded class as a hurdler/chaser, I would like to witness one or two more performances from him before one could make a more affirmative stab at his long term prospects. I liked the way he floated on the ground and I would expect that soft or good/soft may be his preferred underfoot conditions.

SEVEN DE BAUNE (FR) 5 ch g Tiger Groom – Venus De Baune (FR)
Trainer: Ian WILLIAMS Form Figures: 2 -1

French bred chestnut gelding (dam won 4 jumps races): Brian Hamilton travelled south to Borris (Heavy) in December to debut him in a fair four year old maiden. Fifth at halfway, he made steady headway over the final mile, but failed to master the more experienced Reikers Island from the last and was forced to accept a commendable three lengths runners-up berth. Owner Roger Brookhouse paid £75,000 for him at Cheltenham Doncaster Sales five days later and dispatched the horse to Ian Williams. I noted he received several five day entries for bumpers, but did not figure as an overnight declaration until Uttoxeter (Good) in mid May. He left a fine impression as he comfortably outclassed his six rivals to win eased down by half a dozen lengths. He is a horse who is easy to settle and has handled heavy and good ground: the clues are evident that he could be a 130+ middle distance horse and I think he will reach his peak as a chaser in a couple of years and connections would be entitled to harbour aspirations of collecting a tasty prize with this likeable five year old.

SHOT TO HELL (IRE) 4 b g Kayf Tara – Combe Florey
Owner: GIGGINSTOWN HOUSE STUD Form Figures: 31

Strong bay gelding: ran twice in the spring: on his debut at Lismore (Soft/Heavy), Derek O'Connor exercised exaggerated waiting tactics: dropping him a long way behind the pace setting Feel My Pulse: the partnership made steady improvement in the last mile and were within twelve lengths when the horse clattered the second last: in the incident Derek lost his irons and he gave up the ghost and allowed the horse to coast home, beaten 35 lengths in third. Next time at Dromahane (Soft/Heavy), he was the apparent Pat Doyle second string and Derek O'Connor selected another horse over him: ridden by inexperienced John Kenny, Shot To Hell pushed on aggressively from the halfway point and established a big lead: the general verdict would have been he was using too much gas too soon. Racing downhill to the third last he was still fifteen lengths clear, the margin was whittled down to three lengths by the final fence and he looked a sitting duck. To his credit, having popped the final fence, he found extra and galloped honestly to the line and recorded a one and a half lengths win from Cobblers Way. This performance suggested that he has speed and he could be as effective over two and a half miles as three miles. From the family of Young Spartacus, he was purchased on behalf of Gigginstown at the 2017 Derby Sale for a price of €110,000 by Joseph O Brien and I would imagine, said trainer may now have the horse stationed with him for this winter. I doubt if he will be a top notcher: he has sound aspirations of developing into a 130-140 Grade 3 sort, and could win a valuable handicap chase during his track career. He has raced to date on soft/heavy, I have an inkling he will not be inconvenienced by a drier sod, so he may be versatile from a ground preference angle.

TARA WEST 4 b f Kayf Tara - West River (USA)
Trainer: Anthony HONEYBALL **Form Figures: 1**

Created a fine impression as she won arguably the most competitive four year old mares' maiden of the spring session at Loughanmore (Yielding/Soft) in late March. Upwards of six mares were in the mix jumping the second last fence and there was a real injection of pace: Tara West changed gears twice in the final quarter mile and flew the last fence when challenged by Little Light and managed to master that opponent in a driving finish by a head in a photo. The pair looked above average mares. The positives for Tara West are that she illustrated her ability to jump accurately at a high tempo, she stayed the three miles and highlighted that she possessed speed. I did note that she had somewhat of a knee action, and it will be worth watching if this aspect leads to her requiring some measure of juice in the ground. Purchased by the Monbeg team for £24,000 at Doncaster Spring Sales in 2017, they made a tidy profit by selling her for £100,000 inside twelve months at the Aintree April sale. Although a daughter of a National Hunt stallion in Kayf Tara, her dam line (dam by Gone West) majors on Flat performers and that is where she may get that injection of speed. I would be confident that she has the class to win a bumper and should score over hurdles within her own sex and can prosper to become a 120+ hurdler for a handler with a good record with mares.

THE BIG GETAWAY (IRE) 4 b g Getaway (GER) - Saddlers Dawn (IRE)
Trainer: Willie MULLINS **Form Figures: 1**

As his name would hint, this is a powerfully built bay son of Getaway from the Dawn Run family line. He set out to make all at Horse & Jockey (Yielding/Soft) and his task was simplified when his main danger Diol Ker fell at the third last: thereafter he galloped clear from the rest winning by a wide margin. Despite his size, he is nimble and agile and he has the hallmarks of a horse capable of developing into a proper staying Graded chaser. I noted a knee action, and he may prefer some juice in the ground: winning a winter bumper should be a formality: he is a horse with an immense stride and covers ground easily. He secured a tasty payday for the Monbeg team as they bought him for €28,000 at the 2017 Derby Sale and parted with him for £230,000 via the Cheltenham March Sales to Willie Mullins: one of the four year olds from this spring's crop with genuine aspirations of achieving Grade 1 success on the track proper.

TREVELYN'S CORN (IRE) 5 b g Oscar (IRE) - Present Venture (IRE)
Trainer: Paul NICHOLLS **Form Figures: 1**

Another smooth autumn debut winner hailing from the Colin Bowe yard: his success was registered at Borris (Heavy) in mid-December: always travelling in his comfort zone, he drew clear from the second last to win at his leisure. Measuring the merit of the performance is impossible as there was little depth to the race. To the naked eye, he looked an excellent prospect, hence his £400,000 price tag (owner Chris Giles) at the Cheltenham sales a few days later. Trevelyn's Corn is certainly going to be a high class handicap chaser, no one could honestly predict if he could climb to the top of the chasing ladder.

TRUCKIN AWAY (IRE) 5 br g Getaway (GER) - Simons Girl (IRE)
Trainer: Philip HOBBS **Form Figures: 3**

Simons Girl was a very smart pointer back in the 2006 season: she bolted up in the celebrated mares' final at Ballynoe. She has already produced the ill fated 130+ Western Cape and her second produce Truckin Away debuted at Ballynoe (Heavy) in March in a five year old maiden. A well proportioned bay gelding, a little keen, he raced prominently: climbing the hill towards the second last, he was still travelling best: in a bunch finish from the last, he was worried out of it, dropped to third, beaten under two lengths by Speedy Buck. On the day it looked like a hot event, subsequent efforts from other participants calls that verdict into question. With regard to Truckin Away, he did move through the race like the classiest individual on view. Bought privately by Brocade Racing and sent to Philip Hobbs, this horse may have plenty to offer going forward as he has bags of potential. I think he will function to effect on flat tracks such as Wincanton and can build into a 130+ chaser.

UMBRIGADO (IRE) 4 br g Stowaway - Dame O'Neill (IRE)
Trainer: David PIPE **Form Figures: 2**

A tall almost black son of Stowaway, he finished second to Brewers Project at Ballyarthur (Heavy) in March: he kept close tabs on that horse (his market rival) all the way, until that rival injected some pace at the second last and, having yielded a three to four lengths margin, he could not bridge that gap on the climb to the line. Pointed by Scobie Fitzgerald, he paid €37,000 for him at the 2017 Derby sale and more than quadrupled his money as David Pipe stumped up £160,000 just five days after the run at Cheltenham March sales. This youngster will require a season or two to strengthen his frame and reach physical maturity. Winning an ordinary maiden hurdle this winter and earning a tilt at something like the EBF final at Sandown (if rated 120-130) could be a realistic goal. Into the future, he can aspire to a chase mark north of 125 and could be a candidate for feature "Saturday Handicap Chases".

STABLE GOSSIP

Last year's article produced **19 winners** at a strike-rate of 25% showing a £10 level stakes **PROFIT** of £230.50 in the process. The selections included **BALLYMOY (3 wins), GOOD BOY BOBBY (3 wins), I JUST KNOW (4/1), KALASHNIKOV (3 wins** including the ***Betfair* Hurdle @ 8/1)** and **MIDNIGHT SHADOW (11/1 & 25/1 - Scottish Champion Hurdle)**.

Triple Grand National winning owner **TREVOR HEMMINGS** had 24 domestic winners last season. High profile horses **CLOUDY DREAM** and **MOUNT MEWS** joined Donald McCain during the summer and Hemmings has bolstered his team with a number of interesting recruits. I spoke to Trevor's racing manager **MICK MEAGHER** in August who kindly passed on his thoughts regarding the new additions.

"**CHAMPAGNE MYSTERY** ran in two Irish points finishing runner-up last time. He has joined Nicky Henderson having been bought at the Cheltenham May Sale. A tough horse who appears to stay well, he came highly recommended."

"**CHINENSIS** is a lovely straightforward horse who is in training with Nigel Twiston-Davies. A five year old by Well Chosen, he won three of his four Irish point-to-points before we purchased him at the Doncaster Sales in May. He will go novice hurdling and is a smashing horse for the future. I like him a lot."

"We also acquired **DEISE ABA** at the Doncaster May Sales having won a point by four lengths. Very athletic, he is a good moving horse with plenty of size. Philip Hobbs is training him and novice hurdling will be his job this season."

"**DIAMOND BRIG** is only six and is a beautiful type of horse. He won three of his four points, plus a hunter chase at Kelso in the spring. We bought him privately and he has joined Rose Dobbin. Rated in the 120s, he is a good looker and easy mover and we are hoping he will develop into a nice staying chaser."

"**HILL SIXTEEN**, who was bought at the Aintree Grand National Sale, is a gorgeous horse. Trained in Ireland by Colin Bowe, he won his only point-to-point a few days before the sale in April. Measuring 17 hands, he has loads of size and scope and is a lovely horse. He is in training with Sue and Harvey Smith."

"**LAKE VIEW LAD** has some very good form at Haydock (321) and he looks ideal for something like the Peter Marsh Chase (19th January). He stays well and we are hoping he may develop into a Grand National contender one day. The Rowland Meyrick Chase at Wetherby on Boxing Day is another possible target."

"We bought **NINTH WAVE** at the Doncaster May Sales having won a point-to-point bumper for Philip Rowley. A handy horse with a great attitude, he looks a stayer who should have no trouble winning races. He has joined Philip Hobbs and will go novice hurdling this season."

Two others to watch out for include **STONEY MOUNTAIN**. "He did well in bumpers for Henry Daly last season winning at Warwick and Bangor. A five year old by Mountain High, he isn't over big but could be the sort to develop into an EBF Final horse at Sandown in March."

"**VERY FIRST TIME** (Tim Easterby) has only raced six times over fences winning twice at Hexham and Newcastle last season. He is a grand staying sort who is suited by soft ground. Races such as the Rowland Meyrick Chase at Wetherby and the Eider Chase at Newcastle in February could be options."

****

Another high profile owner, namely **ROGER BROOKHOUSE**, paid £150,000 for the impressive Irish bumper winner **RAYA TIME** at the Doncaster Spring Sale in May. A five year old grey gelding by Al Namix, he won the same bumper at Killarney in May, which Sam Curling had landed twelve months earlier with Brookhouse's subsequent Skybet Supreme Novices' Hurdle winner Summerville Boy. A fourteen lengths winner, he has joined **HENRY DE BROMHEAD**.

Brookhouse has transferred **ESPOIR DE TEILLEE** to **TOM GEORGE** during the summer. A faller in his only point-to-point, prior to be being bought for £220,000 in May 2016, the Martaline gelding won a bumper and a novice hurdle for Neil Mulholland. A sixteen lengths winner on his hurdles bow at Catterick last November, the six year old missed the remainder of the season due to injury. No longer a novice, he will be forced to go down the handicap route, unless he is sent chasing, but is a horse of considerable potential and an exciting addition to George's team.

****

I spoke to **DAVID EASTERBY**, father of trainer **MICK**, at Pontefract in August and he told me the plan is to send the stable's EBF Final winner **SAM'S GUNNER** over fences this season. A seven lengths winner at Sandown in March off a mark of 125, he pulled up on his final start at Aintree over three miles. Rated 136, the Black Sam Bellamy gelding has yet to school over the larger obstacles but his trainer's assistant is expecting big things from the five year old.

****

SUE SMITH trained 40 winners last season with her total prize-money reaching £608,624. Wakanda won the Listed Sky Bet Handicap Chase at Doncaster, while Midnight Shadow claimed the Grade 2 Scottish Champion Hurdle. I strongly suggest readers keep an eye out for the unraced **RARE CLOUDS** who is expected to make his mark in bumpers this season. A four year old by Cloudings, he is a full-brother to stablemate and Scottish National third Vintage Clouds and has reportedly impressed in his work at home.

Scottish Champion Hurdle winner Midnight Shadow is the stable's number one hope for novice chases. However, Danny Cook is reportedly also looking forward to partnering the same owner's **JOKE DANCER** over fences this season. The Authorized gelding won three times over hurdles last winter earning an official rating of 128. Effective in testing ground, he is one to keep an eye on.

****

Numerically, **VENETIA WILLIAMS** endured her quietest campaign last season since 1996/1997 with 34 winners. However, the Grand National winning trainer has made some interesting 'signings' during the spring/summer including **BRIANSTORM**. Bought for £46,000 at the Doncaster May Sales, the former winning Irish pointer won twice over hurdles for Warren Greatrex last season. A wide margin victor at Taunton (2m : Soft) in January, the Brian Boru gelding followed up by sixteen lengths at Sandown (2m : Soft) in March, making all the running. Pulled up in Grade 1 company at Aintree (2m 4f) last time, the 132 rated hurdler is a free going sort (worn a hood on every start under Rules) who could be an exciting proposition over fences for his new owners **David & Carol Shaw**.

A novice chase campaign is likely to be on the agenda for another new recruit, **DIDERO VALLIS**. A five year old by Poliglote, he finished third in four French bumpers for Laurent Viel before joining Willie Mullins last season. A four lengths winner on his hurdles debut at Downpatrick (2m 3f : Good) in August 2017, he was placed in four of his next six starts over trips up to three miles. Rated 127, he also cost £46,000 at the Doncaster May Sales and is one to bear in mind for a novices' handicap chase on his fencing bow. He now belongs to **Lady Bolton** and the fact he handles good and heavy ground is a bonus.

APPENDIX

As in previous years, I have attempted to highlight a number of horses, in various categories, who are expected to contest the major prizes during the 2018/2019 campaign.

Two Mile Chasers:

The brilliant **ALTIOR** remains unbeaten over obstacles (5 from 5 over hurdles & 9 from 9 over fences). Forced to miss the first half of last season after Nicky Henderson discovered the eight year old's larynx wasn't operating sufficiently, he underwent surgery on his wind. A four lengths winner of the Game Spirit Chase at Newbury in February, the High Chaparral gelding then won at the Cheltenham Festival for the third consecutive year when beating Min by seven lengths in the Queen Mother Champion Chase with a spectacular display. **"I was in serious trouble the whole way round, but that's solely down to the ground, which is horrific. He's one of a kind: I was blown away by how he finished. He finds an extra gear after the last fence. It's incredible. He's some horse. He's exceptional – and that was sensational,"** enthused Nico De Boinville (12 from 12) at the Festival. A workmanlike winner of the Grade 1 Celebration Chase at Sandown on the final day of the season, his jockey commented: **"He was just lacking that bit of electricity today and it was pretty workmanlike. I think Cheltenham left its mark and it is soft ground here."** The six times Grade 1 winner is likely to reappear in the Tingle Creek Chase at Sandown (8th December) and it will be interesting to see if his connections are tempted to step him up in distance at some stage this season. Yet to race beyond the minimum trip, he was very strong at the line in the Champion Chase.

Willie Mullins has yet to win the Queen Mother Champion Chase but he won his third Arkle Trophy in the last four years when **FOOTPAD** sauntered home by fourteen lengths in March. A dual Grade 1 winner over hurdles, he looked even better over fences last winter winning all five of his races, including four at Grade 1 level. **"The first time we schooled Footpad over fences he was electric. He absolutely loves jumping and again gained lengths at his fences today,"** remarked Mullins at Leopardstown on St Stephen's day. Rated 166, he was a twelve lengths winner at Punchestown in April with his trainer commenting: **"That was some performance, better than Cheltenham I think. He was spring heeled and jumped much bigger than he did in the Arkle. Daryl (Jacob) said that once he settled, it was push button stuff. I'd have no problem going out in trip with him next season. He has plenty of stamina and he could be a future Gold Cup horse."** A Grade 1 winner over two miles three over hurdles, the six year old didn't appear to stay three miles at Punchestown in April 2017 but it was his final run of the season and may not have been at his best. Regardless of his optimum trip, he is a hugely exciting prospect and a major threat to Altior. His form figures at Cheltenham are 341.

Like Footpad, **SCEAU ROYAL** is owned by Simon Munir and Isaac Souede and he, too, developed into a high-class novice chaser last season winning four out of five until injury intervened and ruled him out of the spring Festivals. An eleven lengths winner of the Grade 1 Henry VIII Novices' Chase at Sandown in December, Alan King said afterwards: **"I've always worried, certainly when he was running over hurdles, that he was ten pounds below the very top, but I think fences have improved him. You won't see a slicker round of jumping than that. From the first moment we schooled him, he has been electric."** His record at Grade 1 level is 06461 and the Grade 2 Shloer Chase at Cheltenham (18th November) has been provisionally pencilled in as his likely starting point. The six year old's first time out record since arriving from France is 211 and his form figures at Cheltenham are 10162.

Like Nicky Henderson, Paul Nicholls has won the Queen Mother Champion Chase on five occasions. The former champion trainer is hoping **DIEGO DU CHARMIL** will make an impact in the top two mile chases this season. A two and a half lengths winner of the Grade 1 Maghull

Novices' Chase at Aintee, Nicholls said: **"He's a good horse, he just wants to mature a bit. He's got a load of toe, he jumps well, and there's a lot to come."** His rider at Aintree, Harry Cobden (115), also remarked: **"What impressed me most is that he jumped so slickly. He's a lovely horse and he's improving all the time."** A previous Cheltenham Festival winner, he is rated 157 over fences and could reappear in the Haldon Gold Cup (6th November), a race Nicholls has won six times.

PETIT MOUCHOIR and **SAINT CALVADOS** compromised their chances in the Arkle Trophy at Cheltenham by taking each other on from the outset and therefore setting the race up for Footpad. However, both horses are smart two mile chasers who are capable of winning Graded prizes this season. The former didn't fire at either Aintree or Punchestown but he endured a far from smooth preparation following a joint injury soon after his win at Punchestown on his chasing debut in October. Rated 157 over fences, Henry De Bromhead's grey is a dual Grade 1 winner over hurdles and shouldn't be written off. I think he is the dark horse of this division. Davy Russell was the leading rider at the 2018 Cheltenham Festival with four winners but he didn't excel on the seven year old in the Arkle.

At a lesser level, there is a good two miles handicap chase to be won with **LADY BUTTONS** this season. Phil Kirby's stable star won two of her three starts over fences last term with her sole defeat coming in Grade 1 company at Aintree. Beaten around nine lengths behind the aforementioned Diego Du Charmil, the eight year old looks tailormade for the **Castleford Chase at Wetherby (27th December)**. Rated 141, she relishes testing ground and her record at the A1 track is 115P2.

Two and a half Mile Chasers:

Paul Nicholls has won the Old Roan Chase twice, including with the mighty Kauto Star in 2006, and he is toying with the idea of running his Melling Chase winner **POLITOLOGUE** over the same course and distance (28th October) in the Autumn. The seven year old also won the Haldon Gold Cup, Tingle Creek and Desert Orchid Chases last season before finishing fourth in the Champion Chase. Returning to two and a half miles at Aintree in April, he edged out Min to win by a neck. **"I think a flat track suits him. We always thought he would be a King George horse one day and it's just possible he might end up getting three miles. Every time he gets to the bottom of that hill at Cheltenham, he doesn't finish. I don't think Cheltenham suits him. He loves tracks like this, Kempton, Sandown and Exeter,"** commented his trainer at Aintree. Yet to race beyond two miles five, the 168 rated chaser could be lining up in *Betfair* Chase at Haydock (24th November), if passing his initial test. His form figures at Grade 1 level are 24F141

BENIE DES DIEUX provided Willie Mullins with his ninth win in the David Nicholson Mares' Hurdle at Cheltenham in March. However, it is hoped the ex-French seven year old resumes her chasing career this campaign because she is a tremendous jumper and hugely exciting. Unbeaten in five races since joining Mullins, she won Listed prizes over fences at Carlisle and Naas before edging out Midnight Tour at the Festival. The daughter of Great Pretender rounded off her season with a three lengths win from stablemate Augusta Kate in the Grade 1 Annie Power Mares Champion Hurdle at the Punchestown Festival. Rated 147 over fences and unbeaten in three starts, David Mullins (2 from 2) said at Naas in February: **"Benie Des Dieux nearly travelled too well, but she is so quick over a fence. She's a pleasure to ride and she could do anything."** Her trainer said at Cheltenham: **"When she won the first time I texted Rich (Ricci) and said this could be 'Benie Des Douvan,' that was the sort of vibe she was giving me at home. We'll go way back up in trip and back over fences now, I think that's her job really. She can go to the top over fences."** Mullins added at Punchestown: **"I thought after her first win she had the ability of Douvan. I wondered whether she was a female version of Douvan. She's as good as I thought she was."** Another yet to race beyond two and a half miles, the Ryanair Chase at the Cheltenham Festival could be her main target this season, although it is worth noting all five of her UK and Irish runs have been on soft or heavy ground. A sounder surface is an unknown.

Ireland have won the last three runnings of the Ryanair Chase and it would be no surprise if last season's winning trainer Henry De Bromhead targets **MONALEE** at the event next March. For the second consecutive year, the seven year old ran well in defeat at the Cheltenham Festival. Runner-up in both the Albert Bartlett Novices' Hurdle and RSA Chase behind Penhill and Presenting Percy respectively, both his wins over fences last season were gained over the intermediate trip of two and a half miles. A three parts of a length winner of the Grade 1 Flogas Novice Chase at Leopardstown (2m 5f : Soft) in February, his record over 2m 4f - 2m 6f is 1211. The Milan gelding's form figures at Grade 1 level are 24F12F. He is capable of winning a big prize over fences this season.

The likes of **MIN, SHATTERED LOVE** and **WAITING PATIENTLY** (provided he returns from injury) should all continue to make an impact on the major prizes over two and a half miles plus.

The **BetVictor Gold Cup** at Cheltenham (17th November) is always a terrific spectacle and there are two horses who appeal at this stage for the 2018 renewal. Alan King won the £160,000 added event with Annacotty in 2015 and the plan is to run ex-French trained **FULL GLASS** this time around. Rated 142, the Diamond Green gelding won three times over hurdles and once over fences for Guillaume Macaire. His record in Graded company over the larger obstacles in France is 4424PF3 chasing home former stablemate and Grade 1 runner-up Edward D'Argent on no less than six occasions. The five year old has raced once for King finishing a good third in the Listed Hillhouse Quarry Handicap Chase at Ayr's Scottish National meeting in April, on ground which was considered too lively. Granted some ease underfoot, he could emulate Cyfor Malta (1998) and Caid Du Berlais (2014) by winning this as a five year old. He is a well handicapped chaser and very much one to keep an eye this winter.

No four year old has ever won the two and a half miles event but Paul Nicholls, who has won the race twice (Al Ferof (2012) & Caid Du Berlais (2014)) is contemplating entering another ex-French gelding, **MAGIC SAINT**. Rated 145 over fences, he too plied his trade under the guidance of Macaire in France and was successful in two of his four chases. Both victories were gained at Auteuil (2m 1f & 2m 2f) with his overall CV reading 4 wins from 7 career starts. A gelding by Saint Des Saints, he is owned by John Cotton and it is worth remembering the Nicholls trained Granit Jack (five year old) was travelling strongly when falling fatally at the second last in this race in 2007 on only his sixth run over fences.

Staying Chasers:

The first two home in last year's Cheltenham Gold Cup, namely **NATIVE RIVER** and **MIGHT BITE** look set to play leading roles once again in all the major staying chases. Colin Tizzard has indicated his eight year old will reappear in the *Betfair* Chase at Haydock (24th November) and is likely to clash with stablemate **THISTLECRACK**, who will warm up for the Grade 1 event by tackling the Charlie Hall Chase at Wetherby (3rd November) three weeks earlier. Tizzard has already won the *Betfair* Chase three times, thanks to the recently retired Cue Card.

The 2017 Cheltenham Gold Cup winner **SIZING JOHN** missed the second half of last season having suffered a displaced fracture of his pelvis whilst being prepared for the defence of his crown. Jessica Harrington's eight year old will hopefully be back this season.

King George winner **MIGHT BITE** gained some compensation for his defeat at Cheltenham when capturing the Grade 1 Betway Bowl at Aintree by seven lengths. Nicky Henderson said afterwards: **"That jumping out there was an exhibition round, you won't see better. He's all class and on good ground we'll have to go back and have another crack next year. I'd like to have another go at Native River on good ground, but next year we'll have to get a bit braver and go via the *Betfair* Chase."**

The champion trainer has won the Ladbroke Trophy at Newbury (1st December) on three occasions when the race was known as the Hennessy Gold Cup (Trabolgan (2005), Bobs Worth (2012), Triolo D'Alene (2013)). He is likely to be represented this year by dual Grade 1 winning novice chaser **TERREFORT**. The Martaline gelding joined Henderson last season having won over hurdles and fences for Guillaume Macaire in France. Having won a novices' handicap chase at Huntingdon in January off a mark of 137, he went on to win the Grade 1 Scilly Isles Novices' Chase at Sandown before chasing home Shattered Love in the JLT Novices' Chase at the Cheltenham Festival. Stepped up to three miles one for the first time in the Grade 1 Mildmay Novices' Chase at Aintree (Soft), he stayed on strongly to beat another mudlover Ms Parfois by nearly four lengths. Rated 158, I can't find the last five year old to win the Newbury showpiece but he doesn't lack experience having already had ten outings over fences. He has yet to race on ground quicker than soft.

RSA Chase and dual Cheltenham Festival winner **PRESENTING PERCY** is prominent in the ante-post lists for the Gold Cup and it is not difficult to see why following his devastating display last March. The seven year old, who won the Pertemps Final off a mark of 146 in 2017, made a seamless transition to fences winning three of his five starts last term. An eleven lengths winner of a staying handicap at Fairyhouse (3m 5f : Soft) in December off 145, he then won the Grade 2 Galmoy Hurdle at Gowran Park in January. Sent off 5/2 favourite for the RSA Chase, he stormed to victory under Davy Russell (415116131121) beating compatriot Monalee by seven lengths. **"God he's some horse. He has won with his ears pricked,"** remarked his rider afterwards. Trained by Pat Kelly, who only has 15 horses in training, the Sir Percy gelding is owned by Philip Reynolds who commented: **"To have one as good as Presenting Percy, you need to mind him and look after him and we're going to give him every chance. He was incredible – absolutely unbelievable. He was foot perfect the whole way round and I thought Monalee put up a brilliant performance as well."** There have been five Irish trained winners of the Cheltenham Gold Cup this century and this 165 rated chaser could make it six next March. Denman and Bobs Worth are the last two horses to complete the RSA Chase and Gold Cup double in consecutive years.

Owners Andrea and Graham Wylie and trainer Willie Mullins came within a short head of winning the Cheltenham Gold Cup in 2014 when On His Own was denied by Lord Windermere. The partnership are hoping their Punchestown Gold Cup winner **BELLSHILL** can go one better next spring. A four times Grade 1 winner, he was beaten ten lengths by Might Bite in the RSA Chase in 2017. The eight year old overcame an absence of 346 days to win the Grade 3 Bobbyjo Chase at Fairyhouse in February before finishing a length fifth in the Irish Grand National at the same track. The King's Theatre gelding ended the campaign on a high though when beating the now retired Djakadam at the Punchestown Festival (3m : Yielding). His owner said afterwards: **"Willie (Mullins) did say after Fairyhouse that he thinks I might have a Gold Cup contender for next season."** Mullins himself added: **"He has a huge engine. He could be a Gold Cup horse."** Still lightly raced over fences, his record at the highest level is 0113021F31. His Cheltenham form is the chief concern though – he has finished 10th, 13th and 3rd at the Festival.

Finally in this section re staying chasers, I feel the following THREE horses are worth watching out for in races such as the **Ladbrokes Trophy (formerly the Hennessy Gold Cup)** at Newbury **(1st December), Welsh National (27th December)** or **Grand National**.

BELAMI DES PICTONS (Officially rated 148) is trained by Venetia Williams who won the Hennessy Gold Cup with Teeton Mill (1998) and Welsh National twice (Jocks Cross (2000) & Emperor's Choice (2014)). This lightly raced seven year old, who was included in this article last year, has won three of his four races over fences by an aggregate of nearly fifty six lengths. Forced to miss the whole of last season, he is reportedly back in work now. Unbeaten over three miles, he was a wide margin winner at Warwick and Leicester off marks of 138 and 148. His form figures on soft or heavy ground are 3111411. Bought for €120,000, the Khalkevi gelding has won five of his six races since joining his current yard.

Lucinda Russell won the Grand National in 2017 with One For Arthur and the Kinross based handler may have another live contender in years to come courtesy of **BIG RIVER**. The eight year old, who is rated 143, won twice over fences last season gaining both victories at Kelso. Indeed his form figures at the Borders track are 112111. Runner-up at Uttoxeter in March, he was attempting to concede twenty three pounds to Harry Fry's Behind Time. The Milan gelding has only raced a handful of times over fences and his first time out record is 2121. Given his record on heavy ground (although he has also won on good ground) - 11P112 - races such as the Becher Chase (8th December) and Welsh National could be on his agenda en route to a National bid next April.

Pat Doyle has been associated with some top-class point-to-pointers before they have excelled under Rules. The Co.Tipperary handler may have a Grand National contender on his hands in the progressive **KAISER BLACK**. A seven year old by Germany (the same sire as Faugheen and Samcro), he has won two of his five races over fences, including the Mayo National at Ballinrobe (2m 7f : Good) by fifteen lengths and the Connacht National at Roscommon (3m : Good) by four lengths off marks of 123 and 138 respectively. Raised nine pounds since, he is also a winner on heavy ground and his record over two miles seven plus (including in PTPs) is 221211. Davy Russell (3611) rode him at Roscommon and said afterwards: "**He was always a horse who was crying out for good ground but he is big and raw and I was worried about whether Pat would run him on today's ground. He is a lovely horse and Pat has done a marvellous job with him and is adamant he stays on flat tracks and maybe he might have to go right-handed as well."** His record racing right-handed (under Rules) is 143411 compared to 36422 going left-handed.

Two Mile Hurdlers:

Nicky Henderson won the Champion Hurdle for a seventh time in March with **BUVEUR D'AIR** retaining his crown. A hard fought neck winner, the seven year old was unbeaten in four races last season and is likely to follow a similar path. Officially rated 169, the Crillon gelding has won 10 of his 11 races over hurdles and is already a six times Grade 1 winner. He will be bidding the emulate the likes of See You Then and Istabraq by winning hurdling's Blue Riband three times.

Owners Simon Munir and Isaac Souede will be hoping stablemate **WE HAVE A DREAM** becomes the first five year old to win the Champion Hurdle next March since Katchit in 2008. The Martaline gelding failed to win in three starts over hurdles in France but was unbeaten in five races for Henderson last winter. A dual Grade 1 winner, he was ruled out of the Triumph Hurdle, due to having a temperature, but was back to form with avengeance at Aintree routing his nine opponents by upwards of seven lengths. **"We can dream about the Champion Hurdle. He's got his life in front of him and he's never stopped improving all season. He loves tearing along and his jumping was very slick,"** commented the champion trainer in April. A winner on good and heavy ground, he handles stiff and sharp tracks and remains unexposed. See You Then won the Champion Hurdle as a five year old for the Seven Barrows team in 1985.

Aside from If The Cap Fits and Laurina, who are featured in the *Top 40 Prospects*, the stiffest competition may come from the brilliant novice from last season, **SAMCRO**. Purchased for £335,000 having won his only point-to-point for Colin Bowe, the Germany gelding was unbeaten in three bumpers and was a dual Grade 1 winner over hurdles last term. The six year old arguably produced his best performance in the Deloitte Hurdle at Leopardstown's Dublin Racing Festival in February (2m : Soft) beating Duc Des Genievres by five and a half lengths. Jack Kennedy (1111F) then steered him to a two and three quarters of a length win in the Ballymore Novices' Hurdle at Cheltenham before falling at the third last in the Grade 1 Punchestown Champion Hurdle. His connections have indicated he will remain over hurdles this season with the Champion Hurdle the target. Gordon Elliott commented after his win in the Grade 3 Monksfield Novice Hurdle at Navan in November: **"We've always thought he was very good but that was a bit special. He's a horse for next year so anything he does this year will be a bonus."** Jack Kennedy said at Cheltenham: **"I'd love to ride him over a fence, he'd be utterly brilliant**." Built and bred for chasing, I was hoping he would go over fences this season but there is no doubt Gordon Elliott's gelding has the ability to make a major impact on the Champion Hurdle scene. Having trained Mick Jazz to finish third in last season's race, the dual Grand National winning trainer may feel he has a far superior horse in Samcro to aim at the race this time around.

Stablemate **LABAIK** is reportedly back in training having missed the whole of last season. The former Skybet Supreme Novices' Hurdle winner has only raced eight times over obstacles and he beat subsequent Champion Hurdle runner-up Melon at the Festival in March 2017. The Montmartre gelding isn't straightforward but his talent has never been questioned. Elliott may give the grey a light campaign before heading back to Cheltenham. He is rated 161.

MELON, as discussed, has finished runner-up at the last two Cheltenham Festival. The Medicean gelding produced a career best in March when narrowly edged out by Buveur D'Air. **"It was a terrific performance from Melon and its vindicated what we thought of him. He just didn't face the hood last time and he's a horse who is going to improve. He'll be better next year,"** stated Willie Mullins at the Festival. Rated 165, he also fell at the third last when upsides Samcro at the Punchestown Festival. His record at Grade 1 level is 2252F. Like Labaik, the six year old has only raced eight times over timber.

It is believed Mullins is also training Grade 1 winning novice **DRACONIEN** for the Champion Hurdle. A five year old by Linda's Lad, he finished fourth in a Grade 1 APQS bumper at Saint-Cloud in 2016 before heading to Ireland. A twelve length winner on his hurdles debut at Clonmel (2m 3f : Soft/Heavy) in December, his trainer said: **"He's a nice sort for the future and jumps very slick. He was very sharp over his hurdles, especially out of that ground when a lot of horses couldn't jump out of it. He didn't waste an inch in the air."** Although beaten on his next three starts, the Clipper Logistics owned gelding was back to his very best when winning the Grade 1 Champion Novice Hurdle at the Punchestown Festival (2m : Yielding/Soft). A two and a quarter lengths winner from Vision Des Flos, his connections feel he benefited from a more patient ride by Noel Fehily (21) and the better ground suited him, too. He could be anything and shouldn't be underestimated.

Sizing Europe (2007) was the last Irish trained winner of the **Greatwood Hurdle at Cheltenham (18th November)** but they may have a prime candidate for this year's renewal in the lightly raced and progressive **OFF YOU GO**. A five year old by Presenting and from the family of Irish National winner Shutthefrontdoor, he won two handicap hurdles at Limerick (2m 4f : Heavy) and Leopardstown (2m : Soft) off marks of 107 and 123 respectively. A length and a quarter winner of a €59,000 event at the Dublin Racing Festival at Leopardstown, he hasn't raced since. Raised eleven pounds to a mark of 134, he is owned by J.P.McManus and trained by Charles Byrnes. Yet to be partnered by Barry Geraghty, he looks capable of winning a big handicap hurdle this season starting with a trip to Gloucestershire in November. The five year old has only raced half a dozen times and is open to significant improvement.

INDEX

SELECTED HORSE = BOLD *Talking Trainers = Italics*

Please see pages 162-170
for details of the
One Jump Ahead Updates

Don't forget to read my Diary @
www.mhpublications.couk

ONE JUMP AHEAD UPDATES

I shall be producing **5 One Jump Ahead *Updates*** throughout the 2018/19 National Hunt season. Each *Update* comprises information about the horses in ***One Jump Ahead*, an update from top Bloodstock Agent Anthony Bromley**, **Bumper News**, **Ante-Post Advice** (recommendations for the major races), **Big-Race Previews** and **News from Ireland** from one of the most informed Irish experts Declan Phelan**. Please note, the *Updates* are ONLY AVAILABLE VIA EMAIL (Not Post).**

It is £6 per *Update* (except £10 for the Cheltenham Festival version) or £34 for ALL 5 via **EMAIL**.

Summary of the 2017/2018 *Updates*:

What The Clients Said:

"Very good bonus information in Spring Watch, Festival Update Mark." **K.M.**

"Caribert, the icing on a very big cake. Thank you for another great tip." **D.W.**

"Very impressive 14/1-12/1 second and a 3/1 nice winner today. Top up from Cheltenham much appreciated." **P.H.**

"Thanks for the excellent information in Cheltenham email 1 and 2 in Lincoln no mean feat." **A.P.**

"A wonderful Festival enhanced by the comments of yourself and Declan. A great read and great value - it always pays for itself!!" **D.H.**

"I just wanted to email to say thanks for the Cheltenham Update which provided a number of winners over the week and it proved a great help in narrowing down those big fields in what has been one of the best weeks racing I can remember. The info from the preview nights was great and from which I had Tiger Roll to win the Cross Country." **M.L.**

"Well Mark where do we begin? Outstanding Cheltenham once again. Many thanks. Blow by Blow the icing on a large cake. Well played sir." **S.R.**

"Nice work Mark, pretty incredible given the ground and the near misses too...great week." **M.B.**

"I just wanted to thank you once again for a wonderful Cheltenham Update. Rounded off today with the Newbury result. Great value as always." **M.F.**

The PADDY POWER MEETING 2017

5 WINNERS: APPLE'S SHAKIRA (Evens), FINIAN'S OSCAR (10/11), FOX NORTON (4/5), MELROSE BOY (11/4), ON THE BLIND SIDE (9/2)

Quote: *"**MELROSE BOY** is trained by Harry Fry who has won the last two renewals of this courtesy of Unowhatimeanharry (off 123 in 2015) and Behind Time (115 last year). Bought for 65,000 as a three year old, he is making his handicap debut off 123 having failed to win any of his three starts over hurdles last term. However, the Saint Des Saints gelding ran some good races in defeat bumping into some smart rivals. Third at Uttoxeter a year ago, he then finished seven lengths runner-up to Grade 2 winner and Skybet Supreme NH third River Wylde at Ludlow. Third at Wetherby last time, he was only beaten around two lengths by Eaton Hill* *and Mount Mews (Grade 2 winner and now rated 145) over two miles three. Kieron Edgar will partner him for the first time and he is very much shortlist material."* **WON by 6 lengths @ 11/4**

Plus: **KALASHNIKOV (4/7 & 8/1), PETE SO HIGH (7/1, 100/30), SALDIER (4/9, 10/1)**

Quote: *"**KALASHNIKOV** (see page 128 in One Jump Ahead) looks set to develop into a flagbearer for his promising young trainer **Amy Murphy**. A two lengths winner of a bumper at Wetherby in the spring, the four year old returned to the West Yorkshire track for his hurdles debut on Charlie Hall Chase day and produced a scintillating display. Jack Quinlan's mount jumped quickly and accurately throughout and bounded clear after the second last to register a ten lengths victory. Unlike his full-sister Kalane, he coped well with the slow ground and looks a horse with a bright future. His trainer suggested afterwards that the Kalanisi gelding will run under a penalty in another novices' hurdle at **Doncaster (2nd December)**."* **WON TWICE, including the *Betfair* Hurdle at Newbury (8/1).**

BROMLEY'S BEST BUYS – Part II: WINNERS: **NAYATI (10/11, 8/11), REDICEAN (11/8, 8/13, 10/11) & STYLE DE GARDE (5/4)**.

OWNERS ENCLOSURE: **JARED SULLIVAN**
WINNERS: **CHEF DES OBEAUX (2/5, 11/8, 13/8), CUT THE MUSTARD (3/1), DARIUS DES BOIS (7/2), DIESE DES BIEFFES (4/9, 5/2), GETAREASON (4/6), LAURINA (1/4, 13/8, 4/7, 2/11), MSASSA (1/4), RIO VIVAS (7/2), SAGLAWY (2/5, 13/8), SANDSEND (11/4), STORMY IRELAND (2/7), TURTLE WARS (3/1)**.

CHRISTMAS SPECIAL 2017

The IRISH ANGLE by Declan PHELAN: WINNERS: **BURNING AMBITION (4/6), DANNY KIRWAN (13/8), GILGAMBOA (5/4, 6/4, 8/13), KNOW THE SCORE (1/2), SANDSEND (11/4), SOMETIME SOON (2/1), WHISPERINTHEBREEZE (6/4)**

Quote: *"My banker of the holiday session is in the other hunter chase at Limerick on the 27th: a maiden hunters' chase, most of the runners will never be found guilty of winning a track race. The highly progressive **BURNING AMBITION** can land the prize in comfort. He won his maiden point at Cragmore in February (defeating the recent handicap winner Black Scorpion (won off 109 at Clonmel)): since then Burning Ambition has added another three wins to his tally, including two in the recent autumn session. Last time in his first spin in Open grade he hammered Sambremont at Maralin. The ground at Limerick churns up over the four day festival and the ability to handle tacky/heavy ground is vital. Burning Ambition will have no trouble on that count. Incidentally, his partner Rob James who has been a top 4 point rider for the last two seasons (amassing over 80 winners), has actually to date never partnered a track winner. Burning Ambition will set that record straight. Unfortunately, the odds of reward will not be generous: I would price him up as a comfortable odds on shot to dismiss any of his rivals in a point, if available a price in the 6/4 range should be snapped up, as this horse as upwards of two stone in hand on these modest rivals in this hunter chase (3.10 Limerick 27th)."* **WON by 13 lengths @ 4/6**

Quote: *"The hunter chase scene is about to crank up a notch or two and we have a couple of races in that code in Ireland this Festive period. **GILGAMBOA** has been slow to come to hand this Autumn, disappointing at Castletown Geoghegan in October: however, he dropped a vital clue that he is steadily progressing when losing out in a photo finish at the start of this month at Mainstown. He was placed fourth in the 2016 Aintree Grand National and I gather the Aintree Foxhunters in April is his main target. Race conditions are tailored to suit him in the Down Royal* *hunters' chase (26th) and in a race lacking strength in depth, he should return to the winner's enclosure."* **WON at Down Royal (26th December) @ 5/4**

Quote: *"**SOMETIME SOON**: bay son of Shantou, provided trainer David Christie with his first ever four-year-old maiden winner when bolting up on his debut at Kirkistown (Yielding/Soft) in November: apparently owned then by former bookmaker John Stuart. Middle sized, he seemed to have a lovely racing attitude and was beautifully relaxed during the race for rider Barry O'Neill. Captured by Gigginstown for £225,000 at the December Sales and he will be trained by **Gordon Elliott**. I can see him developing into a Grade 2/3 style chaser for new connections and a likely bumper winner too."* **WON @ 2/1 at Fairyhouse (24/2/18)**

Plus: **BENIE DES DIEUX (Evens, 9/2, 3/1), CAID DU BERLAIS (9/2), DEMI SANG (11/10), DUKE OF NAVAN (6/1), I'M TO BLAME (Evens), KILDISART (5/1), SAYO (8/11), VIRAK (10/11, 5/4), VIVALDI COLLONGES (9/2)**

Quote: **BENIE DES DIEUX**: *"Trained by Willie Mullins, the ex-French six year old has produced two tremendous rounds of jumping on both her starts over fences. A thirty lengths winner on her chasing debut at Limerick a year ago, she was forced to miss the rest of the season. However, the Great Pretender mare returned at Carlisle early this month and barely came out of second gear to beat four rivals by upwards of eight lengths in another Listed chase. I was working for Racing UK at the Cumbrian venue and spoke to her rider David Mullins afterwards. The Grand National winning jockey was very impressed and felt she could be effective from two to three miles and didn't envisage any problems when racing on better ground. Granted luck, she could be something special and a Grade 1 winner in the making."* **Won next three races, including Grade 1 wins at Cheltenham (9/2) & Punchestown (3/1).**

Quote: *"**CAID DU BERLAIS** is rated 143 over hurdles and fences and is a four times winner under Rules and has been placed twice at the Cheltenham Festival (form figures 230F8). The eight year old was eighth in the Pertemps Final last March and made his point-to-point debut at Larkhill earlier this month. Trained by **Rose Loxton**, he ran out an easy 20 lengths winner of a Ladies Open. It will be interesting to see if he returns to **Paul Nicholls** if aimed at the Foxhunters' at Cheltenham this spring. Either way, he should have no trouble winning his share of hunter chases."* **WON the Champion Hunters' Chase at the Punchestown Festival by 21 lengths @ 9/2**

FEBRUARY 2018

CHELTENHAM FESTIVAL HANDICAPS PREVIEW: BENIE DES DIEUX (WON the mares' hurdle (9/2)), THE STORYTELLER (WON the Brown Advisory & Merriebelle Stable Plate Handicap Chase @ 5/1)). Plus: MALL DINI (2nd in the Kim Muir @ 4/1), NUBE NEGRA (3rd in the Fred Winter Hurdle @ 15/2)

Quote: *"This time last year, **THE STORYTELLER** was being aimed at the Martin Pipe Conditional Jockeys' Handicap Hurdle having won twice at Down Royal and Thurles. Indeed, the Shantou gelding was one of the market leaders in the ante-post lists. Unfortunately, Gordon Elliott's charge incurred an injury which ruled him out of the Festival and the remainder of his novice campaign. Rated 142, he finished a creditable runner-up behind Chateau Conti in a conditions hurdle at Fairyhouse in November on his return to action. His connections then decided to send him chasing and the seven year old jumped slickly before beating subsequent winners Sutton Manor and Livelovelaugh by upwards of four and three quarters of a length at the same track less than a month later. Stepping up in class, he contested a Grade 3 novice chase at Punchestown and appeared to have plenty more to offer when pecking badly at the penultimate fence. Although rallying to hold every chance at the final obstacle, his effort petered out on the run-in but Davy Russell's mount was only beaten four and a half lengths by the high-class*

Invitation Only. Elliott will no doubt be keen for The Storyteller to head to the Festival this time around, having missed out twelve months ago. Entered in the JLT and RSA Chases, he is officially rated 147 over fences and could yet end up in one of the handicaps, namely the Ultima Chase on the opening day or the ***Brown Advisory & Merriebelle Stable Plate (2m 5f)****. Stablemate Diamond King was sent off 5/1 favourite for the latter event last year off a mark of 150 as a novice. The Shantou gelding would need to run once more though to qualify for the handicaps and he holds three entries over the weekend – Grade 1 Scilly Isles Novice Chase at Sandown (2.25 Saturday), Grade 1 Flogas Novice Chase at Leopardstown (3.00 Sunday) & Grade A 2m 5f handicap at Leopardstown (4.10 Sunday). He is a horse with a high cruising speed and big engine and the fact he handles good and soft ground is a bonus. Whichever race he contests at the Festival, he is worthy of a second look."* **WON the Brown Advisory & Merriebelle Stable Plate @ 5/1**

Plus: WINNERS: CASSE TETE (6/1), TOPOFTHEGAME (11/2), WESTEND STORY (5/4). Plus: BLEU ET ROUGE (Advised @ 16/1 – 2nd in the *Betfair* Hurdle at Newbury (10/2/18))

Quote: *"Despite only finishing seventh and beaten thirty six lengths, I thought* ***CASSE TETE*** *ran better than the statistics suggest in the Grade 3 two miles five handicap chase at Cheltenham last Saturday. The Poliglote gelding was a ten lengths winner over fences at Auteuil for Guillaume Macaire in October 2016, prior to joining Gary Moore. A twenty seven lengths winner at Sandown's Imperial Cup meeting last spring on his fourth run for his new connections, he jumped badly left at Ascot on his reappearance before Christmas and never got involved. Back in action a month later at the Trials meeting last weekend, he held every chance at the top of the hill but couldn't land a blow before keeping on. Casse Tete is related to a two miles seven winner in France and looks well worth a try over a longer trip. Still only six and lightly raced over fences, I will be surprised if there isn't more mileage in his rating of 133 (dropped four pounds)."* **WON next time at Warwick @ 6/1**

Quote: **TOPOFTHEGAME**: *"Raised three pounds since, he looks well worth a try over three miles for the first time under Rules and the giant gelding gets the opportunity at Sandown on Saturday (3.00) in an ultra competitive eighteen runner handicap hurdle."* **WON at Sandown @ 11/2**

The CHELTENHAM FESTIVAL 2018

8 WINNERS: COO STAR SIVOLA (5/1), BUVEUR D'AIR (4/6), SAMCRO (8/11), ALTIOR (Evens), DELTA WORK (Advised @ 14/1), THE STORYTELLER (Advised @ 10/1), LAURINA (Advised @ 8/11), BLOW BY BLOW (Advised @ 20/1)

Quote: *"****COO STAR SIVOLA*** *is trained by Nick Williams who came agonisingly close to winning the 2009 renewal with Maljimar only to be collared close home by a galvanised Wichita Lineman. Rated 140 over hurdles, the six year old boasts good Festival form having finished third in the Fred Winter Juvenile Hurdle in 2016 and fourth in the Martin Pipe Conditional Jockeys' HH last year. Having run well in defeat against the likes of Finian's Oscar, Kalondra and Frodon over fences earlier in the season, he appreciated the step up to three miles for the first time at Exeter last month when winning a novices' handicap by fourteen lengths off 135. Raised seven pounds since, his record at Cheltenham is 23164324 with his form figures on the Old course reading 233. A handful of novices have won this in the last fourteen years and there is no reason why he won't go close. He handles any ground."* **WON the Ultima Handicap Chase @ 5/1**

Quote: *"****DELTA WORK*** *was a winner on the Flat in France for Emmanuel Clayeux before joining Gordon Elliott. A twenty lengths winner on good ground at Punchestown last May, he has run well in defeat since. The Network gelding was third behind stablemate Samcro in a Grade 3 at Navan before finishing runner-up in a Grade 2 at Limerick. Less than four lengths fourth behind*

behind Total Recall in a three miles handicap at Leopardstown last month, he was conceding eight pounds to Willie Mullins' Ladbrokes Trophy Chase winner. Three and a half lengths third last time in a Pertemps qualifier at Punchestown later the same month, his record over three miles is 243. Still unexposed, it is only 22 days since his last run but he races off 139 compared to 141 in Ireland." **Advised @ 14/1 – WON the Pertemps Final @ 6/1**

Quote: *"**THE STORYTELLER** has only raced three times over fences winning on his chasing debut at Fairyhouse (2m 5f) before finishing third behind Invitation Only at Punchestown – making a crucial mistake at the second last. Seven and a quarter lengths seventh behind Monalee in the Grade 1 Flogas NC at Leopardstown last time, he is officially rated 147. Potentially better than his mark, there are two minor concerns. Firstly, he lacks experience over fences – stablemate Diamond King was sent off 5/1 favourite for this last year off a mark of 150 and pulled up following an early mistake. Secondly, his record on left handed tracks is 4th and 7th. Gordon Elliott's charge handles most surfaces and it is hoped either Jack Kennedy (212) or Davy Russell (3rd) takes the ride."* **Advised @ 10/1 – WON the Brown Advisory Handicap Chase @ 5/1**

Quote: *"**BLOW BY BLOW** is trained by Gordon Elliott who intends to run four in this. The Grand National winning handler is keen to win the event following near misses by Toner D'Oudairies (2012) and Noble Endeavor (2015). A Grade 1 winning bumper horse for Willie Mullins (won 3 out of 4), the Robin Des Champs gelding joined Elliott before suffering an injury which sidelined him from April 2016 until November last year. Twice a winner over hurdles this term, he was successful at Navan (2m 7f) in December before being well held behind Next Destination in Grade 1 company at Naas in early January. However, he was back to form under Rachel Blackmore last time in the Grade 3 Michael Purcell Memorial NH at Thurles (Champagne Classic was third in the same race last year en route to victory here). A fourteen lengths winner from the same connections' Gun Digger, his trainer feels he doesn't want the ground too soft. Rated 144, he is well treated if judged on his bumper form."* **Advised @ 20/1 – WON the Martin Pipe Conditional Jockeys' Handicap Hurdle @ 11/1**

The horse I am most looking forward to seeing run at the Cheltenham Festival:
RICH RICCI: BENIE DES DIEUX (WON the mares' Hurdle @ 9/2)

OWNERS ENCLOSURE: **JARED SULLIVAN**: WINNER: **LAURINA (4/7)**
Quote: **LAURINA**: *"We think she is very good and I know both Willie (Mullins) and Ruby (Walsh) feel she is one of their best chances of the week in the **Trull House Stud Mares' Novices' Hurdle** on Thursday. An easy winner of both her starts since arriving from France, she looked an exceptional filly in the Grade 3 at Fairyhouse last time. Willie doesn't usually talk his horses up but he has been very enthusiastic about her. I don't think the state of the ground matters to her."* **WON by 18 lengths @ 4/7**

TALKING TRAINERS: **GORDON ELLIOTT: WINNERS: BLOW BY BLOW (11/1), THE STORYTELLER (5/1), TIGER ROLL (7/1)**
Quote: *"I am planning to run **BLOW BY BLOW, FLAWLESS ESCAPE, FLAXEN FLARE** and **SIRE DU BERLAIS** in the Martin Pipe Conditional Jockeys' Handicap Hurdle and it is a race I am very keen to win. I think Blow By Blow will go well provided the ground dries out."* **BLOW BY BLOW WON @ 11/1**

Quote: **THE STORYTELLER:** *"His form in Graded company is very good but he lacks experience. That would be my concern but otherwise he must have a major chance."* **WON @ 5/1**
Quote: **TIGER ROLL**: *"He has been to Cheltenham twice recently to school around the Cross Country course and is in very good form. Keith Donoghue will take the ride and his preparation has gone well."* **WON @ 7/1**

The IRISH ANGLE by Declan PHELAN

Quote: *"The Elliott horse that appeals to me is* ***BLOW BY BLOW****: it is conceivable that he may top the weights, though as explained, with a slim weight range than will be insignificant: he was a top class bumper horse, winner of the 2016 Grade 1 championship bumper at Punchestown: in his bumper days he conquered Death Duty and Moon Racer. Beset by niggling injuries, he was parked up for a season. He commenced hurdling this winter and it has been a slow haul back to form: he scrambled home to win a 2m 7f maiden hurdle at Navan in December, and then faded tamely from the second last when sixth to Next Destination in a Grade 1 at Naas. He came alive for the first time this season a fortnight ago at Thurles: the race was the Grade 3 Michael Purcell Memorial: in 2017 Gigginstown/Elliott won this contest with Champagne Classic before arriving at Cheltenham and winning the Martin Pipe. It may have been the persuasive female handling of Rachel Blackmore or the blinkers or both, Blow By Blow picked up the running entering the homestraight and galloped right away: he won by fourteen lengths and it could have been twenty five and it took Rachel two furlongs too pull him up. The sheer power of his stride at the finish was a rare sight. Running as close as 22 days to the Festival is not ideal: the ground at Thurles was not too bad, dead on the good to soft side, than genuine soft and unlikely to have taken as much out of a horse as opposed to heavy ground. The handicapper in the UK has slapped a mark of 144 on Blow By Blow which on the surface looks tight: from that Thurles race, Roaring Bull was running on fumes and a weakening second when falling at the last: the handicapper has given that horse a mark of 138 for this race: not in a million years would Roaring Bull get within an asses roar of Blow By Blow on those terms, hence Blow By Blow may be favourably treated. Without delving into the 141 initial entries for this race, I would imagine that Blow By Blow is the only Grade 1 winner amongst the troop. If Gordon can book a jockey who can humour this big chestnut gelding into action, then he can produce fireworks. He handles all variety of grounds, that Grade 1 win was on good ground. Now, if Blow By Blow does not fancy the task at hand, he will be a beaten docket inside the first half mile. If he settles into a rhythm, his class and staying power may surface at the climax. As risk/reward outsiders go, at 20/1 Blow By Blow is deserving of support."* **WON the Martin Pipe Conditional Jockeys Handicap Hurdle @ 11/1**

SPRING WATCH: Quote: *"Harry Fry won the* ***Goffs UK Spring Sales bumper at Newbury (24th March)*** *last year with Bullionaire and Paul Nicholls' former assistant is set to run the twice raced* ***CARIBERT*** *in the 2018 renewal. The Ballingarry gelding justified strong market support on his racecourse debut at Wincanton in November. Making all, he stayed on strongly to beat Hideaway Vic by four and a half lengths. Ten lengths runner-up behind Time To Move On (won again since) under a penalty at Exeter less than a month later, he has been freshened up since and Fry confirms the five year old in good form at home. His stable are in fine form at present (3 winners at Kempton last Monday) and Caribert should go well at the Berkshire track."* **WON @ 5/2**

Quote: *"Switching codes, I interviewed William Haggas and David O'Meara for Ahead On The Flat last month and both trainers have leading hopes for the* ***Lincoln Handicap*** *at Doncaster on the same day. William feels* ***ADDEYBB*** *is a Pattern horse in the making and the four year old has wintered well. Ideally suited by some ease in the ground, the head of Somerville Lodge thinks a mile is his bare minimum but still expects the four year old to go well. However, I can also pass on a very positive mention for O'Meara's* ***LORD GLITTERS. "A horse with an incredible turn of foot, we purchased him at the Arqana Sale in France in July having watched a replay of some of his races. He showed a lot of speed and is a horse who is best covered up and delivered late. Runner-up at Ascot over seven furlongs in early October on his first run for us, he then produced a super performance to win the Balmoral Handicap over a mile and at the same track on Champions day. Beaten a neck in a Listed race at Newmarket last time, he has only raced on soft ground for us but we don't feel it is a necessity. Bought as a replacement for Mondialiste who has retired, he is a different type of horse to him. We***

have high hopes for him this year over seven furlongs and a mile," *reports his trainer."* **1st & 2nd in the Lincoln Handicap**

The AINTREE GRAND MEETING 2018

4 WINNERS: WE HAVE A DREAM (Advised @ 9/4), MIGHT BITE (4/5), TERREFORT (Advised @ 7/2), SANTINI (Advised @ 9/4). Plus: SHANAHAN'S TURN (Advised @ 40/1 – 2nd @ 14/1)

Quote: *"**WE HAVE A DREAM** is rated 145 having won 4 of his 7 races and is unbeaten since joining Nicky Henderson. The Martaline gelding didn't manage a win in three outings in France but he hasn't looked back since arriving at Seven Barrows. A ten lengths winner at Doncaster in Grade 2 company, he then beat Sussex Ranger by a length and a half in the Grade 1 Finale Hurdle at Chepstow over Christmas. A four and a half lengths winner at Musselburgh in February, he was forced to miss the Triumph Hurdle. A winner on good and heavy ground, he has been off for 67 days, which is an advantage, and the Simon Munir and Isaac Souede owned gelding looks set to play a leading role."* **Advised @ 9/4 WON by 7 lengths**

Quote: *"**TERREFORT** is trained by Nicky Henderson who has won this with Irish Hussar (2003), Burton Port (2010) and Might Bite (2017). A winner over hurdles and fences at Clairefontaine in France when trained by Guillaume Macaire, the five year old has won two of his three races since arriving at Seven Barrows. A ten lengths winner of a novices' handicap chase at Huntingdon off a mark of 137, he then won the Grade 1 Scilly Isles NC at Sandown by a neck from subsequent Grade 2 winner Cyrname. Seven lengths runner-up behind Shattered Love in the JLT NC at Cheltenham last time, he was conceding six pounds to Gordon Elliott's mare, who has since finished an unlucky second in the Grade 1 Powers Gold Cup at Fairyhouse. This will be his first run beyond two miles six but I will be surprised if he doesn't stay. Yet to race on ground quicker than soft, Banjo (1995), Star de Mohaison (2006) and Big Buck's (2008) won this as five year olds."* **Advised @ 7/2 WON the Grade 1 Mildmay Novices' Chase @ 3/1**

Quote: *"**SANTINI** won his only English point-to-point at Didmarton by fifteen lengths last season before being snapped up for £150,000 in March last year. The Milan gelding has won two of his three starts over hurdles for Nicky Henderson and is rated 150. He beat stablemate Chef Des Obeaux by four and a half lengths at Newbury in December before reeling in subsequent Festival runner-up Black Op close home in a Grade 2 novice at Cheltenham's Trials meeting in late January. Four and a half lengths third in the Albert Bartlett NH last time, he has yet to race on ground better than soft but gives the impression he will handle it. The six year old is an exciting prospect and it would be no surprise to see him sign off his novice hurdle career with a Grade 1 victory."* Advised @ 9/4 – **WON the Grade 1 Sefton Novices' Hurdle @ 6/4**

Quote: *"**SHANANHAN'S TURN** is well handicapped off a mark of 134 having won the Galway Plate for Henry De Bromhead off 142 in 2015 (hasn't won since but has only had seven races). Absent due to a stress fracture from July 2016 until November last year, the ten year old has only raced twice for Colin Tizzard. A remote eighth of nine over two miles at Cheltenham in November, he had a wind operation and didn't return to action until the Festival last month. Although beaten twenty three lengths in ninth, the Indian Danehill gelding travelled strongly for a long way and was still in contention turning for home. Dropped three pounds since, he was once rated 153 and will hopefully have Robbie Power on his back for the first time. Despite his age, he has only raced 19 times."* **Advised @ 40/1 – 2nd @ 14/1 in the Topham Chase**

The horse I am most looking forward to seeing run at Aintree: **ANTHONY BROMLEY: WE HAVE A DREAM (WON @ 2/1)**

It is £6 per *Update* (except £10 for the Cheltenham Festival version) or £34 for ALL 5 via **EMAIL.**

ONE JUMP AHEAD UPDATES 2018/2019 ORDER FORM (EMAIL ONLY)

AVAILABLE AT £6.00 EACH (£10 Cheltenham) OR £34 FOR ALL 5

- **CHELTENHAM PADDY POWER MEETING 2018**
  (Will be emailed on Thursday 15th November 2018)
- **CHRISTMAS SPECIAL 2018**
  (Will be emailed on Friday 21st December 2018)
- **FEBRUARY 2019**
- **MARCH 2019 - CHELTENHAM FESTIVAL PREVIEW**
  (Will be emailed on the Sunday before the Festival)
- **APRIL 2019 – AINTREE PREVIEW**
  (Will be emailed on the Tuesday before the Meeting)

Total Cheque / Postal Order value £............. made payable to MARK HOWARD PUBLICATIONS Ltd. Post your order to: MARK HOWARD PUBLICATIONS. 69 FAIRGARTH DRIVE, KIRKBY LONSDALE, CARNFORTH, LANCASHIRE. LA6 2FB.

NAME: ....

ADDRESS: ....

....

.... POST CODE: ....

Email Address: ....

If you have not received your *UPDATE* via email 24 hours before the meeting starts, please contact us immediately.

Available to order via **www.mhpublications.co.uk**

AHEAD ON THE FLAT 2019

The 19th edition of *Ahead On The Flat* will be published in early April for the 2019 Flat season. It will be formulated along the same lines as previous years with a ***Top 40 Prospects*** (the 2018 edition included **AJMAN KING, CRYSTAL OCEAN, DASH OF SPICE, WITHOUT PAROLE & YOUNG RASCAL**), ***Handicap Snips*** (included **DIOCLETIAN (33/1)** in 2018), ***Maidens In Waiting*** (**CRYSTAL HOPE (14/1)** & **PILASTER (3 wins (12/1, Evens, 11/4)**) and ***Significant Sales*** (**GUNMETAL (10/1, 9/2 & 10/1) & MAGIC CIRCLE (8/1 & 11/2)**) In addition, there will be the usual stable interviews with some of the top trainers in Great Britain (this year's included **Andrew Balding, Owen Burrows, Roger Charlton, Keith Dalgleish, William Haggas, Iain Jardine, David O'Meara, Hugo Palmer, David Simcock** and **Roger Varian**). *Ahead On The Flat* will contain 152 pages and the price is £9.99.

I shall also be producing **three *Ahead On The Flat Updates* (EMAIL ONLY)**. There will be a **Royal Ascot Preview** (**8 winners & 11 places** in 2018 including **SETTLE FOR BAY (Advised @ 16/1), AGROTERA (Advised @ 14/1)** and **DASH OF SPICE (Advised @ 10/1)**), a **York Ebor Preview (5 winners** in 2018 including **PHOENIX OF SPAIN (Advised @ 8/1)** and **URBAN ASPECT (5/1))** and an **Autumn *Update***. The Royal Ascot version is £10 with the other two £6 or £17 for the ALL THREE.

ORDER FORM

- **AHEAD ON THE FLAT 2019 (Book ONLY) £9.99**

AHEAD ON THE FLAT UPDATES 2019 (can be ordered individually at £6.00 EACH (£10 ROYAL ASCOT) or ALL 3 updates for £19.00):

- **ROYAL ASCOT PREVIEW 2019 £10.00**
- **YORK EBOR MEETING PREVIEW 2019 £6.00**
- **AUTUMN PREVIEW 2019 £6.00**
- **ALL 3 UPDATES (EMAIL ONLY) £19.00**
- **AHEAD ON THE FLAT + 3 UPDATES £27.99**

Total Cheque / Postal Order value £............. Made payable to MARK HOWARD PUBLICATIONS Ltd. Please send to: MARK HOWARD PUBLICATIONS Ltd. 69 FAIRGARTH DRIVE, KIRKBY LONSDALE, CARNFORTH, LANCASHIRE. LA6 2FB.

NAME: ....

ADDRESS: ....

....

.... POST CODE: ....

Email Address: ....